STUDIES IN IMPERIALISM

general editor John M. MacKenzie

When the 'Studies in Imperialism' series was founded more than twenty-five years ago, emphasis was laid upon the conviction that 'imperialism as a cultural phenomenon had as significant an effect on the dominant as on the subordinate societies'. With more than ninety books published, this remains the prime concern of the series. Cross-disciplinary work has indeed appeared covering the full spectrum of cultural phenomena, as well as examining aspects of gender and sex, frontiers and law, science and the environment, language and literature, migration and patriotic societies, and much else. Moreover, the series has always wished to present comparative work on European and American imperialism, and particularly welcomes the submission of books in these areas. The fascination with imperialism, in all its aspects, shows no sign of abating, and this series will continue to lead the way in encouraging the widest possible range of studies in the field. 'Studies in Imperialism' is fully organic in its development, always seeking to be at the cutting edge, responding to the latest interests of scholars and the needs of this ever-expanding area of scholarship.

Visions of empire

MANCHESTER
1824

Manchester University Press

Visions of empire

PATRIOTISM, POPULAR CULTURE AND THE CITY, 1870–1939

Brad Beaven

MANCHESTER UNIVERSITY PRESS

Published by Manchester University Press
Altrincham Street, Manchester M1 7JA, UK
www.manchesteruniversitypress.co.uk

British Library Cataloguing-in-Publication Data is available

Library of Congress Cataloging-in-Publication Data is available

ISBN 978 1 5261 0669 8 paperback

First published by Manchester University Press in hardback 2012

This edition first published 2017

Printed by Lightning Source

This book is dedicated to my partner Becky, our sons George and Sam, and my parents Martin and Gail Beaven

CONTENTS

LIST OF ILLUSTRATIONS

LIST OF TABLES

ACKNOWLEDGEMENTS

My thanks to John MacKenzie and the anonymous readers who commented on the original proposal and draft manuscript. Thanks also to the MUP publishing team whose professionalism is second to none.

I'm fortunate to work with a group of talented social and cultural historians whose friendship and collegiality has made working in the team such a rewarding experience. A number of colleagues (past and present) whose work overlaps with mine generously gave their time reading and commenting on drafts. Thanks to Ken Lunn for his detailed comments, Karl Bell, Rob James, James Thomas and Sue Bruley. Dave Andress, in particular, has always been happy to discuss ideas despite his heavy Faculty work load. I've also had the benefit of discussing and writing with John Griffiths, a collaborator in the field of social and cultural history for almost twenty years. John's recent research on empire and popular culture in the Antipodean colonies has proved a useful contrast.

My research has taken me principally to three city archives, and my thanks go to the staff of Coventry History Centre, Leeds Archives and Local Studies Library and the Portsmouth History Centre. I collected a wide range of material from these archives including statistical evidence that, thanks to my Dad's expertise with spreadsheets, I've been able to present in the form of charts and tables. I am grateful to Gina Harrison, who valiantly battled against the office equipment to print out the manuscript.

I have been fortunate to test my ideas out in a number of seminars and conferences including staff seminars in Winchester and Portsmouth Universities, the Urban History Conference at University of Warwick 2009 and the Social History Conference in Glasgow 2010. I am particularly grateful to Susie Steinbach and Stephen Miller for their invitation to join the 'Victorian Culture and Identity during the South African War' panel in the North American Conference on British Studies, Denver, USA, 2011.

The Centre for European and International Studies Research generously funded my research and conference attendance. I am also grateful to the Centre for funding the teaching relief I was awarded to complete the writing of the book.

Finally, my thanks to Becky my partner and our two sons George and Sam for all their love and support. Becky has, as always, been very supportive and patient while I've locked myself away in my office to write the book. While George has taken an early interest in history, I'm under no illusion that this book can ever compete with his *Horrible Histories* series. Sam's recent arrival has livened things up as his early interests have centred on grabbing anything at ground level (including the cat). George was born just before I finished my first book and Sam was born just before finishing this one. It's with some trepidation that I embark on my third book!

GENERAL EDITOR'S INTRODUCTION

A nation's cultural history is clearly made up of many local components. National and local interact in a two-way process in which the centre influences the peripheral cities, towns and villages in which the populace resides, but these localities then adapt and modify such cultural phenomena, even transmitting some aspects of their socio-cultural characteristics back to the capital. As Brad Beaven points out in this book, many of the studies of imperial culture have been top-down in their character, attempting a national focus lacking a true grounding in regional centres. Moreover, many such studies have concentrated on London and too often that great city has been seen as a synecdoche for the whole of Britain. The other problem is that the British Isles, Pocock's 'Atlantic archipelago', are in reality made up of four nations, England, Ireland, Scotland and Wales, each with its own cultural and ethnic make-up, itself complex and hard to unravel. Beaven, perhaps sensibly, has chosen to concentrate on one of these, England, and examine imperial patriotism and popular culture in three contrasting cities, Portsmouth, Coventry and Leeds, one in the south, one in the midlands, and one in the north (as it is usually regarded). In doing so, he taps into the now extensive series of studies that have emerged over the past thirty years or so while adding much local variation and detail, all dependent on the geographic location, the economic foundation and the social profile of these three places.

The roots of an imperial and patriotic culture have to be identified in a whole range of civic phenomena – in the churches, the schools, the press, the societies, the entertainment and sporting forms, the companies and other sources of employment, as well as the military and naval connections of each place. Moreover, the very fabric of British towns and cities carried expressions of civic imperialism and patriotism – in the architecture and decoration of its buildings, in its statuary, in civic ceremonies, in parades and pageants, as well as through travelling troupes of actors, bands or other entertainers. The study of all of these phenomena raises many issues of the relationships between national and local politics, of the connections with economic and commercial issues, of the local repercussions of international events, of aspects of class strife or alleged conciliation, the heightening or amelioration of social tensions. All of these are of course subjected to the dynamic of historic changes through the late nineteenth and early twentieth centuries, including the fever points of imperial excitements (for example in competitive conflict with other European powers), of colonial wars and of major world conflicts. Of these the Anglo-Boer of 1899-1902 and the First World War are obviously the most important.

Beaven analyses all of these with great acumen. What emerges is a highly complex picture with many local variations. While it is true that anti-imperialism seems to be a relatively muted phenomenon, the imperial dimensions of patriotism vary according to time, place and the particular social or culture medium examined. The picture that is built up is a very mixed one which reveals the essential heterogeneity of these phenomena. It may well be that the various 'factions' that have emerged in the historiography will find something to comfort them in these pages, but there is certainly no sure and simple answer to the questions posed about popular culture and its relationship with imperial patriotism. And, as Beaven himself convincingly argues, a truly national picture can be built up only through local contexts.

My own work in this field spans some thirty years of activity, while punctuated by many excursions into other areas (including environment history, Orientalism, migration and settlement studies, museums, four nations theory and much else). My original publications did indeed adopt an essentially national focus. But the realisation of the need for the local study arose with my consideration of Glasgow as an imperial city. More recently, I have been looking at aspects of imperial culture in Dundee and the manner in which these interacted with the social deprivation and labour troubles of that city. It is abundantly apparent that much more needs to be done, that we need to examine imperial and patriotic cultures in cities and towns elsewhere in England, as well as in Ireland, Scotland and Wales. The great joy of history is that the more it is explored the more do its expanses seem limitless. Beaven's study will surely help to inform and stimulate all future local studies. It is to be hoped that there will be many more of them.

John M. MacKenzie

Introduction

In the midst of the Boer War the Reverend C.G. Lang, Vicar of Portsea, organised a meeting for working men who did not usually attend church or chapel. His lecture, which was on the lessons of both municipal and national elections, was entitled 'The Imperial Instinct'. He informed his large audience, in the words of the local newspaper, that

> It was a most remarkable time, because it marked the first appearance in the country of entirely new force. There had been occasions when other forces and passions had aroused the nation, but they had passed away. This time, though, they had a new force, and one which carried with it an enormous responsibility because he did not think that it would go back or pass away – that force was the Imperial instinct. There was no doubt that a great future was before this force. The country had been preparing for it during the last 300 years, ever since the great Spanish Armada.[1]

For Lang, the 'imperial instinct' would soon have a distinct presence, not only at a national but also at a municipal level. His audience was left in no doubt that Portsmouth, the Empire's principal naval base, had been destined for its pivotal role in preserving and energising the Empire in a new imperial age.[2] Lang's recognition of how an 'imperial instinct' could flow from local institutions which had tangible meanings to a local populace has all too often been overlooked by historians who have viewed empire as a monocultural phenomenon. In presenting an imperial culture as a singular entity there is a tendency to neglect the complex layers of society through which the imperial message was transmitted and filtered. Indeed, proponents of this approach are invariably silent on the dissemination process and how it was consumed by the public at large.[3] This book instead focuses on this process of dissemination of imperialism, the form it took and its consumption by those living in contrasting English cities. Analysis of the city and its institutions provides perhaps the most consistent test of whether the urban environment acted as an effective conduit for an aggressive imperial culture, a pervasive force that had the potential to impinge upon working-people's daily urban lives between 1870 and 1939.[4]

Current historiography in the history of empire

For over twenty years the nature, impact and importance of Britain's domestic imperial culture has been the subject of intense academic debate. J.M. MacKenzie's pioneering research on the relationship between British society and the Empire encouraged a rich seam of work on the subject that was fostered by Manchester University Press's *Studies in Imperialism* series that began in the mid-1980s.[5] This research generated an invaluable body of work that sought to illustrate the pervasive influence of empire in cultural institutions such as the theatre, music, advertising and the cinema. The launch of *Studies in Imperialism* helped initiate a vigorous debate that continues to this day on whether the consumption of this culture impacted upon individual lives during the late nineteenth and early twentieth centuries. For example, over the past forty years historians have consistently identified the Boer War as the litmus test for popular imperialism. Richard Price's seminal monograph in 1972 challenged the orthodoxy, claiming that the popular manifestation of jingoism on the streets of Britain was largely limited to the lower and middle classes.[6] This position of distancing working-class communities from the jingoism of the Boer War has been repeated in a number of studies, most recently by Bernard Porter and Andrew August.[7] Significantly, both historians arrive at their conclusions through material drawn from Price's original text, despite MacKenzie's intervention in the mid-1980s that seriously questioned Price's vision of a working class disengaged with a jingoistic popular culture.[8] However, fresh research on the domestic consequences of the Boer War has generated further scepticism that the working class exhibited apathy towards the Empire. Stephen Miller's exhaustive account of Boer War volunteers published in 2007 draws from a wide range of working-class autobiographies to argue that 'this imperial mission was inculcated in children through a variety of modes including Sunday sermons, aggressive advertisements, after school instruction, and weekend participation in any of a wide array of "paramilitary" organisation such as the Boys' Brigade'.[9] Historians, then, have reached something of a stalemate on the success or otherwise of the imperial inculcation of popular culture. Those whose findings have identified a successful imperial hegemony in British society through song sheets and propaganda have difficulty in proving that the imperial messages in the music hall or schooling were consumed unquestioningly by the recipients.[10] Likewise, historians who intend to absolve the working class of any noteworthy engagement with the imperial project have difficulty in accounting for the significant numbers of volunteer soldiers and the immense popularity of music hall and cinema entertainment that was immersed in imperial meaning and imagery.[11] What is perhaps missing here is an examination of popular culture that sustains a comparative analysis over differing urban and chronological contexts.

In recent years another strand of imperial history has challenged both the conceptual and methodological approach of historians of empire. Within the last twenty years, 'new imperial' historians have argued for a broader analysis of empire that questions the concepts of nation and identity by exploring the 'metropole and periphery' through the same analytical perspective. For historians such as Antoinette Burton, who have focused on the formulation of identity, 'Empire and nation were mutually constitutive'.[12] She challenged a tendency in '"imperial studies" to shore up the nation and re-constitute its central-ity, even as the legitimacy of Great Britain's national boundaries are apparently under question'. Burton argues that such a conservative approach would run the risk 'of remaking Britain (itself a falsely homogenous whole) as the centripetal origin of empire, rather than insisting on the interdependence, the "uneven development" . . . of national/imperial formations in any given historical moment'.[13] However, as James Thompson has pointed out, this preoccupation with the relationship between nation and empire raises important questions:

> Did empire undercut or consolidate the 'nation' and for whom? Sec-ondly, in foregrounding the relationship between 'nation' and 'empire', there is a danger of producing a monolithic, even contested, notion of the nation. New Imperial historians have examined contestation of the 'nation' in terms of gender, class and 'race' but perhaps ironically, this has sometimes served to privilege national identities and downplay region, city, town and neighbourhood.[14]

Certainly, by narrowing the focus to the elite networks between the metropole and the periphery, there is no sense of *how* imperialism worked in practice in Britain. Imperial hegemony is perceived as a 'given' and there is no consideration of the complexities of dissemina-tion that were often shaped by time and place. Indeed, the decontexu-alisation of subject matter and the dearth of empirical evidence are fault lines that seem to run through 'new imperial' histories. In this light, Price offered a damning analysis of the 'new imperial' history as he was struck by 'how much of the existing scholarship is far better at stating the proposition of a mutually constituted history between Britain and the empire than executing it'.[15] Likewise, Andrew Thompson accused postcolonial theorists of 'failing to deconstruct the European "centre" in the way it has so successfully deconstructed the extra-European "periphery"'. Indeed, he concluded from his own research that there is 'no big theory' that underpins imperialism, 'no uniform imperial impact, no joined-up monolithic ideology of imperialism, no single source of enthusiasm or propaganda for the empire'.[16]

A consistent trait in 'new imperial' history is an absence of *how* empire and imperial hegemony were constructed in British culture.[17] Thus we are left with little historical context or discussion on how imperial hegemony was constantly compromised and filtered through a variety of late nineteenth- and twentieth-century agencies. The lack of an empirical base from which to evaluate the influence of empire has led Bernard Porter to take issue with the notion that an imperial culture dominated society and particularly working people's lives between 1800 and 1940. He maintained that at the height of imperial fervour entrenched divisions in social class meant that there was no shared meaning of nation or empire. 'Out of separation arose a very different political culture (or cultures), with priorities and values of its own, which the imperialists were very unlikely to be able to penetrate.'[18] Porter argued that the 'new imperial' history or postcolonial work in particular lacked a sensitivity to historical contexts. In short Porter accused these historians of searching for imperial events and meanings at the expense of identifying the more mundane everyday experience of living in British society during the nineteenth and twentieth centuries. The accusation of uneven source selection and over-generalisation could, however, be levelled at Porter himself, whose evidence for the minuscule impact of imperial popular culture is largely drawn from working-class autobiographies from a variety of industrial and urban backgrounds. Moreover, *Absent-minded Imperialists* was so concerned in dismantling an argument that it does not present a model to replace it, something that Porter later acknowledged.[19]

Recent research, then, on the impact of imperialism has allowed assumptions of the hegonomic power of imperialism to become embedded in analyses of the metropole–periphery relationship, while those challenging 'new imperial histories' have immersed themselves in a wealth of primary evidence drawn from multifarious sources across Britain. This book adopts a rather different perspective through inves-

[4]

tigating how imperial ideas were disseminated through three urban communities between 1870 and 1939. It addresses recent calls to assess the social and cultural processes that went into the construction, diffusion and reception of an imperial culture in Britain.[20] The book focuses upon how a town's urban elite was a significant conduit of empire, while recognising that differing urban contexts were vital in shaping the imperial message in terms of its form, tone and reception in the larger community. In this sense, it is the book's intention to advance MacKenzie's recent observations that a four-nation approach to the British Empire is becoming an increasing necessity. He argues that 'simple bilateral metropole–periphery relations can no longer be sustained as a basis for analysis: empire constituted sets of multilateral relationships'.[21] This book takes this perspective further by examining the provincial town and how imperial ideas were filtered through a range of institutions, elites and urban popular culture.

The city and empire: research parameters

Analyses of the city, its institutions and the dissemination of citizenship during this period provide perhaps the most consistent test of whether an aggressive imperial culture impinged upon working people's daily urban lives between 1870 and 1939. Indeed, Robert Colls and Richard Rodger have shown that, in themselves, cities and towns added an extra dimension to social, cultural and economic relationships.[22] Historians of empire have begun to map out the way in which cities were interconnected socially, economically and politically and the part they played in an 'imperial system'.[23] Other essays have explored how imperialism imprinted indelible marks on city landscapes, architectures and cultures.[24] However, despite the city acting as a significant cultural conduit for dominant contemporary ideas, the relationship between the modern city, empire and its citizens has largely been neglected.[25] National discourse on the nature of civic life, particularly during the Edwardian period, was inevitably influenced by anxieties stemming from conditions at the heart of the British Empire. In examining the relationship between the city and empire, London, or, to put it more precisely, the East End, has dominated both contemporary and historical analysis. From the 1870s, social observers were concerned that the East End was devoid of any civic leadership and that squalid and degenerate conditions were effectively nurturing a human residuum. For imperialists, there was a danger that this social crisis would escalate into a crisis of empire in which urban 'inferior stock' would fail to compete in an era of 'national efficiency'.[26]

Given how the East End has dominated both contemporary and subsequent historiographical accounts of the pervasive influence of imperialism, this book focuses on three communities from the south, midlands and north of England. The case studies are drawn from England, rather than Britain, since the four nations had separate relationships with empire that developed distinct ethnic and sectarian engagements with the imperial project.[27] The three English cities or towns – Portsmouth, Coventry and Leeds – were chosen primarily for their contrasting civic, industrial and cultural identities and differing geographical locations.[28] The significant physical and cultural naval presence in Portsmouth ensured that its local economy and national portrayal were bound tightly to imperial grandeur.[29] Alongside the naval influence, the city possessed a strong civic culture and an increasingly important skilled working-class sector employed in the Royal Dockyard. If London was the heart of empire, Portsmouth was surely the imperial flagship since the city's architecture and street furniture had an unmistakable imperial imprint.[30] Coventry, on the other hand, had neither an obvious imperial identity nor a strong civic culture. Between 1870 and 1939, the city emerged as an industrial boom town owing to the bicycle and car trades that employed vast armies of migrant semi-skilled workers. This was a manufacturing town at the centre of the 'new' industries producing mass-consumer goods for domestic and imperial markets. In such circumstances, working-class affluence and consumerism rather than poverty were the chief characteristics of this city.[31] Finally, Leeds represents the older manufacturing city that was at the forefront of disseminating the civic ideal through architecture and schemes of social citizenship.[32] For some historians this civic identity was immersed in an imperial culture that counteracted the divisions of class and race within Leeds.[33] The city developed rapidly through the industrial revolution and built its manufacturing base and wealth on the dress trades and mechanical engineering.[34] Whereas 'new' workers and 'new' industries were the key features of Coventry, Leeds's industrial background fostered more 'traditional' working-class communities.[35] In addition, Leeds had a greater ethnic diversity than either Portsmouth or Coventry since the city accommodated a significant Eastern European Jewish community by 1914.[36]

These three cities drawn from the south, midlands and north exhibited contrasting civic and industrial contexts, and possessed a range of working-class communities with differing cultures and levels of affluence and poverty. Commentators and subsequent historians have linked a working-class celebration of empire to a variety of causal factors such as the cultures of skilled and conversely unskilled workers, the beginnings of mass consumerism, and civic and national leadership. The following chapters investigate whether, why and how an imperial culture was successfully transmitted by local and national agencies. They will explore whether we can talk of 'an imperial culture' and whether the imperial message was diffused and interpreted differently according to contrasting urban contexts.

In addressing the impact of imperialism on popular culture, this book draws on a consistent set of themes that influenced urban life between 1870 and 1939. As Simon Gunn has noted, the full consequences of urban modernity were not fully recognised until the second half of the nineteenth century when the city was reimagined through the promotion of civic culture and architecture. This book, then, investigates whether after 1870 imperial values became enmeshed with urban renewal and whether civic institutions imparted an imperial message to working communities.[37] In this respect, a town's civic elites' involvement in education, military recruitment and national celebrations provide an insight into the relationship between working people, the city and notions of patriotism, nation and empire. The urban elite, then, lay at the crux of the relationship between the city and Empire and so some clarification of its composition and definition is necessary.

In line with similar research on power and authority in towns during the nineteenth and twentieth centuries, this book defines urban elites as those individuals, from any social background, who held leadership positions in the key institutions in the town. Rick Trainor has noted that this approach avoids a narrow focus on one particular social class and instead widens the perspective to explore how authority was exercised in Victorian society.[38] Those cited as an urban elite, then, will have assumed leadership roles such as councillors, guardians, school board members and JPs. Moreover, both John Garrard and Trainor established that there was considerable overlap between municipal representatives and a town's social leaders in their respective studies of northern and midland industrial towns.[39] Garrard discovered that Rochdale, Bolton and Salford 'were each municipally presided over by men who substantially combined political, economic and social leadership', with local manufacturers and merchants comprising the largest occupational group.[40] Likewise, Andy Croll found that those involved in Merthyr's civic project were almost exclusively drawn from the ranks of the social elite.[41] This is not to assume that the urban elite was an homogeneous social grouping with clear political or ideological positions. While town councils in the late nineteenth century typically exhibited little political divide or clear political mandate, specific civic initiatives did often divide the civic elite into 'progressives' and 'economic' factions.[42] Furthermore, by the early twentieth century, representatives of labour organisations were joining the ranks of the urban elite through election to councils and local boards.

Historians have also arrived at a broad consensus on the key periods in which there were significant shifts in the social composition of urban elites between 1830 and 1939. Garrard, and F.M.L. Thompson have noted that the upper middle class, the municipal leaders of the early nineteenth century, took flight from civic responsibilities from around the 1870s. According to Thompson, 'leadership of the work-town then passed by default to those who lived there at the time: the local builders, traders [and] shopkeepers'.[43] From the 1870s through to the interwar period, British local government was the stronghold of small businessmen and shopkeepers, who, in certain regions after the First World War, vied for power with an emerging labour movement.[44] This national trend resembles the composition of the urban elite in the three case study communities. While Coventry and Leeds attracted a scattering of powerful manufacturers to the Council, the urban elite in the three towns were dominated by a 'shopocracy' of small local tradesmen.[45]

The urban elites' involvement and response to civic projects were further complicated by the role of the local press, which often championed the civic cause but was not slow to criticise the town's population or indeed the urban elite if they failed to embrace the civic ethos.[46] Undoubtedly, then, the press was the main conduit for the diffusion of the civic message.[47] Conversely, during this period in which there was mass education and literacy, newspapers were concerned to capture popular opinion and so the readership had some influence over newspaper coverage through published letters and their ultimate sanction – their purchasing power.[48]

Themes and sources

The urban community provides the framework from which to assess the flow of imperial ideas, sentiment and propaganda. However, while urban elites were adept in disseminating their ideas through urban institutions and the local press, popular reactions and receptions to the imperial message are, of course, more difficult to fathom. However, the analysis of civic institutions, work and leisure patterns can provide an insight into the relationship between working people and empire. Provincial newspapers, trade directories and the periodical press during this period offer detailed accounts of civic and national issues, events and rituals. While working people were often not party to writing these accounts, their numbers and significantly *behaviour* at events such as Mafeking or Empire Day celebrations were recorded. Indeed, this book argues that, alongside a head count at civic and national celebrations, the crowd's behaviour and engagement with an event can provide a clue to the acceptance or otherwise of the imperial message. Together with the national and local press, other key sources include extant oral histories, autobiographies and contemporary literature on citizenship, empire and the urban landscape.

Finally, the book presents a consistent thematic analysis of these three urban communities through examining popular responses to empire. These themes were selected for their long historiographical pedigree and their capacity to gain an insight into how imperial ideas were filtered through an urban setting. Chapters 1 and 2 deal with the socio-cultural and political contexts of the three urban communities and ask whether the questions raised by contemporaries about the East End's imperial decline and degeneration had any currency in the provincial towns of England. Did the shock of urban degeneration and its social-Darwinist connotations radiate from the 'Heart of Empire' or were provincial towns consumed with more pressing matters? These chapters assess the formation of civic identities and how or whether imperial ideas became enmeshed in their construction. Chapters 3 and 4 explore the local and imperial nexus and whether imperial wars in the far reaches of the Empire were translated into tangible localised issues. Here we shall examine the role of volunteerism and patriotism through two important conflicts – the Boer War and the First World War. It is shown that the social and political turmoil of the Edwardian period placed strains on the civic project that in turn weakened working-class patriotism at both a local and an imperial level. Chapters 5 and 6 explore the complexities of propagating an imperial message through schooling and national institutions or events such as Empire Day, public radio broadcasts and the 1924 Wembley Exhibition of Empire. Pressing local anxieties, the role of teaching staff and how national events were filtered through local elites and presented to the public are examined. Finally, Chapter 7 focuses on the changing face of popular leisure between 1870 and 1939. It considers how music hall, theatre and cinema entered differing phases of engagement with the imperial message and whether societies advocating empire commanded popular support. Of crucial importance here is whether overtly imperial entertainment was absorbed by an eager audience and appropriated in more informal popular celebrations on the main thoroughfares of the three communities under consideration.

Notes

1 *Hampshire Telegraph*, 10 November 1900.
2 The navy had, by the Edwardian age, come to symbolise Britain's imperial strength; see M.A. Conley, *From Jack Tar to Union Jack. Representing Naval Manhood in the British Empire, 1870–1918* (Manchester, Manchester University Press, 2009), ch. 1.
3 See my analysis of the 'new imperial' history below.
4 R. Colls and R. Rodger, *Cities of Ideas: Civil Society and Urban Governance in Britain 1800–2000. Essays in Honour of David Reader* (Aldershot, Ashgate, 2004), p. 1.
5 J.M. MacKenzie, *Propaganda and Empire* (Manchester, Manchester University Press, 1986); J.M MacKenzie (ed.), *Imperialism and Popular Culture* (Manchester, Manchester University Press, 1984); C. Hall (ed.), *Cultures of Empire. Colonizers in Britain and the Empire in the Nineteenth and Twentieth Centuries: A Reader* (Manchester, Manchester University Press, 2000); J. Richards, *Imperialism and Music. Britain 1876–1953* (Manchester, Manchester University Press, 2001).
6 R. Price, *An Imperial War and the British Working Class. Working-class Attitudes and Reactions to the Boer War* (London, Routledge, 1972), p. 216.
7 B. Porter, *Absent Minded Imperialists. Empire, Society and Culture in Britain* (Oxford, Oxford University Press, 2004, 2006 edn), p. 216; A. August, *The British Working Class 1832–1940* (Harlow, Longman, 2007), p. 151.
8 MacKenzie, *Propaganda and Empire*, pp. 61–2.
9 S.M. Miller, *Volunteers on the Veld. Britain's Citizen Soldiers and the South African War, 1899–1902* (Norman, Oklahoma Press, 2007), p. 22.
10 Richards, *Imperialism and Music*.
11 Price, *An Imperial War and the British Working Class*.
12 E. Said, *Culture and Imperialism* (London, Vintage, 1993). See for example, G. Russell, 'Entertainment of Oddities', in K. Wilson (ed.), *A New Imperial History: Culture, Identity and Modernity in Britain and Empire 1660–1849* (Cambridge, Cambridge University Press, 2004), pp. 48–70.
13 A. Burton, 'Who Needs Nation? Interrogating "British" History', *Journal of Historical Sociology*, 10, 3, September 1997, pp. 229, 231.
14 J. Thompson, 'Modern Britain and the New Imperial History', *History Compass*, 5, 2, 2007, p. 459.
15 R. Price, 'One Big Thing: Britain, Its Empire and Their Imperial Culture', *Journal of British Studies*, 45, July 2006, p. 603.
16 A. Thompson, *The Empire Strikes Back? The Impact of Imperialism on Britain from the Mid-nineteenth Century* (Harlow, Longman, 2005), pp. 241–2.
17 Price, 'One Big Thing: Britain, Its Empire and Their Imperial Culture', p. 610.
18 Porter, *Absent minded Imperialists*, p. 224.
19 B. Porter, 'Further Thoughts on Imperial Absent Mindedness', *Journal of Imperial and Commonwealth History*, 36, 1, March 2008, p. 103.
20 Quoted in Porter, 'Further Thoughts on Imperial Absent Mindedness', p. 110.
21 J.M. MacKenzie, 'Irish, Scottish, Welsh and English Worlds? A Four-nation Approach to the History of the British Empire', *History Compass*, 6, 5, 2008, p. 1224.
22 It has been shown that cities and towns themselves added an extra dimension to social and economic relationships; see Colls and Rodger, *Cities of Ideas*, p. 1.
23 S. Haggerty, A. Webster and N.J. White (eds), *Empire in One City? Liverpool's Inconvenient Imperial Past* (Manchester, Manchester University Press, 2008).
24 F. Driver and D. Gilbert (ed.), *Imperial Cities* (Manchester, Manchester University Press, 2003).
25 Driver and Gilbert, *Imperial Cities*, p. 4.
26 To some extent this contemporary view has been taken up uncritically by subsequent historians; see M. Brodie, *Politics of the Poor: The East End of London 1885–1914* (Oxford, Clarendon Press, 2004).

27 MacKenzie, 'Irish, Scottish, Welsh and English Worlds?', p. 1244. I was reminded of the sensitivities of this issue when giving a paper at the Social History Conference in Glasgow in 2010. Thank you to my Scottish colleagues who corrected my slippage between English and British when describing the nineteenth-century city.

28 By the end of the chronology of this book all three communities had gained city status. Coventry had become a city in 1345, Leeds in 1893 and Portsmouth in 1926.

29 J. Field, 'Wealth, Styles of Life and Social Tone amongst Portsmouth's Middle Class 1800–75', in R.J. Morris (ed.), Class, Power and Social Structure in British Nineteenth Century Towns (Leicester, Leicester University Press, 1986).

30 K. Lunn and R. Thomas, 'Naval Imperialism in Portsmouth, 1905–1914', Southern History, 10, 1988.

31 B. Beaven, Leisure, Citizenship and Working-class Men in Britain, 1850–1945 (Manchester, Manchester University Press, 2005), p. 2.

32 R.J. Morris, Class, Sect and Party. The Making of the British Middle Class, Leeds 1820–1850 (Manchester, Manchester University Press, 1990).

33 E.D. Steele, 'Imperialism and Leeds, c. 1850–1914', in D. Fraser (ed.), A History of Modern Leeds (Manchester, Manchester University Press, 1980), p. 327.

34 S. Gunn, The Public Culture of the Victorian Middle Class. Ritual and Authority and the English Industrial City, 1840–1914 (Manchester, Manchester University Press, 2000), p. 12.

35 R. Hoggart, The Uses of Literacy (Harmondsworth, Penguin, 1957).

36 J. Buckman, Immigrants and the Class Struggle. The Jewish Immigration in Leeds, 1880–1914 (Manchester, Manchester University Press, 1983).

37 Gunn, The Public Culture of the Victorian Middle Class, p. 37.

38 R.H. Trainor, Black Country Elites. The Exercise of Authority in an Industrialized Area 1830–1900 (Oxford, Clarendon Press, 1993), p. 18.

39 J. Garrard, Leadership and Power in Victorian Industrial Towns, 1830–80 (Manchester, University Press, 1983), 4; Trainor, Black Country Elites, p. 246.

40 Garrard, Leadership and Power in Victorian Industrial Towns, p. 4.

41 A. Croll, Civilizing the Urban. Popular Culture and Public Space in Merthyr c. 1870–1914 (Cardiff, University of Wales, 2000), p. 5.

42 Garrard, Leadership and Power in Victorian Industrial Towns, p. 82; F.W. Carr, 'Engineering Workers and the Rise of Labour, 1914–1939' (PhD thesis, University of Warwick, 1978), p. 18.

43 F.M.L. Thompson, 'Town and City', in F.M.L. Thompson (ed.), The Cambridge Social History of Britain 1750–1950, 3 vols (Cambridge, Cambridge University Press, 1990), vol. 1, p. 47.

44 Thompson, 'Town and City', p. 72; J.K. Walton, 'The North West', in F.M.L. Thompson (ed.), The Cambridge Social History of Britain 1750–1950, 3 vols (Cambridge, Cambridge University Press, 1990), vol. 1, p. 410.

45 B. Beaven, 'Challenges to Civic Governance in Post-war England: the Peace Day Disturbances of 1919', Urban History, 33, 3, 2006, p. 376; V. Fulder, 'Space, Civic Pride, Citizenship and Identity in 1890s Portsmouth' (unpublished PhD thesis, University of Portsmouth, 2006), p. 58; Steele, 'Imperialism and Leeds Politics, c. 1850–1914', p. 327.

46 Garrard, Leadership and Power in Victorian Industrial Towns, pp. 27–31.

47 Croll, Civilizing the Urban, p. 43.

48 For a full analysis of the newspaper in the three communities see Chapter 1.

CHAPTER ONE

Cities in context: civic culture, 'New Journalism' and the creation of localised imperial identities, 1870–1939

In 1907, Lord Curzon, one of the leading imperialists of his day, visited Birmingham to deliver a speech on the spirit of empire and the moral basis for imperialism. Birmingham, which thanks to Joseph Chamberlain possessed impeccable imperial credentials, was in many ways a natural setting from which to outline the meaning of empire. However, the decision to speak from a provincial town hall had a deeper symbolic resonance in a society that had invested heavily in celebrating civic culture towards the end of the nineteenth century. According to Curzon, a town hall was 'almost the central altar of the British democracy' as there was no better place to address his countrymen on 'what it was that Empire meant, in what sense it was vital to them, why it ought to be deep in their hearts and fervent, though never boastful, on their tongue'.[1] The emergence of monumental buildings fostering a civic culture and identity was perceived by some contemporaries as the ideal conduit in shaping the exemplary citizen in the modern city. For imperialists like Curzon, the dissemination of civic culture was also a convenient conduit for the imperial message. Indeed, historians have argued that, by 1900, the English city was awash with imperial sentiment. Jonathon Schneer asserted that 'because London was the seat of a great empire, imperial markers were everywhere' and that 'imperial themes and messages saturated daily life'.[2] If London was the undisputed heart of the British Empire, Glasgow had bestowed upon itself the title of the 'Second City of Empire'. John MacKenzie noted that by 1900 contemporaries began using the 'Second City' title which represented attempts to weld 'its disparate population into a specifically civic and imperial identity'.[3] Other studies have downplayed the uniqueness of London and Glasgow and stressed that major British cities operated within an 'imperial system'. Sheryllyne Haggerty and others have argued that Liverpool's imperial past was not exceptional but was part of an urban network 'working both commercially and politically in collaboration with other cities in Britain and the empire'.[4] By investigating, as far as we can, the ebb and flow of daily life in Portsmouth, Coventry and Leeds, this book endeavours to identify the diffusion of and engagement with imperial values within the three communities. The late Victorian era proved a critical period for urban elites' attempts in establishing a sense of civic identity. Supported by an enthusiastic local press, rebuilding schemes created civic spaces while public displays and rituals were reinvented to accompany and legitimise this 'civic gospel'.[5] These civic initiatives occurred when towns and cities were undergoing unprecedented demographic growth and political changes, and when imperial grandeur was at its height. As we shall see, an exploration of local contexts is paramount since they determined the degree to which empire permeated the urban elites' narrative of their community's civic identity.

Demographic and industrial change

On one level the three towns, despite their southern, midland and northern locations in England, experienced similar demographic pressures, political patterns and civic questions. The striking feature of the period 1851 to 1911 was the rapid population growth that stretched these medium-sized communities to their limits. In Leeds the population recorded in the census increased from 172,270 in 1851 to 445,550 in 1911 while similar increases over the same period were experienced in Coventry, from 48,120 to 117,985, and Portsmouth, from 72,096 to 188,123.[6] The tripling of Portsmouth's population figures must be taken with some caution since the presence in the town of the extensive military personnel complicates assessments of the town's actual growth in size.

The doubling of Coventry's population was largely due to the establishment of the bicycle and motor industries in the city from the 1870s. The number of cycle firms increased from 16 in 1881 to 70 by the mid-1890s, employing over four thousand workers.[7] Bicycle and motor car production was essentially assembly work and required semi-skilled labour and, consequently, by 1914 Coventry had become a magnet for the young semi-skilled male worker migrating from the midlands and the south-east of England.[8] Originally, the cycle workers' factories and housing were confined to the Gosfort Street area in the heart of the city because of lands owned by Freeman which surrounded the north-west and west side of Coventry.[9] However, the cycle and motor industry's expansion before the First World War saw large concentrations of workers and firms spreading to the surrounding districts of Stoke, Radford and Foleshill.[10] Furthermore, work in cycle and motor industries was reasonably well paid, ensuring that Coventry was awash with relatively affluent young male workers.[11] The *Coventry Herald* noted that

> No midland town has grown so rapidly as Coventry has in the course of two years . . . there is an air of prosperity about local life which was not formerly expressed. Wealth increases among the general of the inhabit- ants and there is ample proof in the receipts of the savings banks that the careful artisan can put money by.[12]

While stopping short of building a new civc centre, the formation of new neighbourhoods and the rapid transformation of Coventry's social structure led the urban elite to initiate schemes of social citizenship in a bid to encourage a sense of civic identity among the new migrants. Indeed, social commentators in the city were quite aware that a young, relatively affluent and transient workforce may well have exhibited little in the way of civic, national and imperial pride. Thus as we shall see, the notion of civic pride was often conceived within a broader framework of devotion to empire.[13]

In Portsmouth, a comparable population increase triggered similar responses by the town's civic elite. The town comprised three inter- locking communities. The middle-class enclave of Southsea, with its large villas and high-class shops, made for a stark contrast to Landport, an area that surrounded the dockyard and suffered severe social and economic deprivation. While casual dockyard workers often resided in Landport, the skilled artisans, such as shipwrights, began settling in the new and expanding eastern and northern districts of the town such as Eastney and Kingston. It was these relatively newly enfranchised workers that both politicians and the local press were keen to influ- ence.[14] The expansion of the dockyard had largely been responsible for Portsmouth's population growth. By 1901, the dockyard employed almost eight thousand workers, representing 53 per cent of all male industrial workers in Portsmouth.[15] Not only was a large proportion of the population dependent on the navy but the town's physical envi- ronment was unmistakably stamped with a military character. By the mid-1870s, the dockyard occupied over 300 acres of the west side of Portsmouth while the 1901 census recorded that over seven thousand men were stationed in army barracks or navy ships in the harbour.[16] The main thoroughfares through Landport were, as E.S. Washington noted, 'full night and day of men in naval uniform', while 'many large barracks with parade grounds were constant reminders of the naval and military presence in the town'.[17]

While Coventry and Portsmouth's population increases were largely due to migration internal to Britain, in Leeds the populace grew significantly through the immigration of Jews from Eastern Europe. Leeds had long enjoyed a tradition of manufacturing, with the woollen industries dominating its economy in the eighteenth and early nineteenth centuries. However between 1850 and 1911, the woollen trade was usurped by the clothing and footwear industries and it was these semi-skilled mass-production trades that principally attracted Eastern European Jews to Leeds. Jews migrated to Leeds setting up clothing businesses or providing the labour for the new factories and sweat shops that began emerging in the Leylands region of the town.[18] While there had been an established Jewish community in Leeds dating back to the eighteenth century, the most important immigration occurred after 1881, when Jews fled the Russian pogroms. The *Lancet* noted that 'the greater part came from the province of Knovo; and at starting they are often acquainted with but one word of English, and that word is Leeds', adding that 'the name of Leeds was a modern term for an El Dorado'.[19] The eastern European Jews were concentrated in the Leylands district where in some streets 85 per cent of the residents were Jewish. Despite the government's restrictions on immigration imposed in 1905, the six thousand foreign-born Jews in 1891 had increased to approximately fifteen thousand on the eve of the First World War, representing about 12 per cent of the Leeds population.[20] The Leylands district's rapid population growth aggravated the already poor sanitary conditions and the area became relatively cut off, materially and culturally, from the city centre. The Leylands district became regarded by contemporaries as the 'Other', raising concerns among the urban elite that 'civilising' influences of the town hall were failing to penetrate the parts of Leeds that needed it most. In an ironic twist, Eastern European Jews had escaped from one ghetto to reside in another in Leeds.[21] The rapid influx of Eastern European Jews marked an important difference from the population rises in Portsmouth and Coventry and had a profound impact upon how the civic elite in Leeds engaged with matters of empire. Convinced that the Eastern European Jews lacked a sense of patriotism, the civic elite and local press ensured that the Jewish community's commitment to the British Empire became a point of contention in local discourse at points of imperial crises.

National and municipal political patterns

In investigating political patterns in the late nineteenth and early twentieth centuries, a number of historians have confidently claimed that formal political movements not only set imperial agendas but also cultivated a degree of social and cultural harmony in English society. E.D. Steele has argued that

> Imperialism, understood as an amalgam of interests and sentiment, of trade, politics and religion, bolstered the hegemony of the urban patriciate by counteracting the divisions of class, sect and race within Leeds. Moreover, in Leeds as elsewhere, empire deeply affected the entire local community's relationship with the historic rulers of the nation, the landed class, whose primacy proved so enduring.[22]

These are bold claims that are largely drawn from political speeches, biographies and formal political movements. Steele offers little in the way of specific examples of *how* imperialism created greater social cohesion, relying instead on the language and tone of political speeches and manifestos. Here we adopt an alternative approach which understands formal municipal and national political patterns as contexts to an investigation on the relationship between popular culture and empire in local communities.

There can be little doubt that most local political leaders in Portsmouth, Coventry and Leeds employed rhetoric that stressed their own community's strong links to nation and empire. Clearly in Portsmouth, the home of the Empire's navy, councillors and MPs had the easier task of demonstrating the town's contribution to the imperial cause. A succession of Tory candidates from the 1880s had 'played the imperial card', linking British naval supremacy with a strong and growing empire. In 1906, for example, the independent Fred T. Jane, author of *Jane's Fighting Ships*, stood as a 'Naval Interest' candidate. The *Hampshire Telegraph* noted Jane's insistence that 'the maintenance of the navy at full strength was the only way Portsmouth could be kept going. In seeking election he appealed for votes to all who manned our ships, or built our ships or lived by providing for those who did.'[23] In 1910, the nationally recognised Admiral Charles Beresford successfully took the seat for the Conservatives in January and retained it in the December election of the same year.[24] After the First World War, the importance of the navy did not dominate election campaigns as it had done earlier, though the Conservatives continued to select national naval figures for candidates during the interwar period. Interestingly, while the Liberals had tended to favour local professionals to stand for Parliament, the Labour Party was also willing to select naval candidates. For example in 1923 and 1931, Labour selected a Brigadier-General and a Rear Admiral in a bid to gain support from the dockyard worker.[25]

In Leeds, Steele noted a consensus over the importance of empire but differences between Tories and Liberals over the ways and means of promoting it. Not surprisingly given Leeds's manufacturing base, controversy centred on tariff reform and empire. The increasing international competition of the Edwardian period, and the general anxieties surrounding the future of the British Empire, placed pressure on the Liberals' campaign to retain a free trade, policy. The local Liberal MP James Kitson, while acknowledging that his own business interests had suffered through international competition, maintained that imperial tariff walls would damage the town's trade. Kitson cited the Argentine purchase of Leeds-built locomotives as an example of the virtue of free trade, claiming that 'the Argentine was practically keeping . . . some workshops going'. Once again, the navy proved an imperial badge of honour since, when Leeds Tories derided their opponent's lack of imperial enthusiasm, the local Liberals boasted that Lloyd George's 1909 budget made ample provision for an enlarged navy programme.[26] The belief that the navy and empire would elicit votes from the general public was evident across the political spectrum. In 1906, James O'Grady, Leeds's first Labour MP, declared in a debate on the navy in the House of Commons that 'I have not a word to say against the expansion of empire and the acquisition of overseas markets.'[27]

Political discourse during general elections in Coventry mirrored that of Leeds, with empire and particularly the navy figuring prior to the First World War. For example, the Liberal A.E.W. Mason, author of the highly successful imperial novel *The Four Feathers*, brought a colourful vision of empire to the local electorate while his radical Liberal successor David Mason (no relation) courted controversy with his criticism of militarism and empire building.[28] The naval expansion programme was brought directly into focus in Coventry when David Mason declared that he was opposed to naval rearmament, siding with the pacifist movement. From his election in 1910, the Conservative local press played upon Mason's pacifism and stoked up much resentment towards the sitting MP. In August 1914, the *Coventry Graphic* pointed out that Coventry had close associations with the navy as one of Coventry's key munitions factories relied on naval orders and had recently produced the largest ever gun to emerge from the city, weighing 100 tons.[29] The issue of free trade also haunted the Liberals and Labour parties in the interwar period when the Conservative protectionist candidate Sir Archibald Boyd-Carpenter successfully campaigned against Labour's removal of the McKenna duties in the 1920s. These McKenna duties effectively protected the British motor industry from foreign competition and it was widely reported that their permanent removal would have had dire consequences for Coventry firms.[30] Unlike in Leeds, however, parties of all persuasions in Coventry tended to recruit candidates from beyond the city. Possibly owing to a weaker municipal culture than Leeds and a smaller pool of middle-class professions connected with the city, candidates were almost all national

[17]

career politicians from a range of professional backgrounds including authors, journalists, merchant bankers and academics.[31]

Given these contrasting urban and political contexts, we must move on to consider their impact upon voting patterns in Portsmouth, Coventry and Leeds. Politicians and the national media had little doubt on the impact of the Royal Dockyard's influence over workers' voting preferences. By the 1880s, dockyard workers were considered to have harboured 'war-like traits'. One Liberal-leaning article in the *Fraser's Magazine* declared that

> among the boroughs Portsmouth was pre-eminently warlike, and it was reported from more than one of the other dockyard towns that, while the towns-folk were favourable to peace, the men in the yards could not be trusted, as there was a natural impression that war brought work into the yards.

Indeed, royal dockyard towns in general were dismissed as wanting 'gunpowder' and militarism with little hope of returning a Liberal MP.[32] The Liberal newspaper the *Hampshire Telegraph* responded by pointing out that, although a Conservative MP was returned in the 1880 election, his majority had been reduced by over half and that

> It is beyond dispute that at the recent election the Dockyard vote in this town was given largely in favour of the Liberal candidates. No doubt the Services stood by the 'gunpowder and glory' policy, as in truth they were bound to do; but where political considerations had free play it is unquestionable that a very large Liberal vote was cast.[33]

Significantly, then, the *Hampshire Telegraph* drew an important distinction between the voting habits of the military personnel and the dockyard workers. However, by the early twentieth century, Liberal and Labour candidates often strayed beyond party lines to curry favour with the dockyard workers. In 1909, the Labour Party condemned Chatham dockyard workers for 'combining self-interest with patriotism' and compelling their Labour representative to attack the government for reducing munitions work, a demand that contravened Labour policy. The prominent Labour MP Will Thorne was so incensed that he vowed never to represent a dockyard constituency as it would have compromised his socialist principles.[34] Nevertheless, it would be misleading to assume that Portsmouth's dockyard workers exhibited jingoism and naturally fell into the Tory fold. After one bitter defeat in 1895, the losing Tory Candidate Evelyn Ashley complained that

> Elections were now swayed by a dense mass of Dockyard men and dwellers in the northern portion of the town to whom politics and imperial considerations and even their own self-interest, were as nothing com-

pared with their socialistic and unreasoning hatred of everything that, rightly or wrongly, they considered superior to themselves either in position or intelligence.[35]

Clearly, the aristocrat Ashley had difficulty coming to terms with a mass electorate but his observations of the capricious nature of dockyard workers' voting habits suggests that a good proportion did not have strong political allegiances. Indeed, the town's voting patterns did not stray far from the national trend throughout the late nineteenth and early twentieth centuries. G.J. Ashworth has noted that, although Portsmouth followed national patterns, the most noticeable feature of the town's parliamentary seats was their overall volatility. For example, while the Conservatives nationally lost approximately 7 per cent of their vote in the 1906 election, Portsmouth Conservatives experienced a loss of 23 per cent. However, in the following 1910 election, the Conservative's national gain of 3 per cent, contrasted with an impressive 24 per cent gain in Portsmouth. Ashworth concluded that while naval issues might account for the size of majorities in the town, 'in no case, however, can it be demonstrated that local issues generated a swing against the national trend'.[36]

Coventry had a long tradition of parliamentary representation courtesy of an Elizabethan Act that secured the city's apprenticed freemen the franchise. Thus, unusually, Coventry's artisans had been part of the political process from the early modern era.[37] The 1867 Reform Act extended the franchise to £7 householders which had the effect of doubling Coventry's electorate from around four thousand to almost eight thousand voters and ensured that the respectable artisan was in the preponderance.[38] The politicisation of artisans helped foster a vibrant and partisan local press and, with only one parliamentary seat in the city, political rivalry sometimes spilled over into violence. Until the First World War, the seat oscillated between the Tories and Liberals.[39] As with Portsmouth, Coventry parliamentary elections mirrored national trends which saw the rise of Labour Party at the expense of the Liberals after 1914. With only one seat, however, the splitting of the traditional Liberal base secured victory for the Conservatives in five of the seven elections between 1918 and 1935. Labour took the seat on the two other occasions, following national trends and winning the seat in 1923 and 1929.[40]

In Leeds, voting patterns appear to have been less volatile, almost certainly owing to the distinct and less socially heterogeneous constituencies. Arthur Taylor noted that 'Leeds in 1914 was no less two cities than England was two nations'.[41] The 1867 Reform Act increased the town's electorate fivefold, ensuring that working-class voters dominated the political landscape providing the basis for Liberal ascendancy until the First World War. The Liberal Party had enjoyed a long tradition in Leeds and this was set to continue into the early twentieth century. On a national level, Leeds ousted Birmingham as the official focal point for Liberalism in Britain when in 1883 the local manufacturer Sir James Kitson assumed chairmanship of the National Liberal Federation. By 1885, the town had five seats with the three in the south's solid working-class areas consistently returning Liberal MPs.[42] The Leeds Liberal Party operated a flexible approach to the electorate, campaigning for welfare reforms in its working-class constituencies and dissent and free trade in the middle-class northern districts. Nevertheless, the Liberal Party dramatically declined after the First World War since voters in the southern constituencies switched their allegiance to the Labour Party while Leeds North became a firmly Conservative ward throughout the interwar period.[43]

Celebration of local identity: the construction of civic space and monuments

If the pattern of parliamentary political discourse and election results largely reflected national trends in Portsmouth, Leeds and Coventry, there were notable differences in three communities' civic culture. The Liberal traditions in Leeds made for a vibrant civic culture that was embodied in monumental buildings that had been built from the mid-nineteenth century. The celebrated Town Hall, built in 1858, was the first of an array of impressive municipal buildings such as the reference and public library in 1871–72 and the Art Gallery in 1888.[44] The new Town Hall contained the council and law courts and was used for public meetings and festivals, and surrounding buildings were gradually cleared to create the sense of a dedicated civic space or centre.[45] In 1905, the installation of a statue of the late Queen Victoria gave the civic authorities an opportunity not only to demonstrate the town's loyalty to the crown but also to confirm the Town Hall as the principal civic space in the city. Rejecting the offer to contribute to a national monument in London, the Leeds Council elected to commission a statue of its own. The *Leeds and Yorkshire Mercury* proclaimed that the event confirmed that 'Leeds is fast evolving an artistic atmosphere' while Councillor Lawson, chairman of the Memorial Committee, boasted that 'there is no other statute like it in Great Britain'.[46] Simon Gunn persuasively argued that 'the centre was progressively emptied of population and recreated as a monumental, moral and aesthetic space and a site of consumption and spectacle'. While separate from the hustle and bustle of town life, the civic space was designed to symbolise a unity that would cultivate a bond with the city's growing periphery.[47]

The creation in Leeds of new civic spaces defined by municipal buildings, statues and monuments was part of a national trend within English cities of separating the civic from commerce and industry.[48] In Portsmouth, the completion of a new Town Hall and civic square represented attempts to establish an identifiable centre and an alternative space and power base to the Admiralty that owned much of the land on the west side of Portsmouth. The original Town Hall in Old Portsmouth was considered too small and too close to the dockyard and an inadequate symbol for the unification of the differing but interlocking districts of Portsmouth. On the day the new Town Hall was opened, the *Evening News* observed that 'one by one the old institutions of Portsmouth have gravitated towards the centre of the borough at Landport'.[49] However, the Town Hall was not merely built for its more convenient central position. A significant driving force behind the project was the desire to forge a new dynamic relationship between the urban elite and the people. William Gates, the editor of the *Evening News*, noted that

> those who have visited the midlands, who have lived in Leeds, Manchester, Bolton and other great industrial centres where the masses are most considered and vehemently assert their right to consideration, cannot fail to have been struck by the magnificent buildings in which the municipalities conduct their business.[50]

Viv Fulda has recently argued that Portsmouth's Town Hall was 'placed in a newly created centre of the town, a space that belonged to the municipal' and that it was designed as a 'symbol of unity'.[51] Indeed, Sir William King, the Mayor, proclaimed that the Town Hall had removed 'all divisions' and that 'there was now no Portsea, no Landport, no Kingston, no Buckland – only the grand town of Portsmouth'.[52] Portsmouth's pivotal role in the defence of the Empire offered another important justification for its construction. William Gates informed readers that the decision to build a new hall was vindicated on the grounds that Portsmouth was the gateway to the empire and regularly hosted leading colonial subjects and foreign dignitaries. Gates claimed that Portsmouth's 'dockyard attracts, as if by a magnet, the leading men of other nations. No eminent foreigner who visits our shores feels that he has seen England if he does not visit Portsmouth.'[53] In 1903, this new space in Portsmouth was confirmed as the civic and imperial hub of Portsmouth with the erection of the statue of Queen Victoria, the Empress of India, close to the Town Hall.[54]

During the late nineteenth and early twentieth centuries, Coventry's urban elite were dominated by 'economistic' councillors who were not prepared to preside over public investment into civic amenities. As a consequence, the city avoided any civic rivalry with its near neighbour Birmingham and refrained from committing funds to build a town hall.[55] The closest Coventry councillors came to constructing a monumental civic building before 1918 was the new Council House, built in a grand gothic style between 1913 and 1917. However, controversy surround this development as the fiscally conscious councillors had their first plan of including shops on the ground floor to generate income rejected by President of the Local Government Board for being 'unworthy of Coventry'.[56] Moreover, this building was essentially a place of council business and not the public space, such as a town hall, museum or art gallery, where the residents of Coventry could be drawn into the civic ideal. It was not until the interwar period, when Coventry's medieval streets were unable to cope with the increased population, traffic and workshops, that Councillors began to embrace broader municipal schemes. By 1937, an array of narrow thoroughfares into the city were cleared to make way for Corporation Street and Trinity Street, two major roads that became the main arteries to the city centre.[57] Alongside this public investment, attempts were made to promote a cultural heritage and energise a civic spirit. The City Guild, a group of young architects, worked with the Council on plans to build a civic centre complete with museum and art gallery.[58] Such was the renewed interest in civic patriotism that the Council established a committee to promote it and gave the *Coventry Herald* an opportunity to define its meaning:

> An honest pride in the town of one's birth or adoption, a determination to speak well of it, an inclination to do our best to forward good government, if not personally, at least by helping to secure the best men and the best methods to bring this about, and last but not least, by personal service.[59]

Unfortunately, Coventry Council's belated attempt to construct both a physical and a cultural edifice to celebrate civic identity was out of step with the changing social nature of urban leadership. Whereas the Victorian industrial leaders were often based locally and engaged in civic initiatives, the emergence of large company takeovers of the 1930s saw a preponderance of a managerial class of business leaders with little interest in local affairs.[60] The *Coventry Herald* lamented that

> It demands the best brains of the community, and it is regrettable to find not only in Coventry but elsewhere, that leaders in the industry, who

have so much at stake in the matter, are generally disinclined to shoulder the burden of municipal responsibility.[61]

Although very little came of Coventry's Local Patriotism Committee its definition of 'local patriotism' and celebration of local identities helps us gain an insight into how local government and the press attempted to make sense of the significant demographic change that cities like Coventry experienced during the interwar period.

The celebration of local identity: civic ritual and becoming cities in the age of empire

The belief that a community could positively project itself through municipal works and civic culture had become adopted by progressive local councillors as a riposte to the bleak view of urban degeneration that had been propagated by novels, parliamentary enquiries and socio-religious pamphlets from the 1870s. Thus John Griffiths has argued that in 'reviving ancient notions of civic duty, citizens were supposed to interact with city institutions in the development of self'.[62] Thus, alongside the monumental buildings, civic ceremony was invented and employed to embody a public sense of identity and social position in the city. As Simon Gunn has noted, the public procession culture was very much a nineteenth-century phenomenon in which 'social groups and institutions staked their claim for a place in the social body of the town'.[63] The Victorian parade also exuded a sense of social hierarchy with the sequential order of the procession that gave a physical form to the urban elites' legitimacy and authority. The parade was also designed to engender a sense of inclusiveness by incorporating diverse social identities, though every effort was made to ensure that social hierarchy was not infringed. Moreover, the procession also sent clear signals to onlookers that certain groups or institutions not included in the procession were deemed to have no significant role in the social body or civic culture of the town.

In Portsmouth, the second half of the nineteenth century saw an increase in the number of Fleet Reviews and military parades. Significantly, by the 1880s these events had become transformed from purely military affairs to royal, imperial and public spectacles. Thus, between 1773 and 1887, there were only eight Royal Reviews in Portsmouth compared to 27 Royal or Fleet Reviews between 1888 and 1914.[64] The zenith of this public ceremony came with the *Dreadnought* launches in the Edwardian period when up to sixty thousand people witnessed a public spectacle that, according to one historian, 'expressed deep-seated authoritarian values'.[65] The civic leaders' desire to promote and

[23]

disseminate a civic culture, then, merged seamlessly with the late Victorian trend of treating the public to theatrical displays of military and imperial strength. The opening of the Town Hall in August 1890 was the first opportunity for the municipal authorities to impose a civic meaning on the military pageantry that was becoming commonplace in the town. Indeed, Portsmouth's familiarity with the public theatre of military parades provided a template for the event both for the organisers and spectators. Press reports indicate that the event was highly choreographed and tightly policed with clearly defined roles designated for the participants and the crowd. The Town Hall was opened by the Prince of Wales, who arrived in Portsmouth on the royal yacht at the Royal Dockyard. The order of the procession from the dockyard to the Town Hall represented the delicate balance of military and civic power in Portsmouth with the Admiralty leading the Prince from the dockyard to the Town Hall steps from where the Mayor assumed the leading role in the proceedings. This was a symbolic handing over of responsibility and power between the military and civil authorities and encapsulated the sometimes uneasy relationship between the urban elite and Admiralty. Given the imperial significance of the naval dockyard, civic leaders had little option but to embrace the town's naval heritage. This was recognised by Alderman Pink, who, at the banquet to celebrate the opening of the Hall, realised that, as the newspaper reported,

> While it would be futile to hold out a hope that Portsmouth would commercially rival Liverpool and other great centres of trade in the north, they could not forget the advantages conferred by the great position occupied by the town as the first naval port and as a great military centre. He rejoiced that the growth and prosperity of the Portsmouth were but a miniature of the growth and prosperity of the Empire.[66]

However, although civic leaders were keen to exploit the glories of empire and military pageantry, it was not to be at the expense of the town's civic identity and the recognition that the power in civic institutions rested with themselves.[67] Despite the guarded relationship between the civic authorities and the Admiralty, the Town Hall pageant resembled a well-drilled military parade viewed by a crowd familiar with Fleet Reviews and naval spectacles. The *Evening News* described the scene at the point when the procession left the dockyard:

> As the Dockyard gates were thrown open to allow the cavalcade to leave, an extraordinary spectacle presented itself. Dense crowds were assembled on Common Hard, whose enthusiastic cheering quite drowned the music of the military bands . . . Troops lined each side of the way right

from the Dockyard Gates, through Edinburgh-road to the Town Hall . . . A special feature was the perfect ease with which the authorities were able to enforce the regulations, which had been made with the sole view of making the pageant successful. At no point along the line of route was there anything like a hitch, and even at the points that the crowd was thickest the greatest good-humour prevailed.[68]

While Portsmouth's civic and military pageantry developed in a symbiotic fashion, municipal public spectacles in other provincial towns were still in their infancy in the 1880s.

Given that Leeds had developed a vibrant civic culture and built impressive municipal buildings from the 1850s, one might have assumed that by the late 1880s the urban elite would have had developed elaborate public displays on the scale seen in Portsmouth. However, a public celebration of the civic and efforts to align the town with the empire was surprisingly late in materialising. Leeds Town Hall was opened in 1858 by Queen Victoria and was marked by an elaborate ceremony *within* the Town Hall. Significantly the occasion was both organised and reported in a very different fashion from the Portsmouth celebration 32 years later. While the Portsmouth ceremony was designed as a public spectacle, the Leeds event was very much focused on the Queen and urban elites. There was no carefully constructed procession from the railway station to the Town Hall nor did the local press make any reference to the gathering crowds when the Queen entered the building. Only on the Queen's departure did the *Leeds Mercury* mention the 'cheering' general public that had been kept at some distance from the Town Hall. Indeed, since the ceremony was designed to facilitate the Queen's confirmation of the status, power and legitimacy of an urban civic elite, the spectators were viewed as little more than royal watchers.[69] Indeed, even by the mid-1880s, the urban elite had yet to draw Leeds's population into an organised and structured civic spectacle. This is still more surprising given the relentless pace and expenditure that had gone into constructing impressive municipal buildings for public use. In 1884, Leeds Town Council opened lavish municipal buildings housing meeting rooms, a public library and civic offices. However, the *Leeds Mercury* noted that prior to the opening of the Hall an observer 'would never have leaned from the dress and demeanour of passers-by that any unusual event was about to happen in our midst', adding that 'we English have a poor reception for ceremony'. The journalist complained that the crowd's part in the event was limited to viewing a procession of councillors since the actual ceremony took place within the Town Hall and municipal buildings. It may explain why only a 'modest' crowd assembled in which the 'rotund well-to-do' rubbed shoulders with 'loafers'. This, then, remained a 'civic' rather than a public event that continued to internalise ceremony and where the protocols of municipal ritual and the role and segregation of the crowd had yet to be routinely established. This understated approach to the opening of this grand municipal building was compounded by a rather shambolic speech by John Bower the Mayor. He stated that he was not aware that he was expected to make a speech until he arrived in the hall and read the official programme. The *Leeds Mercury* reported that:

> He had no indication as to the nature of the address expected of him and he hardly knew what to say to them. What he had to say would be of a very simple character. He had other duties to perform before he went to bed, and in all probability his strength would be severely taxed; therefore they would excuse him if he did not occupy their attention for any great length of time. There was nothing very special in connection with the history of Leeds. Its history was much the same as that of a large number of great manufacturing towns.[70]

Even in 1893, when Leeds achieved a city status, the celebrations and press coverage were rather muted. Advertisers capitalised on Leeds's new status, Brooke Bond Tea proclaimed 'three cheers for the city of Leeds, and one cheer for the cup that cheers!', but the newspapers covered the event rather more soberly.[71] The *Yorkshire Factory Times* declared that 'Leeds is at last a city but is no more civilised for that', while the *Leeds Daily News* also gave a matter-of-fact assessment of the status, free from the civic aggrandisement one might have expected:

> The new honour may not amount to much in a practical way. It will, as has been carefully pointed out, do little for the material advancement of the newly-fledged citizens. The whole thing is a matter of sentiment; and, fundamentally, there is still sentiment even in these days . . . And if the new honour has the effect, as it has in other newly-created cities, of making the inhabitants take a deeper interest in everything municipal, and if it raises the dignity and general tone of the Leeds Council and infuses something approaching public spirit into that body, then it will have accomplished something really valuable, even in a practical sense.[72]

However, despite these downbeat assessments of civic culture, between 1890 and 1900 public civic events multiplied in Leeds and were transformed from rather elite and functional affairs to elaborate public spectacles. For example, in 1894, the opening of a new hall in the Yorkshire College (later Leeds University) was an event sufficient to draw a procession of royalty and veterans of the Crimean War and Indian Mutiny. Significantly, it was carefully choreographed to parade through the main thoroughfares of Leeds, thereby drawing the people into a celebration both of the municipal and of soldiers from a former imperial adventure.[73]

While Coventry may have lacked grand civic monuments and a redesigned civic space prior to the Second World War, the city did have a rich tradition in public ceremony courtesy of the Godiva Pageant. The Godiva Pageant had begun as early as 1678 and continued largely on an annual basis until the mid-nineteenth century.[74] The annual processions were halted from the 1850s after sections of the clergy denounced the Pageant as a 'vile and monstrous show' in which the main attraction was a 'strumpet' on a horse.[75] Between 1862 and 1939, there were fewer than 15 processions, though there was a spate of pageants during the Edwardian period.[76] It was no coincidence that the Pageant was revived so regularly during this period since the Godiva procession was the most obvious attempt at promoting a local patriotism and social harmony through staging a lavish civic spectacle. The lead figures in the procession were the city's Mayor, Aldermen and senior councillors donning costumes to portray the city's connection with national and imperial history.[77] For example, in the 1919 procession leading councillors paraded as St George, who legend had it was born in the city, Charles II, George IV and Nelson. The procession comprised a clearly defined social stratum as following the Councillors were the Friendly Societies followed by representatives of the city's traditional artisanal trades. However, this essentially Victorian procession, with its associated social hierarchies, proved hopelessly dated immediately after the First World War as the Pageant was condemned as 'an absolute farce' by disgruntled munitions workers and unemployed soldiers in 1919.[78]

As we have seen, the clearance of residents from town centres for the construction of monuments and the celebration of the civic through ritual and procession occurred in all three towns to varying degrees. This civic space and monumental building was an unambiguous signal to the populace of where the power, culture and authority lay in a town. By the late nineteenth century, this civic space became increasingly used to celebrate events of empire, fusing both civic and imperial messages. For the civic elite, a direct association with empire could only strengthen their own authority and legitimacy within the town and nation generally. This was never so more apparent than during the second Boer War in which, for perhaps the first significant time, the civic arena was officially given over to matters of empire. As we shall see in Chapter 3, Portsmouth, Coventry and Leeds, to varying degrees, marked troop departures and returns, celebrated victories and commemorated the fallen through the official civic events. Moreover, these new civic buildings had become established in the minds of the populace since unofficial celebrations often spontaneously gathered at these recently constructed civic spaces.[79] Likewise, during the First World War, the civic and military spheres of influence in towns became blurred, particularly in Portsmouth where large army and naval bases dominated the west side of the town. To mark the end of the war, both the military and civic leaders hastily arranged a 'Portsmouth Pageant' comprising the civic elite, navy and army. Only eleven days after peace was officially declared, a civic and military procession was routed through the main thoroughfares of the town, ending symbolically at the Town Hall. At the head of the procession was positioned a captured German gun and the town's civic elite. The gun was deposited in the Town Hall Square where an estimated thirty thousand people had turned out, with 'children in great force'.[80] The *Hampshire Telegraph* reported that

> when comparative order had been gained, Major-General Douglas Smith said he had pleasure in handing over to the temporary custody of the Mayor the captured guns, so that the citizens of the town might have an opportunity of inspecting them. He congratulated Portsmouth on the magnificent way it had helped in the war, and said it had contributed in no small degree to the great victory achieved by the allies. The Mayor, accepting the guns said he hoped at no distant date to receive permanent souvenirs of the Great War. He thanked the General for his remarks, adding that Portsmouth stood second to none in the Kingdom in the way it helped in men and money during the late war (hear, hear).

The ceremony closed with a musical medley comprising 'Tipperary', 'Old Contemptibles', *Carmen*, 'Our Empire' and the 'National Anthem'.[81] By exhibiting military hardware in the heart of the Portsmouth's civic arena, the Mayor sought to cultivate the notion that the recent victory and the preservation of the empire was not merely a military achievement but also due to the town's loyal support of men and money that 'was second to none'.[82]

The desire of the civic elite to associate themselves with the glory and trappings of empire was evident also in their choice of freemen during the late nineteenth and early twentieth centuries. The practice of creating freemen or burgesses was originally calculated to enhance a town's political power in the early modern period. The 1835 Municipal Corporation Act swept away the political advantages associated with the creation of Freemen and, as a result, most towns simply abandoned the practice. However, a Parliamentary Act, passed in 1885, enabled towns to confer honorary Freeman status on men of distinction providing that two-thirds of the Council supported the candidate and that the holder would not secure a financial or political gain.[83] The celebration of the civic in the late nineteenth century had done much to rekindle demand for the practice of honouring Freemen, particularly if the ceremony aligned the town with patriotic and nationally known personalities. For example, Portsmouth's civic leaders conferred the honorary title on Lord Roberts in 1898 and in return Roberts spoke of the town's key role in defending the empire since Portsmouth 'exemplified the relationship of the Army and Navy to each other. (cheers). Portsmouth contained the largest naval dockyard in the world, and was the most strongly fortified place in Great Britain.'[84] A further three men from military backgrounds (but with few connections to Portsmouth) were to be made Freemen by 1939, while the Prince of Wales was given the title in 1926 when Portsmouth was awarded city status. Indeed, the ceremony that marked the recognition of Portsmouth as a city was consciously and intrinsically bound with notions of empire. For the civic leaders, the celebration was the culmination of civic culture-building that had begun a generation earlier. Moreover, Portsmouth could now take its rightful place as a pivotal city within the world's greatest empire. The *Hampshire Telegraph* caught the mood of the occasion when it proclaimed that 'Friday July 23 1926, will ever remain a red letter day in the history of the city of Portsmouth, the world's premier Naval port', adding that 'the history of Portsmouth has been bound up intimately with that of the British Empire from the earliest times'.[85] The Prince of Wales was driven through streets lined with schoolchildren, accompanied by the Grammar School Cadet corps. When he arrived at the Town Hall, the Mayor, Councillor F.J. Privett, delivered a speech which is worth citing at some length for its consistent reference to empire and its positive influence on social relations in the city:

> In this great city, the home of the Royal Navy and the gateway of the empire, it has, in the past, often been the privilege of our civic fathers to welcome and admit as Freemen who had by their devotion and service to the motherland, played an important part in the foundation and history of the Empire, of which we are proud members . . . During your Royal Highness' tours through the Dominions and Colonies of the Empire and foreign countries, for which Portsmouth was your starting point, you were so acclaimed; and your progress, which was followed with deep interest by the people of the Empire, was an unqualified success'.

Thus, the Mayor explicitly aligned Portsmouth's elevation to city status with the empire, a port not only defending Britain but a 'gateway' to the colonies and beyond. Moreover, the Mayor, succeeded in 'localising' the vast British Empire, viewing the passage to and defence of the colonies through a Portsmouth lens. Indeed, Privett believed that the occasion would foster a social bond between citizen, city and empire:

> To-day there are assembled in the great hall, men, women and children of all classes of the community. Men and women who in other gatherings would be possibly, in thought as wide apart as the poles; but gathered together as we are in your honour, we are united and can sing with heart and voice 'God Save the Prince of Wales!'[86]

Thus, in the minds of the civic elite, the influence of the British Empire fed back into British society, providing a sense of civic and imperial pride that would help smooth over tensions between differing social groups. In the late nineteenth century the English urban elites embarked on a mission to create strong municipal identities. In a period of 'New Imperialism', this quest for the celebration of the civic naturally drew strength and legitimacy from the British Empire, co-opting imperial glory within narratives of their own towns and cities. Portsmouth's unusual power structure, an axis of civic and military authority in the town, ensured that the civic leaders were perhaps most successful in drawing the town into imperial associations. Likewise, Leeds's thriving civic culture drew on empire and acted as a conduit for imperial values. While Coventry's weaker civic culture could not match the municipal buildings of Leeds, civic leaders adopted a similar practice of viewing the empire through a localised perspective. However, while civic elites worked hard to foster prestigious civic and imperial urban profiles, their attempts would have foundered without the participation of the local press.

The provincial press and the 'new journalism' of the 1880s

By the beginning of the twentieth century, the newspaper press enacted a duel role in a local community. At one level, the newspaper provided day-to-day coverage of the town's events and activities. However, on another level, the press also created multiple identities about community and, as Jeff Hill has noted, brought 'into play a sense of the interrelated loyalties of locality, region and nation'.[87] The newspapers, then, played a significant role in projecting a sense of locality and identity in a community. In addition, the local press, depending on the issue, could act as a commentator, critic or propagandist for the civic authorities. Andy Croll has shown that, political affiliations aside, the press could perform an important surveillance role that scrutinised the urban elite under the guise of 'local patriotism'.[88] The other significant characteristic of the regional press during this period was its political affiliation since most towns and cities supported two or three weekly or daily newspapers that were staunchly Tory or Liberal during this period. Indeed, Matthew Roberts has recently noted that in Leeds the press helped forge distinctive party political cultures that attracted both working and middle-class support during the 1890s.[89] Furthermore, John MacKenzie has argued that the rise of new imperialism and the emergence of the popular daily press during the late nineteenth century ensured that politics at a national and local level was polemicised by empire. Thus, according to MacKenzie, this manifested itself in a 'dominant ideology, the ideological cluster that embraced militarism, monarchism and Social Darwinism'.[90]

In all three towns, the 1890s marked a watershed in working-class reading habits with the arrival of a cheap daily popular press that focused attention more keenly on creating a sense of local identity. Prior to the late Victorian era, Portsmouth, Coventry and Leeds had been dominated by long-established weekly newspapers that reflected the Tory and Liberal divide. Until the 1890s, the long-established newspapers such as the conservative-oriented *Portsmouth Times*, *Coventry Standard* and *Yorkshire Post* largely shared their respective towns' readership with their liberal counterparts *The Hampshire Telegraph*, *Coventry Herald*, *Leeds Times* and *Leeds Mercury*. All of these newspapers presented material in traditional formats that had changed little from the 1860s, with long in-depth reports on business, stock markets and international relations. Parliamentary sessions were reported in full and carried speeches reproduced verbatim. Local news was often confined to the town council and the board of guardians. The leaders' comment on the major issues of the day was at the heart of the traditional newspaper and took precedent over news coverage. Indeed, it was 'views rather than news' that defined the character of the newspaper established in the mid-nineteenth century.[91] These traditional newspapers modelled themselves on the national press, particularly *The Times*, even to the extent that both the *Hampshire Telegraph* and the *Yorkshire Post* both had pretensions that went beyond the local. Thus the *Hampshire Telegraph* could boast impressive circulation figures that dwarfed *The Times*, while the *Yorkshire Post* proclaimed itself to be 'the *Times* of the North of England'.[92] In a formulaic sense there was little to differentiate between the Tory and Liberal press since the layout and linguistic style reflected the professional classes that they had long catered for.[93] However, while the traditional Tory newspapers, such as the *Yorkshire Post* and the *Coventry Standard*, remained fairly stable, the *Coventry Herald*, *Leeds Mercury* and the *Leeds Times* had begun to struggle and look rather dated and unresponsive to the new readership markets that were emerging in the 1890s. The slow decline of these once influential newspapers mirrored a similar downturn in the liberal press generally and it was only the intervention of philanthropists such as Rowntree that saved much of the regional liberal press from extinction.[94] Despite evidence of this national decline, the liberal press in Coventry and Leeds continued to preach a doctrine of artisan self-improvement more suited to a mid-nineteenth-century era.[95] Indeed in 1901 the Baines family, who owned the *Leeds Mercury*, freely admitted that the newspaper had regularly been criticised for its puritanical and moralistic views. Liberal newspapers tended to shun the reporting of popular sport because of its perceived association with gambling.[96] Similarly, while less evangelical with regard to self-improvement, the *Hampshire Telegraph* limited its coverage of popular sports to one short column.[97] It was left, then, to the new newspapers in the late nineteenth century to fully exploit the popular demand for coverage of the mass commercial leisure industries that emerged in the late nineteenth century.[98]

While the national newspapers enhanced news coverage through improved transport and communication links, a new style of journalism seized upon regional news as way of distinguishing themselves from older provincial or national publications. Mark Hampton has usefully defined the characteristics of this new genre as journalism with 'lightness of tone, an emphasis on the personal and the 'sensational,' and reliance on gimmicks to sell newspapers in high-stakes circulation wars'.[99] Significantly, through an emphasis on 'personal' and 'local' news, newspapers were able to tap into a new and growing market of working-class readers.[100] These newspapers were, in effect, serving the first generation of adults that had undergone mass education through the 1870 Forster Education Act.[101] The new journalism's ability to engage with elements of local popular culture enabled them to serve a growing working-class desire for sports and coverage of their locality. Indeed, the new daily local press capitalised on the football craze of the late nineteenth century to exploit a popular manifestation of town pride and civic identity. Supporting a football team was an expression of a town identity that helped forge a collective allegiance and reinforced a sense of 'otherness' towards those people and institutions not connected with the town.[102] Indeed, Andrew August has recently concurred with this view and argued that, despite a common British leisure culture, local identities remained strong and were reinforced by sporting triumphs on the football and rugby fields.[103] This phenomenon was identified by *The Times*, which embarked on an investigation into the 'North/South divide' in the 1890s. Whereas *The Times* recorded some regional differences in street-life etiquette, a more significant discovery was that in both northern and southern towns there was a growing sense that working-class men were identifying themselves with their own locality through sporting and civic activities. The *Times* journalist noted that the northern artisan was drawn to football matches in their thousands in support of their own town's team. In addition:

> They are deeply attached to the town or even to the manufacturing village in which they have been born. Events affecting its reputation or the welfare of its inhabitants move them in a very genuine fashion . . . though it is true that in the East End local patriotism has been developed in considerable vigour.[104]

In short, while class remained a constant, it coexisted with other forms of identification found in the local and regional setting. The newly formed civic spaces, then, proved important landmarks for both official and more spontaneous events that helped forge a resident's identity and relationship with their town.

The Coventry reading public's first experience of a new form of journalism came in 1885 with the publication of the short-lived *Athletic Reporter*. The *Reporter*, a weekend newspaper costing only a halfpenny, was clearly out to capitalise on the working class' growing interest in organised sport, an activity that had hitherto been conspicuously ignored by the city's traditional newspapers. Indeed, the *Athletic Reporter*'s first edition leader noted that, while similar journals existed in Birmingham, Leicester and Nottingham, 'there was no reason why Coventry with its extensive population should be without its athletic organ'.[105] Significantly the founder, Thomas Vaughan, pledged that reports would be 'terse and business like' and that its politics would be 'imperialist'.[106] This mixture of local sport and imperial sentiment was continued in more subtle terms by the publishing magnate William Iliffe, who, after acquiring a number of small newspapers in Coventry and Warwickshire, established the *Midland Daily Telegraph* in 1891. For a halfpenny, readers were promised a 'bright and chatty' newspaper with a focus on local features and reports and, through the extensive use of the telegraph, 'hot news'.[107] National news was usually selected for its sensational character, and murders and crime reporting featured heavily. For example in 1891, after a gruesome murder in Whitechapel, the editor speculated that the culprit was Jack the Ripper, 'the monster who made Whitechapel reek with blood'.[108] Although initially liberal, by 1897 it had become firmly conservative and had adopted new innovations to capture sports 'fanatics' such as producing a 'pink' edition on Saturday evenings that would carry all the latest sporting results.[109] The sports coverage undoubtedly improved circulation figures and by 1906 daily sales stood at ten thousand copies.[110]

While some commentators suggested that new journalism abruptly revolutionised the newspaper industry in the 1890s, it is clear that there was a more gradual transformation that had begun in the 1870s.[111] One of the earliest and most successful newspapers that embraced the principles of new journalism was the *Leeds Daily News* that first appeared in 1872 and priced at a halfpenny. By 1885, it claimed to have an average circulation of 28,600, rising to 75,578 by 1894. This newspaper had clearly set itself apart from its traditional rivals with its focus on sport, local issues and sensational reports at the expense of the in-depth political analysis found in the older broadsheets. Football in particular proved an attraction to readers, with the Saturday edition doubling in price and length to accommodate sporting stories. Furthermore, a special football edition was produced on Saturday evenings carrying the latest results and reports.[112] In 1882, these developments prompted the *Yorkshire Post* to experiment in producing the *Yorkshire Weekly Post*, a more 'popular'-oriented supplement to the 'quality' daily. However, more fundamental changes were required and in 1890 the *Yorkshire Post* founded the *Yorkshire Evening Post*, priced at a halfpenny with over half of the newspaper given over to advertisements and sport. The proprietors rightly envisaged that the *Yorkshire Post* and the *Yorkshire Evening Post* would complement one another, attracting quite separate readerships from differing social backgrounds.[113] The style and content of the *Yorkshire Evening Post* placed it in direct competition with the *Leeds Daily News* for working-class readers. As Roberts has pointed out, in contrast to the *Yorkshire Post* that had a large postal circulation among the more affluent reading public, the evening press was available from mid-afternoon and 'was more likely to be bought on the street either from newsboys and newsagents or from horse-drawn dog carts which made their way through the outlying districts'.[114] Indeed, by adding to their existing title, the proprietors were able avoid compromising their more exclusive *Yorkshire Post* while at the same time tapping into the evening mass readership market.[115]

In Portsmouth, the first popular daily was the *Evening News*, founded in 1877 by James Graham Niven. The newspaper, though fairly successful, was restricted to small runs of around two thousand owing to a lack of capital investment.[116] However, in 1883 a triumvirate of leading Liberals, Samuel Storey MP, Andrew Carnegie and Passmore Edwards, purchased the *Evening News* and the *Hampshire Telegraph* in a bid to further the liberal cause and disseminate ideas on republicanism and radicalism.[117] In a move not dissimilar to the pattern of ownership in Leeds, the proprietors hoped to secure two separate markets of readership; the quality weekly and the popular daily.

Although Samuel Storey soon assumed control of the group after the syndicate was dissolved, the *Evening News* became firmly established as the most popular daily with nightly sales topping sixty thousand by 1914, rising to over 150,000 during the First World War.[118] There were significant challenges to the *Evening News*, however, in what was a highly competitive market. The year 1882 saw the launch of the short-lived *Evening Star*, a newspaper that clearly targeted working-class readers and was successful in attracting correspondents from dockyard workers in particular. For example, early editions were dominated by feverish reports on Britain's hostilities with Egypt along with coverage of the sale of allegedly adulterated tobacco in Portsea. Local news was selected with the working man very much in mind to the extent that one editorial was entirely devoted to the poor quality of beer in Portsmouth. The newspaper closed only a year later, blaming the end of hostilities with Egypt. An editorial reminded readers that the newspaper had been launched in the expectation of 'bloody and protracted hostilities in Egypt' and the cessation of hostilities had meant that the war 'did not last sufficiently long enough to enable us to secure a foundation in the borough'.[119]

Following the demise of the *Evening Star*, Arthur Holbrook founded a conservative-oriented newspaper, the *Evening Mail*, in 1884. This newspaper proved a more serious challenge to the *Evening News* after it was relaunched by the Harmsworth family who purchased the title for £25,000 in 1894.[120] Alfred Charles Harmsworth (later Lord Northcliffe), who had previously worked on publications with the Iliffe family in Coventry, transformed the *Evening Mail* into a profitable newspaper, adopting the chatty and direct style of journalism that had been the bedrock of the *Midland Daily Telegraph*'s success.[121] The *Evening Mail*'s profitable circulation figures prompted Harmsworth to launch the first daily national newspaper priced at a halfpenny, catching the tide of the new wave of journalism at a national level.[122] Named after his Portsmouth publication, the *Daily Mail* was launched in 1896 and embodied the new format and writing style designed for 'busy men in a time of hurry'.[123] The success of the *Daily Mail* enabled Harmsworth to concentrate his newspaper portfolio on a national level and consequently sold the *Evening Mail* to the *Evening News* in 1905.[124]

In all three towns, then, newspaper proprietors were making a play for the newly developing mass readership market. Indeed, by 1900 increased coverage of local news was becoming a feature in even the more traditional newspapers. This development, however, was hardly surprising since in Portsmouth, Coventry and Leeds the traditional newspapers were owned by proprietors who had established sister papers that had pioneered this new type of journalism (see Appendix 1). Thus by 1900, formats, contents and linguistic styles were similar, though notably only Portsmouth had a strong liberal daily owing to the continued commitment of the Storey family to the liberal cause. However, it would be unwise to overstate the political content of the 'popular' newspapers as it would appear that it was the local focus and sports coverage that really attracted working-class readers. As Stephen Caunce has observed, the real growth in circulation was 'now among new readers who had little interest in politics and responded to new methods of presentation and a more sensational approach'.[125] One of the first critics of new journalism was Matthew Arnold, who in 1887 noted that it was geared towards the 'new voters' who, as a group, did not think seriously and cheerfully embraced the newspapers' sensational and 'feather-brained' contents.[126] Likewise, J.A. Hobson despaired that the 'jingo' press was exploiting a naive and newly literate working class and plying its readership with a sub-rational imperial sensationalism. According to Hobson, the press helped 'capture the mind of a nation, arouse its passion and impose a policy'.[127] While contemporaries were convinced of the power of the press, historians have rightly been a little more sceptical. For example, Aled Jones has argued that the reader possessed a relative autonomy and 'was capable of remaining critical of the new medium while engaging with it'.[128] For example, an early twentieth-century letter published in the *Yorkshire Evening Post* amply illustrates the complexities of the working-class consumer since political loyalties did not seemingly detract from the general enjoyment of the newspaper's format and content:

> I have read your paper for a good many years although opposed to me politically, for it is always bright and readable, and deals with such a variety of subject that the reader is always kept posted with current events. But why do you always oppose me as a worker when a dispute is threatened?[129]

Clearly this working man took the *Yorkshire Evening Post* for its lively reporting on local issues and news. Thus the more the popular press immersed itself in the local community, the more working-class readership it could attract regardless of political standpoint.

Conclusion

The evidence drawn from Portsmouth, Coventry and Leeds suggests that differing social, political and cultural contexts helped determine both a community's civic identity and, significantly, its engagement with national and imperial perspectives. The late nineteenth and early twentieth centuries witnessed the urban elite in towns and cities consciously constructing civic identities that placed their own community at the heart of national and imperial narratives. Indeed, for many readers of the provincial press, the Empire became significant only when imperial issues were fused with the local. For Portsmouth's civic elites, the close proximity of the Royal Dockyard had for some time provided an opportunity to proclaim the town as the 'Gateway to the Empire' when constructing their civic identity. In contrast, Leeds belatedly introduced an imperial character to public ceremony in the 1890s, while Coventry's limited civic culture remained fairly stunted during the height of imperial fervour prior to the First World War. The enthusiasm for local patriotism and the celebration of civic culture occurred during a period when, conversely, conditions in towns and cities deteriorated to unprecedented levels. London, the capital of the empire, had begun to be seen as an urban jungle in which intrepid explorers catalogued and 'civilised the city-savages'. Thus, just as urban elites appropriated empire to further a local patriotism, other social explorers and philanthropists applied the language and techniques of the imperial explorer to understand the dark and dangerous underbelly of the modern city. The following chapter will examine the extent to which the imperial metaphor, so liberally applied to people and the environment of the East End of London, entered into the discourse of social observers in the slums of Portsmouth, Coventry and Leeds.

Notes

1 *The Times*, 27 March 1907.
2 J. Schneer, *London 1900. The Imperial Metropolis* (New Haven, Yale University Press, 1999), p. 10.
3 J. M. MacKenzie, ''The second city of the empire'. Glasgow – Imperial Municipality', in F. Driver and D. Gilbert (eds), *Imperial Cities* (Manchester, Manchester University Press, 1999), p. 233.
4 S. Haggerty, A. Webster and N.J. White (eds), *The Empire in One City? Liverpool's Inconvenient Imperial Past* (Manchester, Manchester University Press, 2008), p. 13.
5 S. Gunn, *The Public Culture of the Victorian Middle Class. Ritual and Authority in the English Industrial City, 1840–1914* (Manchester, Manchester University Press, 2000, 2007 edn), pp. 163–86; D. Cannadine, 'The Transformation of Civic Ritual in Modern Britain: the Colchester Oyster Feast', *Past and Present*, 94, 1982; D. Fraser, *Urban Politics in Victorian England* (London, Macmillian, 1976).
6 www.VisionofBritain.org.uk; statistics for Coventry, Leeds and Portsmouth. Accessed 13 December 2010.
7 P. McLeay, 'The Wolverhampton Motor Car Industry 1896–1937', *West Midlands Studies*, 2, 1969, p. 100; D.W. Thoms and T. Donnelly, 'Coventry's Industrial

Economy', in B. Lancaster and T. Mason (eds), *Life and Labour in a 20th Century City. The Experience of Coventry* (Coventry, Cryfield Press, 1986), p. 13.

8   B. Lancaster, 'Who's a Real Coventry Kid? Migration into Twentieth Century Coventry', in Lancaster and Mason (eds), *Life and Labour*, pp. 58–60. For a study on the impact of migration into a light industrial region in the 1930s see M. Stacey, *Tradition and Change: A Study of Banbury* (London, Oxford University Press, 1960); J. Zeitlin, 'Emergence of the Shop Steward Organisation and job control in the British car industry', *History Workshop*, 10, 1980, p. 127.

9   K. Richardson, *Twentieth Century Coventry* (Burgay, Chaucer Press, 1972), p. 11.

10 Thoms and Donnelly, 'Coventry's Industrial Economy', p. 15.

11 B. Beaven and J. Griffiths, ' Urban Elites, Socialists and Notions of Citizenship in an Industrial Boomtown: Coventry *c.* 1870–1914', *Labour History Review*, 69, 1, April 2004, p. 13.

12 *Coventry Herald*, 2 May 1907.

13 Beaven and Griffiths, 'Urban Elites, Socialists and Notions of Citizenship in an Industrial Boomtown', p. 13.

14 V. Fulda, 'Space, Civic Pride, Citizenship and Identity in 1890s Portsmouth' (unpublished PhD thesis, University of Portsmouth, 2006), pp. 1, 33.

15 R.C. Riley, *The Industries of Portsmouth in the 19th Century* (Portsmouth: Portsmouth Papers, 1976), p. 9.

16 R. Riley, *Portsmouth: Ships, Dockyard and Town* (Stroud, Tempus, 2002), p. 41.

17 E.S. Washington, *Local Battles in Fact and Fiction: The Portsmouth Election of 1895* (Portsmouth, Portsmouth City Council, 1985), p. 6.

18 E.J. Connell and M. Ward, 'Industrial Development', in D. Fraser (ed.), *A History of Modern Leeds* (Manchester, Manchester University Press, 1980), pp. 143, 159.

19 Quoted in C.J. Morgan, 'Demographic Change 1771–1911', in D. Fraser (ed.), *A History of Modern Leeds*, (Manchester, Manchester University Press, 1980), p. 62.

20 Morgan, 'Demographic Change', p. 62.

21 L. Vaughan and A. Penn, 'Jewish Immigrant Settlement Patterns in Manchester and Leeds 1881', *Urban Studies*, 43, 3, March 2006, p. 667.

22 E.D. Steele, 'Imperialism and Leeds Politics, *c.* 1850–1914', in D. Fraser (ed.), *A History of Modern Leeds* (Manchester, Manchester University Press, 1980), p. 327.

23 Quoted in K. Lunn and R. Thomas, 'Naval Imperialism in Portsmouth, 1905–1914', *Southern History*, 10, 1988, p. 147.

24 G.J. Ashworth, *Portsmouth's Political Patterns 1885–1945* (Portsmouth, Portsmouth City Council, 1976), p. 9.

25 Ashworth, *Portsmouth's Political Patterns 1885–1945*, p. 12.

26 Steele, 'Imperialism and Leeds Politics', pp. 346–8.

27 Quoted in Steele, 'Imperialism and Leeds Politics', p. 344.

28 Richardson, *Twentieth Century Coventry*, p. 190.

29 *Coventry Graphic*, 6 March, 7 August 1914.

30 Richardson, *Twentieth Century Coventry*, p. 196.

31 Richardson, *Twentieth Century Coventry*, pp. 196–201.

32 *Fraser's Magazine*, May 1880, pp. 714–15.

33 *Hampshire Telegraph*, 3 May 1880.

34 *Evening News*, 15 May 1909.

35 Quoted in Washington, *Local Battles in Fact and Fiction*, p. 20.

36 Ashworth, *Portsmouth's Political Patterns*, p. 10.

37 B. Beaven, 'Custom, Culture and Conflict. A Study of the Coventry Ribbon Trade in the First Half of the Nineteenth Century', *Midland History*, 15, 1990, p. 96.

38 *Victoria County History*, Warwickshire vol. VIII, on-line: www.british-history. ac.uk. Accessed 10 January 2010.

39 *Victoria County History*, Warwickshire vol. VIII, on-line: www.british-history. ac.uk. Accessed 10 January 2010.

40 http://visionofbritain.org.uk. Accessed 10 January 2010.

41 A.J. Taylor, 'Victorian Leeds: an Overview', in D. Fraser (ed.), *A History of Modern Leeds* (Manchester, Manchester University Press, 1980), p. 405.

CITIES IN CONTEXT

42 Taylor, 'Victorian Leeds: an Overview', p. 403.
43 http://visionofbritain.org.uk. Accessed 10 January 2010.
44 R.J. Morris, 'Middle-class Culture, 1700–1914', in D. Fraser (ed.), *A History of Modern Leeds* (Manchester, Manchester University Press, 1980), p. 219.
45 M. Beresford, 'The Face of Leeds', in D. Fraser (ed.), *A History of Modern Leeds* (Manchester, Manchester University Press, 1980), p. 110.
46 *Leeds and Yorkshire Mercury*, 18 November 1905.
47 Gunn, *The Public Culture of the Victorian Middle Class*, pp. 50–3.
48 See J.R. Griffiths, 'Civic Communication in Britain: a Study of the *Municipal Journal*, c. 1893–1910', *Journal of Urban History*, 34, 2008.
49 Quoted in Fulda, 'Space, Civic Pride, Citizenship and Identity in 1890s Portsmouth', p. 57.
50 *Evening News*, 16 August 1890.
51 Fulda, 'Space, Civic Pride, Citizenship and Identity in 1890s Portsmouth', p. 58.
52 *Evening News*, 16 August 1890.
53 *Evening News*, 9 August 1890.
54 *Hampshire Telegraph*, 1 February 1903.
55 Beaven and Griffiths, 'Urban Elites, Socialists and Notions of Citizenship in an Industrial Boomtown', p. 8.
56 F. Smith, *Coventry Six Hundred Years of Municipal Life* (Coventry, Coventry Evening Telegraph, 1945), p. 167.
57 Richardson, *Twentieth Century Coventry*, p. 279.
58 Richardson, *Twentieth Century Coventry*, p. 281; *Coventry Herald*, 1 November 1935.
59 *Coventry Herald*, 8 March 1935.
60 B. Beaven, 'The Growth and Significance of the Coventry Car Component Industry, 1895–1939, (unpublished PhD thesis, De Montfort University, 1994), ch. 5.
61 *Coventry Herald*, 13 September 1935.
62 Griffiths, 'Civic Communication in Britain', p. 777.
63 Gunn, *The Public Culture of the Victorian Middle Class*, p. 174.
64 J. Ruger, *The Great Naval Game. Britain and Germany in the Age of Empire* (Cambridge, Cambridge University Press, 2007), p. 21.
65 R. Thomas, 'Empire, Naval Pageantry and Public Spectacles', *Mariners Mirror*, 88, 2, May 2002, p. 202.
66 *Evening News*, 16 August 1890.
67 Fulda, 'Space, Civic Pride, Citizenship and Identity in 1890s Portsmouth', p. 58.
68 *Evening News*, 16 August 1890.
69 *Leeds Mercury*, 9 September 1858.
70 *Leeds Mercury*, 18 April 1884.
71 *Yorkshire Evening Post*, 11 February 1893.
72 *Yorkshire Factory Times*, 10 February 1893; *Leeds Daily News*, 7 February 1893.
73 *Leeds Mercury*, 6 October 1894.
74 A. Smith and D. Fry, *Godiva's Heritage: Coventry Industry* (Coventry, Simanda Press, 1997), p. 4.
75 Coventry City Archives, T. Collins, 'Brief reflections suggested to those persons who patronized the procession at Spon Street Wake July 8th 1844' (Coventry, Stephen Knapp, 1845), p. 16, 1.
76 Smith and Fry, *Godiva's Heritage*, p. 5.
77 For accounts of processions from the nineteenth and twentieth centuries see *The Times* 7 August 1883; 21 July 1919.
78 B. Beaven, 'Challenges to Civic Governance in Post-war England: the Peace Day Disturbances of 1919', *Urban History*, 33, 3, 2006, p. 382.
79 See Chapter 7 on the spontaneous street celebrations during the Mafeking celebrations.
80 *Hampshire Telegraph*, 22 November 1918.
81 *Hampshire Telegraph*, 22 November 1918.
82 *Hampshire Telegraph*, 22 November 1918.

83 Richardson, *Twentieth Century Coventry*, pp. 7–10.
84 *The Times*, 7 December 1898.
85 *Hampshire Telegraph*, 30 July 1926.
86 *Hampshire Telegraph*, 30 July 1926.
87 J. Hill, 'Rite of Spring: Cup Finals and Community in the North of England', in J. Hill and J. Williams (eds), *Sport and Identity in the North of England* (Keele, Keele University Press, 1996), p. 86.
88 Fulda, 'Space, Civic Pride, Citizenship and Identity in 1890s Portsmouth', p. 68.
89 M. Roberts, 'Constructing a Tory World-view: Popular Politics and the Conservative Press in Late Victorian Leeds', *Historical Research*, 79, 2006, p. 115.
90 J.M. MacKenzie, 'The Press and the Dominant Ideology of Empire', in S. Potter (ed.), *Newspapers and Empire in Ireland and Britain* (Dublin, Four Courts Press, 2004), p. 27.
91 M. Hampton, *Visions of the Press in Britain 1850–1950* (Chicago, University of Illinois Press, 2004), p. 38.
92 S. Caunce, 'Yorkshire Post Newspaper Ltd: Perseverance Rewarded', in J. Chartres and K. Honeyman (eds), *Leeds City Business 1893–1993: Essays Marking the Centenary of Incorporation* (Leeds, Leeds University Press, 1993), p. 30.
93 Roberts, 'Constructing a Tory World-view', p. 122.
94 P. Gliddon, 'The political importance of provincial newspapers, 1903–1945: the Rowntrees and the Liberal Press', *Twentieth Century British History*, 14, 1, 2003, pp. 25–6.
95 Beaven, *Leisure, Citizenship and Working-class Men*, ch. 1.
96 Roberts, 'Constructing a Tory World-view', p. 123.
97 For example see *Hampshire Telegraph*, 10 March 1900, for a typical week's coverage.
98 Beaven, *Leisure, Citizenship and Working-class Men*, ch. 2.
99 Hampton, *Visions of the Press*, p. 36.
100 Caunce, 'Yorkshire Post Newspaper Ltd', p. 30.
101 K.O. Morgan, 'The Boer War and the Media (1899–1902)', *Twentieth Century British History*, 13, 1, 2002, p. 2.
102 J. Williams, 'One Could Literally Have Walked on the Heads of the People Congregated There', in K. Laybourn (ed.), *Social Conditions, Status and Community, 1860–c. 1920* (Stroud, Sutton, 1997), p. 130; R.J. Holt, 'Football and the Urban Way of Life in Nineteenth Century Britain.'. in J.A. Mangan (ed), *Pleasure, Profit and Proselytism. British Culture and Sport at Home and Abroad, 1700–1914* (London, Frank Cass, 1988); M. Savage and A. Miles, *The Remaking of the British Working Class, 1840–1940* (London, Routledge, 1994), pp. 62–8; Beaven, *Leisure, Citizenship and Working-class Men*, p. 74.
103 A. August, *The British Working Class, 1832–1940* (Harlow, Pearson, 2007), p. 49.
104 Quoted in *Leeds Mercury*, 7 November 1896.
105 *Athletic Reporter*, 31 October 1885.
106 *Victoria County History*, Warwickshire vol. VIII, on-line: www.british-history.ac.uk. Accessed 10 January 2010.
107 *Midland Daily Telegraph*, 9 February 1891; *Victoria County History*, Warwickshire vol. VIII, on-line: www.british-history.ac.uk. Accessed 10 January 2010.
108 *Midland Daily Telegraph*, 13 February 1891.
109 *Midland Daily Telegraph*, 10 February 1941.
110 *Midland Daily Telegraph*, 9 February 1951.
111 Hampton, *Visions of the Press*, p. 37.
112 Roberts, 'Constructing a Tory World-view', p. 126.
113 Caunce, 'Yorkshire Post Newspaper Ltd', p. 30.
114 Roberts, 'Constructing a Tory World-view', p. 127.
115 Caunce, 'Yorkshire Post Newspaper Ltd', p. 31.
116 *Evening News*, 24 April 1952.

117 A.J.A. Morris, 'J.P. Edwards: Newspaper Proprietor and Philanthropist', *Oxford Dictionary of National Biography*, Oxford University Press, on-line edition (www.oxforddnb.com). Accessed 10 January 2010. *Evening News*, 27 April 1977.
118 *Evening News*, 27 April 1977.
119 *Evening News*, 24 January 1969.
120 D. Boyce, 'Harmsworth, ACW', *Oxford Dictionary of National Biography*, Oxford University Press, on-line edition (www.oxforddnb.com). Accessed 10 January 2010.
121 Boyce, 'Harmsworth, ACW'.
122 Washington, *The Battles in Fact and Fiction*, p. 21
123 Boyce, 'Harmsworth, ACW'.
124 *Evening News*, 28 April 1952.
125 Caunce, 'Yorkshire Post Newspaper Ltd', p. 38.
126 M. Arnold, 'Up to Easter', *Nineteenth Century*, XXI, 1887, pp. 638–9.
127 J.A. Hobson, *The Psychology of Jingoism* (London, Grant Richards, 1901), p. 107.
128 A. Jones, *Powers of the Press. Newspapers, Power and the Public in Nineteenth Century England* (Aldershot, Scolar Press, 1996), p. 97.
129 *Yorkshire Evening Post*, 29 January 1915.

[41]

CHAPTER TWO

The city and the imperial mission, 1850–1914

In 1901, C.F.G. Masterman reflected on the close relationship between England's capital city and the Empire, declaring 'that increased inter-communications' helped not only to spread British values to the dominions but also effectively to 'bring colonial ideas to London'.[1] Moreover, in exploring the interconnections between the English city and empire, contemporaries drew explicit parallels between the impe-rial explorers in Africa and the investigators of the urban slum. Between 1850 and 1914, the exploration of the African continent shepherded the Empire into a new and exciting phase during a period in which urban conditions at home were deteriorating at an alarming rate. With good reason, London became the focus of this anxiety as the imperial project could not afford decay and degeneration to spread to the 'Heart of Empire'.[2] Recently historians have made significant strides in mapping out how the East End became part of the imperial project through assessing how journalists, priests and researchers projected imperial metaphors onto the peoples and conditions they witnessed in London.[3] What is less well documented, however, is whether the assumptions and analysis of London's East End explorers were adopted by missionaries in the provincial towns and cities. While there has been a preponderance of historical enquiries that have focused on the East End case study, it does raise the question of whether this has distorted our perception of the relationship between city and empire. The chapter explores whether the imperial metaphor and symbolism deployed by researchers in the East End influenced those who sought to investigate the slums in Portsmouth, Coventry and Leeds. Indeed, these three communities endured very different degrees of slumdom and diverse social problems. First, however, we turn to the East End and examine the contemporary explorers' assumptions and analysis of slumdom to consider whether this acted as a template for social inves-tigators in the provinces.

Exploring the heart of empire: London, 1850–1914

The Victorians' propensity to liken the chaotic jungle environment of empire with the rapidly growing English city became a recognisable trait in slum writing by the mid-nineteenth century. For social commentators the city became a place of fascination where, just as imperial expeditions had uncovered new human 'species', urban investigations had revealed similar primitive peoples. These discoveries and comparisons were made even more startling when descriptions of both colonial and urban 'savages' appeared in the popular press. Charles Dickens left readers in no doubt of the 'wickedness' of the colonial savage, criticising the very concept of the 'noble savage'. For Dickens, the 'savage' should be civilised out of existence since 'he is a savage – cruel, false, thievish, murderous; addicted more or less to grease, entrails, and beastly customs; a wild animal with the questionable gift of boasting; a conceited, bloodthirsty, monotonous humbug'.[4] He made similar observations on his frequent jouneys into the poorest parts of London, noting the savergy of the district and employing bestial descriptions for the inhabitants he encountered. After strolling through one poverty-stricken part of London, Dickens noted that the children

> are the very dregs of the population of the largest city in the world – human waifs and strays of the modern Babylon; the children of poverty, and misery and crime; in very many cases labouring under physical defects, such as bad sight or hearing; almost always stunted in growth, and bearing the stamp of ugliness and suffering on their features. Generally born in dark alleys and backcourts, their playground has been the streets, where the wits of many have been prematurely sharpened at the expense of any moral they might have. With minds and bodies destitute of proper nutriment, they are caught, as it were, by the Parish officers, like half-wild creatures.[5]

However, these 'half-wild creatures', like their colonial counterparts, were not beyond social redemption through a civilising programme administered by schooling. In one school praised by Dickens, he declared that he could judge how long a pupil had been educated through their shedding of the bestial characteristics that had been etched on their face and demeanour:

> As they stand ranged in their classes, the diversity of countenances which they exhibit is as striking as are the contrasts presented by the raiment. In some faces you can still trace the brutal expression which they wore on entering. In others, the low cunning, begotten by their mode of life, was more or less distinguishable. You could readily point to those who had been longest in the establishment, from the humanis-

ing influences which their treatment had had upon their looks and expressions. The faces of them were lit up with new-born intelligence.[6]

Significantly, Dickens believed that both the colonial and urban 'savage' were redeemable through the civilising effects of education and religion. However, while Dickens's voyages into the underworld made good copy for his *Household Words*, it was Henry Mayhew who most consistently cast his role as the intrepid urban explorer, deploying the language of the imperial voyager in describing the street scenes of London.[7] Through his articles in the *Morning Chronicle* and his collected essays in *London Labour and the London Poor*, Mayhew aimed to enlighten his readers of the 'wandering tribes' of London, their peculiar language, customs, morals and physical appearance.[8] However, while Mayhew was influenced by contemporary ideas of race, he did not formulate a consistent racial analysis that informed his work. The mass of empirical data he collected, and the array of social groups and characters described, led Mayhew to use the term 'race' rather loosely.[9] Indeed, for both Dickens and Mayhew, their journeys into the underworld convinced them that the poor had the potential to be civilised and did not entertain the idea of any form of biological determinism. However, as John Marriott has pointed out, in the post-Mayhew era, researching the city entered a new and more disturbing phase. In the period around 1860, sensational journalists such as James Greenwood offered the reading public narratives of pauper districts that fused observations of dirt and biological degeneration that began to racialise the poor.[10] This new departure in how the poor were perceived gave further credence to those researchers who saw parallels with the Empire and imagined the city as an urban jungle that was spawning a new and dangerous race. Furthermore, as Bill Luckin has recently argued, scientists, medical men and social commentators had 'convinced themselves that the *city itself* possessed a malign and deadly agency' that would, in due course, turn on and punish the residuum masses it had created.[11] Just as the primitive jungles in the empire had created stunted and brutal uncivilised races, the modern city generated a different species – a dangerous and subhuman underclass. The view was expressed by C.F.G. Masterman and a number of his liberal contemporaries in publications such as *The Heart of Empire* (1901) and *From the Abyss* (1902). Writing in the aftermath of the Mafeking and Boer War celebrations, Masterman described, with some horror, a new city-bred people who were leaving their 'dens' in the East End and causing disturbances in central London. Describing them emerging from the London underground tube station as 'like rats from a drain, blinking in the sunshine', he continued:

They could have looted and destroyed, plundered and razed it to the ground. We gazed at them in startled amazement. Whence did they all come from, these creatures with strange antics and manners, these denizens of another universe or being? . . . As darkness drew on they relapsed more and more into bizarre and barbaric revelry. Whence they whispered now they shouted; where they had pushed apologetically, now they shoved and collisioned and charged. They blew trumpets; they hit each other with bladders; they tickled passers-by with feathers; they embraced ladies in the streets laughing genially and boisterously. Later the drink got into them, and they reeled and struck and swore, walking and leaping and blaspheming God.[12]

Read in contextual isolation, Masterman's description of a strange people who exhibited brutal and uncivilised customs could easily have been mistaken for a piece of colonial exploration in darkest Africa. What made these and similar observations more disturbing was that these strange and threatening peoples lived at the heart of the Empire rather than on its periphery. Masterman's sense of fear as darkness closed in was palpable since, for Masterman, these troglodytes were nurtured in the dark rookeries and alleys of the East End and with nightfall they confidently took possession of the streets of central London. After 'it has crept out into the daylight', Masterman warned, 'how long before, in a fit of ill-temper, it suddenly remembers its tremendous and unconquerable might'?[13] This belief that dark and degenerate urban districts were nurturing a separate race seemed to contemporaries a natural process of evolutionary development and something akin to a neo-Lamarckian analysis of the city.[14] Similar perspectives can be found in H.G. Wells's *The Time Machine*, which featured the Eloi, a gentle upper-world civilisation that, during darkness, was preyed upon by the Morlocks, underworld creatures that were both degenerate and barbarous.[15]

By the late nineteen century, the representation of London's poorer districts had developed from the occasional published insight into urban conditions of the 1840s and 1850s to a distinct genre of slum travel writing published in journals, surveys and, importantly, the new and popular press. The East End had become a literary construct with authors inviting their readers to imagine a labyrinth of dark, filthy rookeries that harboured a residuum population to both repel and fascinate.[16] Authors consciously compared their work with the social explorers of the empire which had proved increasingly popular with a public eager to devour the strange and exotic scenes described in the African continent. For example, sensational journalists such as George Simms spoke of a 'dark continent that is within easy walking distance of the General Post Office', adding that he hoped it would prove as interesting as the Royal Geographical Society's research into recently explored lands and the 'savage tribes' that inhabited them.[17] James Greenwood, in his most infamous work, 'A Night in a Workhouse', explicitly racialised the tramps he met, likening them to the 'brutes' depicted in books he had read on the African colonies. Indeed, Seth Koven has convincingly shown that Greenwood saw the East End of London and the mysterious outpost of empire as 'interchangeable sites of adventure and heroism'.[18] The urban explorers' symbiotic perspective of the English city and empire was never more obvious than in the writings of William Booth. In his book *In Darkest England and the Way Out*, Booth lamented that 'as there is a darkest Africa is there not also a darkest England?', complete with 'barbarians' and 'pygmies'. He added that 'may we not find a parallel at our own doors, and discover within a stone's throw of our cathedrals and palaces similar horrors to those which Stanley has found exiting in the great Equatorial forest?'[19] Troy Boone has recently argued that the Salvation Army was an active movement in what he describes as hegemonic imperialism – that the classes, sexes and generations were united around the imperial nation.[20] However, like those of his contemporaries, Booth's analysis of the poor was littered with contradictions. His belief that the Salvation Army could reform 'lawless lads and licentious girls' was tempered by a neo-Lamarckian perspective. He considered that a combination of the city and a godless working-class culture had fashioned a degenerate people. Thus, even those who were transformed from 'wild animals' living in 'dens' to Salvationists were deemed inferior to their more respectable counterparts in the Salvation Army.[21]

William's namesake, Charles Booth, the more sober and 'scientific' researcher of the poor, did not fully dismiss the notion that a section of the working class was beyond reformation. Charles Booth's monumental research into the poor influenced both government enquiries into poverty and subsequent historians alike. In his 17 volumes entitled *Life and Labour of the People in London*, between 1889 and 1903 Booth's research was both a departure from the preceding sensational journalism of the 1880s and yet a confirmation of some of the fears and anxieties the press generated. Booth's detailed charts and statistics seemed to challenge the view that poverty was a failure of an individual's morality and instead pointed to the casualisation of employment as a fundamental cause. He also dismissed the view that political unrest was the product of the 'residuum' population, showing that it was the skilled artisans who organised workers and challenged the political status quo.[22] Moreover, Charles Booth's production of colour-coded maps based on an evaluation of the condition of the streets he and his researchers visited were cast as an example of 'scientific' exploration. However, although Booth's assessment of an area began with the condition of the streets, he and his researchers could not help but include moral assessments of the residents. Thus the lowest streets coloured black were described as the 'very poor, lowest class, the vicious and semi-criminal'.[23] Like Mayhew, Greenwood and William Booth, Charles Booth and his researchers were excited by the journey into the underworld, employing a moralising dimension to his analysis of the 'Other'. Indeed, the mapping of mysterious and hitherto unexplored regions had parallels with African adventurers and this would not have been missed by the researchers themselves or those who read their work. Indeed, as Judith Walkowitz has pointed out, Booth 'could not resist the temptation to transform his findings into a story, with vivid characters, drama, and moral significance'.[24] While, Booth's published research was laden with statistics and tables which provided it with a 'scientific' veneer, the notebooks used to describe street scenes were not subjected to such constraints. Often accompanied by a policeman for local information and protection, Booth or his researcher would slip into social stereotypes and adopt a style of writing similar to that of the sensational press.[25] In one account, Booth, who was accompanied by a policeman, cycled around a notorious district of Woolwich named the 'Dusthole' and noted 'smell of dirt, dark stains along the pavement on either side where men and women have relieved nature. Badly lighted figures emerge suddenly from the dark corners and disappear again mysteriously as they had come.'[26]

This style of writing, shorn of its scientific pretence, rivalled the sensational journalist for its use of gothic horror in conjuring-up the depiction of the dark foreboding streets and the 'vicious' and 'semi-criminal' people he might encounter. Moreover, just as Booth slipped into sensationalist language, his stereotyping of the Irish, Jews and poor reflected his Lamarckian and Spencerian evolutionary theory of slum life.[27] To Booth and his fellow researchers, there was little to merit the Irish since they were cast as drunken, disorderly and lazy and, accordingly, an Irish presence in a street invariably condemned it to a darker colour on the map.[28] The Jewish community posed different problems since they did not share a disorderly, lazy or drunken categorisation with the Irish. Booth was puzzled by Jews as, while they appeared industrious, well-attired, sober and family-oriented, they could not be deemed respectable owing to their dirty habits, dishonesty and strange physical appearance. Booth noted that 'no one will deny that the children of Israel are the most law abiding inhabitants of East London'. It was, however, their competitive nature in industry which exhibited 'no personal dignity' or no 'feeling of class loyalty and trade union integrity' that was a character flaw in the Jewish race.[29] Booth's work clearly influenced others as, for example, Walter Besant credits Booth for informing his own views on London's 'alien races'. In his study on East London, Besant believed that 'as soon as the Polish Jew has got his head a little above water he begins to exploit his countrymen'. He added that 'these Jews all succeed, unless they are kept down by their favourite vice of gambling'.[30] Booth saw Jews as an 'urban primitive' race that developed in the slums which, according to Walkowitz, 'saw his blurring of social and biological causation.'[31] Charles Booth also extended the concept of the existence of primitive races to the working class by advocating the establishment of labour colonies that would separate the 'residuum' from the respectable working class.[32] As Felix Driver has pointed out, there was not such an unbridgeable gap between the social imperialist William and the scientific empiricist Charles Booth as there were 'striking points of conversion'.[33]

The book which perhaps represents the apex of research that evaluated the biological consequences of the imperial city was Jack London's *The People of the Abyss*, published in 1902. The book was a culmination of the growing literature on the city and borrowed the research techniques and writing styles of Mayhew and Greenwood and employed the social Darwinist perspectives of William and Charles Booth. In 1902, the American author Jack London was commissioned by the American Press Association to report on the after-effects of the Boer War. However, on arriving in London en route to South Africa, he discovered that the venture had been cancelled. Without a project and with time on his hands, London decided to turn his gaze from the colonial subjects in South Africa to the imperial subjects at home. Like his forebears, Jack London presented a dramatic, compelling and often confused portrait of the East End poor, which was littered throughout with political and social contradictions.[34] On the surface, London differed from his predecessors as he was an American, with working-class origins and a socialist critical of capitalism and imperialism. Jack London's *People of the Abyss* is essentially a devastating critique of industrial capitalism and the British Empire since, for London, it was these processes that had produced the nightmarish conditions he described in the East End. In a stark contrast, British social investigators such as William Booth, Charles Booth and C.F.G. Masterman sought to prevent the crumbling of the Empire from within by calling for religious and social reform. However, despite these very different starting points, Jack London's social investigation had much in common in method and assumption with both earlier and later explorations in the city. Like Greenwood, London disguised himself as one of the poor, in his case a stranded American sailor, in a bid to be accepted by and become one of the people of the abyss. According to London, a mere change of costume transformed his relationship with the poor; he noted that 'no sooner was I out on the streets than I was impressed by the difference in status effected by my clothes. All servility vanished . . . I had become one of them.'[35] This form of ethnographic research was becoming increasingly popular since it was believed that through mixing and living like the subjects, learning their language and experiencing their hardships, a new understanding of the poor would emerge.[36] Moreover, despite his working-class origins, Jack London found the East End and its inhabitants an alien environment on a number of levels. Like his middle-class predecessors, Jack London was an outsider to English popular culture and was equally indifferent to the lives of working-class East Enders. Indeed, his analysis of how capitalism and imperialism had produced a disfigured and primitive 'race', a throwback to a primeval age, led him to exhibit little sympathy for the poor. The people of the abyss did not resemble a working class that was familiar to Jack London and he certainly did not regard them as fit to assume a role in any future socialist project. For a committed socialist, London's lurid descriptions of the people he met in the East End may seem somewhat surprising. However, his damning and insensitive depiction of the poor is explained by the influences of social-Darwinsm and eugenics that run through his work.[37] In describing the poor, Jack London litters his text with bestial metaphors that were matched only by the celebrated imperial explorations of Stanley's *In Darkest Africa* and Booth's *In Darkest England*. In describing the imperial city, Jack London declared that 'a new race has sprung up, a street people. They pass their lives at work and in the streets. They have dens and lairs into which to crawl for sleeping purposes and that is all.'[38] While social commentators from the 1850s had employed the language of the urban jungle, Jack London takes this metaphor further by conjuring up an image of a 'savage human zoo' at the heart of the British Empire. While commentators such as William Booth and C.F.G. Masterman had described the urban jungle as a somewhat chaotic phenomenon, Jack London's human zoo or jungle had some physical boundaries (the East End) and an agency to keep the inhabitants in check (the police). London described the people of the East End as 'a menagerie of garmented bipeds that looked something like humans and more like beasts, and to complete the picture, brass buttoned keepers kept order among them when they snarled too fiercely'. He added that he was thankful for the presence of the keepers as he was not wearing his 'seafaring clothes' and would undoubtedly been a 'mark' for the 'creatures' that 'prowled' along the street.[39] In one passage, London transforms the English working class of the East End into bestial savages who had evolved from the depths of the slum, the product of an aggressive capitalism and imperialism system:

> They reminded me of gorillas. Their bodies were small, ill-shaped, and squat. There were no swelling muscles, no abundant thews and wide-spreading shoulders. They exhibited, rather, an elemental economy of nature, such as the cave-men must have exhibited . . . They possess neither conscience nor sentiment, and they will kill for a half-sovereign, without fear or favour, if they were given half a chance. They are a new species, a breed of city savages. The streets and houses, alleys and courts, are their hunting grounds. As valley and mountain are to the natural savage, street and building are the valley and the mountain to them.[40]

The revelation that a new 'race' or 'breed' had evolved in the city slums featured to varying degrees in the work of Greenwood, Charles and William Booth, and Masterman. These authors saw the city savages as a threat to stable social relations at home and ultimately would undermine the empire through the dilution of the Anglo-Saxon stock. Jack London concurred with this biological analysis, particularly in their ability to defend the Empire. However, he was less convinced of their capacity to destabilise the social or political institutions in Britain. Just as the Empire held its colonial peoples in check with a mixture of military force and pomp and ceremony, the East End 'savages' were subjected to similar bouts of repression and imperial ritual. In one passage, Jack London recounts how he witnessed the King's Coronation pageant complete with its glorification of empire and its show of military power. For Jack London this military power was wielded by 'a totally different race of men' whose only function 'is blindly to obey, and blindly to kill and destroy and stamp out life'.[41] Their role was to preserve order over conquered peoples, be it the 'savages' in the colonies or the home-bred 'primitive' subjects of the East End. The pageant brought empire to the streets of London where the watching crowds witnessed a spectacle imbued with a mixture of power and menace. The parade was led by the 'War Lords of Empire' such as Kitchener of Khartoum and Lord Roberts of India, 'bronzed and worn . . . fighting men of England, masters of destruction, engineers of death'.[42] However, while the military strength of the parade might serve a warning to the disaffected, according to London, imperial pro-paganda swept the dispossessed into a jingoistic frenzy. As the King in his carriage passed by, London recalled that

> Everybody has gone mad. The contagion is sweeping me off my feet – I too want to shout, 'The King! God save the King!' Ragged men about me, tears in their eyes, are tossing up their hats and crying ecstatically.

'Bless 'em! Bless 'em! Bless 'em!' . . . And I check myself with a rush, striving to convince myself that it is all real and rational, and not some glimpse of fairyland.[43]

Thus while Jack London's imagined East End shared many character- istics with social explorers that pre- and postdated his work, the sense that the imperial project could continue unabated was a departure from his liberal counterparts. Here was an empire that created a degen- erate, vicious race of people that required the same dose of discipline and pomp and ceremony as their colonial cousins.

While Jack London's desire to research the East End may have been a result of a cancelled trip to South Africa, his socialism and eugenic convictions clearly supplied the impetus to his research. However, the motivations that drove other philanthropists to the East End were perhaps more obscure and have been the subject of recent historical discussion. To the public, men such as William Booth and W.T. Stead were social imperialists keen to save both the poor and empire, whereas Greenwood, Charles Booth and other social researchers campaigned for better conditions among the poor. However, historians have begun to question their attraction to the slum and speculated that they may well have been drawn to an underworld that subverted Victorian moral codes. W.T. Stead, the moral campaigner against child prostitution and the editor of the *Pall Mall Gazette*, reported his journey into London sin in the style of a 'Gothic Fairytale'. In 'The Maiden Tribute of Modern Babylon', Stead seemingly uncovers the black market for young virgins and demonstrates to his readership how easy it was to procure a girl by actually purchasing a child for £5. As Walkowitz has pointed out, Stead 'seems to have gone over the edge in his attempts to authenticate and document criminal vice'. Stead attempted to live the role as a sexual libertine and explorer and explained that 'I had been visiting brothels and drinking champagne and smoking' in order to ensure that his research and experience was genuine.[44] Even after his conviction for child abduction resulting from the 'Tribute of Modern Babylon' story, Stead continued to explore the city and associ- ate himself with street walkers and vice.[45]

However, it was the university and religious settlements in London that institutionalised the exploration of the East End. In these institu- tions, university men could live among the poor and help evangelise the district. Indeed, such settlements were viewed as beacons of light amidst the heathen population and would prove a useful experience for those intent on missionary work in the Empire. In addition, Koven has argued that these institutions also tested 'heterodox conceptions of masculinity and male sexuality'.[46] During the 1880s, the East End was subjected to a number of settlements; the High Anglican Oxford House, Toynbee Hall and the Oxford House Movement run by Anglo-Catholic slum priests.[47] The homosocial aspect of settlement life clearly attracted university men who desired to escape middle-class moral conventions and bond with fellow male missionaries and even the 'rough' lads from the East End. Some volunteers, such as the homosexual socialist C.R. Ashbee, saw the settlement movement as an opportunity to explore their sexual desires with boys from the East End. According, to Ashbee's diary, the time he spent with 'his boys' at Toynbee Hall moved beyond the classroom where they shared 'love time'. While no evidence of sexual scandal surfaced, it was clear that Ashbee pushed the boundaries of what was acceptable in Toynbee Hall and left after clashing with its founder, Cannon Barnett. Ashbee accused Barnett of being a 'eunuch in spirit and heart' and for being unwilling to lead or be led by the boys.[48] Ashbee was not alone in his fondness for Cockney boys. Residents of Oxford House such as Hugh Legge would refer to them as 'my boys' and would admire their roughness, coarseness and physical strength.[49] Likewise, the slum priests in the Oxford House Movement such as Father Dolling and Father Osborne Jay would mix freely with the boys, establishing gymnasiums and attending music halls and even inviting 'rough' boys into their own homes. The university settlement men, then, like their journalist and social scientist counterparts, were attracted to the moral freedoms that appeared to operate in an enclosed netherworld far removed from polite society. The settlements exposed men to a life of service and sin. Just as colonial missionaries, based in artificial homosocial environments, were tempted by the exotic natives and customs of the indigenous peoples, so too were their domestic equivalents. As we shall see, these institutions not only provided ideal preparation for civilisers of the empire, they also proved an excellent training ground for philanthropists keen to disseminate their imperial missionary zeal to the slums of the provincial cities.

Widely regarded as the heart of empire, London was the repository for an array of social imperialist anxieties that informed urban explorers and underpinned their research methodology and assumptions. Slum dwellers were cast in social, sexual and racial constructs, troubling the social explorers who encountered them as this residuum population was deemed to have been the product of urban and imperial decay. Given London's central importance to the empire, the question remains how far these anxieties were disseminated to the provincial cities. Were social explorers in Portsmouth, Coventry and Leeds similarly consumed with imperial anxieties during the late nineteenth and early twentieth centuries?

Exploring the provincial city

Bill Luckin has recently observed that historians' interest in the social conditions of the late nineteenth century city and their analysis of the 'biologically rooted perceptions of an urban underclass' have been dominated by studies on London.[50] This imbalance may well distort our view of the relationship between the city and imperial anxiety, particularly since London's role at the heart of the empire was recognised by those social explorers who ventured into the East End. It would be a mistake, then, for historians to assume the pervasiveness of an urban and imperial anxiety in England's provincial cities on the basis of the London experience alone. By the 1860s, the provincial centres began developing their own network of environmental agencies such as Improvement Commissioners and Medical Officers of Health who would produce annual reports for public consumption.[51] Inspired by the reporting of Greenwood and Stead in the *Pall Mall Gazette*, the local popular press also shone a light on the darkest slum districts of their respective towns. Given that the rise of the provincial popular press coincided with the sensational reporting in London, there can be little doubt that the style, method and language employed by local reporters owed much to the discourse on London. Barry Doyle's detailed analysis of Norwich's slums presents one of the few recent studies on reporting the provincial slum and noted that social investigators 'delighted in the sense of danger' consciously making parallels with London's East End.[52] Authors drew contrasts with the bourgeois home, shocking readers with stories of the slum dwellers' drunkenness, immorality and filth. In a similar style to East End reporting, provincial reports on slums were often littered with bestial allusions to the poor, describing their 'herding' together in 'rabbit warrens' or 'sties'. However as Dolye has shown, although representations of provincial slums shared characteristics with London's East End, they were not entirely monolithic and reflected the peculiarities of particular urban contexts.[53] Moreover in the provincial city, the civic elites' desire to provide a monumental space directed attention to the municipal heartland rather than the West–East fissure in London. Thus, Medical Health Officers and the media focused on the slum dwellers who resided close to the central zone as these inhabitants were effectively the antithesis of everything that the 'civic gospel' movement hoped to achieve.[54]

All three communities – Portsmouth, Coventry and Leeds – had districts that contemporaries had condemned as slum areas between 1860 and 1914. However, as we shall see, the form that imperial anxiety took in the urban explorers' narratives of the slums was neither uniform nor entirely inspired by the slum travel writing of the East End. Thus, while often employing the language of the London slum traveller, the provincial explorer filtered the potential damage that slumdom was wreaking on the Empire first and foremost through local concerns and contexts. The local press and urban elites, like their London counterparts, were both drawn to and repelled by the slum areas that existed. In late nineteenth-century Portsmouth, Portsea, an area that encompassed the royal naval base and dockyard, had become renowned for its low entertainment venues, public houses and brothels. Indeed, during an attempted crack-down on the many public houses that inundated the district in the 1890s, anti-drink campaigners labelled the area the 'Devil's Acre'.[55] During the same period in Coventry, poor-quality housing and courts encircled the city centre so that the Chauntry and Rope Walk became synonymous in the city with slumdom. In other slum areas it was calculated that rates of consumption were eight times higher in St John's Street than the rest of the city, while in Much Park Street infant mortality was four times higher than the figure for Coventry as a whole.[56] In Leeds, the Leyland district was marked out for special attention, for not only did it contain some of the worst housing and sanitary conditions, it was also home to a substantial Eastern European Jewish community. For Leeds's urban elite, the monumental civic architecture was an island of civilisation, encircled by slums where 'prostitution, assault and larceny were seen as rife'.[57]

Of the three communities, Portsmouth, the town closest to London, was also the community that shared the most characteristics with the capital. As in London, contemporaries perceived that Portsmouth possessed a special connection with the Empire and, as with the capital, it also brought some unwelcome repercussions. One commentator noted that, from its connection to the navy, Portsmouth's

> relationship to the life of the Empire is of an unrivalled description, and the fact that so many of its adult male population are, in one sense or another, servants of the State, and are not under private employment, seemed to direct special attention to its crying needs on the part of the National Church.[58]

Just as there was an absence of an indigenous philanthropic leadership in the East End, the state's dominance as an employer meant that Portsmouth lacked a cluster of wealthy philanthropic industrialists from the private sector who were common in the manufacturing districts. Portsea itself had, until the early nineteenth century, been a walled community for military defence purposes which had increased its isolation and 'Otherness' from the rest of the town. Tightly packed with poor-quality housing, inadequate sanitation and a labyrinth of courts that lay behind the main thoroughfares, Portsea became the focus of religious missionaries who undoubtedly took their cue from their counterparts in London and the wider Empire. The Reverend Reginald Shutte was one missionary whose work in Portsea appears heavily influenced by the sensational explorers of the 1860s such as Greenwood. After completing a degree in Cambridge and being ordained in 1854, Shutte established the Mission of the Good Shepherd in Portsea in 1866 to save fallen women.[59] Shutte was a flamboyant ritualist and was not afraid to court either religious controversy or publicity for his cause.[60] Indeed, Shutte's pamphlets spoke directly to his middle-class readership in sensational terms that would both intrigue and appal them. An imperial theme ran through Shutte's texts as he placed himself as both daring explorer and saviour of the Empire's reputation. Shutte first demanded from his readers whether they 'know Portsea' or 'walked up and down the leading streets' near the dockyard. If so he noted that they would be familiar with the

> Bloated, draggled women in dirty print frocks, who lounge along in twos or threes without bonnet or shawl, and who in broad daylight make your flesh creep with their loathsome words and gestures. These are some of the companions of our soldiers and sailors, in whose society they spend their hours of leisure. They are just now sunning themselves on the Hard or Queen Street, and are waiting to pick up the latest gossip about the Channel Fleet, or drink a dram with a friend. Their name is legion, and, as you look into their faces, each one seems fouler than the last.[61]

Shutte, then, described these prostitutes in Portsea in bestial terms and depicted their public displays of immorality as bringing disgrace to the main thoroughfares of Portsea. Moreover, their presence also had repercussions for the Empire since they drew the armed forces into their depravity. The brothels of Portsea, according to Shutte, had become 'infamous from the Baltic to Japan'.[62] Shutte then took on the role of urban explorer to venture into the 'rookeries' where his readership would have feared to tread:

> All I can say, is that if you have penetrated into the dens of lust and violence which are closely packed within the slice of brick and mortar that lies between St George's Square and Queen Street, your heart will have been sickened, and you will be giddy with sights and sounds which your brain refuses to forget . . . our work is to deal with the poorest and most depraved of the classes that haunt these lanes and alleys.[63]

One can only speculate at the excitement that Shutte and his readership experienced when he 'penetrated' the 'dens of lust and violence' in a bid to save Portsea's fallen women. However, there can be little

doubt that Shutte's mission was fuelled by a sense of imperial exploration as he invited African imperial missionaries to speak to his con-
gregation to mark the official opening of his new chapel buildings.[64]
Indeed, the African explorers were in popular demand in Portsea since
a similar chapel in Penny Street also invited the group, which included
the Bishop of Maritzburg in South Africa and the African explorer
Commander Cameron. After the Bishop had outlined some of the
'heathen' superstitions and immoral practices, Cameron urged his
audience to support the quest of civilising inferior populations since
'these people [Africans] might go forward without seeing a church or
clergy-man, and it was highly important, therefore, that the English
people should, by every measure in their power, seek to develop their
Christian missions'. It could not have escaped the Portsea missionaries
in the audience that they were charged with a similar task in the
empire's chief naval port.[65]

The missionary zeal in Portsmouth's slums did not end with
Shutte's death in 1892.[66] Inspired by the University settlements in the
East End, Winchester College established St Agatha's Mission in
Portsea, which was led by Father Dolling from 1885.[67] As we have
seen, Dolling was apprenticed in missionary work in the East End and
recognised in Portsea a similar urban and immoral decay that he had
witnessed in Stepney. However, for Dolling the significance of empire
was even greater in Portsea owing to its naval strategic importance,
and he saw the symbols of navy and empire inscribed into his new
environment. He noted that 'the streets are, most of them, very narrow
and quaint, named after great admirals and sea-battles, with old world,
red-tiled roofs, and interiors almost like cabins of ships'. Turning his
attention to the inhabitants, Dolling remembered 'sailors everywhere,
sometimes fighting, sometimes courting' and 'slatternly women creeping out of some little public house'. However, like his African missionary counterparts, he found it important to describe in some detail
the shocking heathen customs of the natives both to appal the reader
and to illustrate how the mission eventually brought light and civilisation to a dark and corrupted area. Dolling recounted that on his first
Sunday afternoon stroll through the district he witnessed 'a Landport
Dance':

> Two girls, their only clothing a pair of sailors' trousers each, and two
> sailor lads, their only clothing the girls' petticoats, were dancing a kind
> of breakdown up and down the street, all the neighbours looked on
> amused but unastonished, until one couple, the worse for drink toppled
> over. I stepped forward to help them up, but my endeavour was evidently
> looked upon from a hostile point of view, for the parish voice was trans-
> lated into a shower of stones.[68]

In another passage, Dolling complained that the poor lighting in Portsea courts and the abundance of slaughterhouses in the area had helped foster a savage population. Indeed, he likened Portsea's conditions to those of the East End and warned of the terrible dangers (meaning the Whitechapel murders) that might call upon Portsmouth if nothing was done.[69] He claimed that among the Portsea boys 'it is no uncommon thing to find one who eats raw meat and drinks blood'. These descriptions of the native with their mysterious semi-naked dances, primitive rituals and implicit references to cannibalism glamorised Dolling's mission and drew readers into an unknown underworld which paralleled contemporary African expeditions. It was perhaps no accident that reviewers of the book and biographers of Dolling consistently cited the 'Landport dance' incident as it firmly set Dolling in the role of intrepid imperial slum explorer.[70] He was successful cultivating this image since one biographer likened him to an imperial adventurer, reclaiming his heathen brethren street by street. The Reverend Charles Osborne marvelled at his

> wonderful record, and not one word of it is an exaggeration. It is wonderful as a witness to that spirit of statesmanship which enabled Dolling like a capable general to grasp position after position. Truly from his watch-tower in that extraordinary 'parsonage' he was like an ecclesiastical Cecil Rhodes, planning ever fresh developments.[71]

Dolling was a liberal imperialist, firmly supporting the Boer Wars in the 1890s, asserting that 'it is hard to maintain Imperialism without a military autocrat'.[72] Indeed, his work in London and Portsmouth had led him to believe the modern city fostered alarming levels of vice and decay which were undermining the English stock. In London, Dolling singled out the Jews for their overly competitive nature, a view shared by his biographer, who believed them to be the 'greatest rack-renters' among the 'swarms of aliens' who inhabited London.[73]

For Dolling, an imperial war 'with its defeats, was a great corrective to national indulgence', and Portsea provided the ideal base to contribute to a national rejuvenation. Situating the mission in the heart of Portsea, Dolling's chief objective was to 'save' young boys from Portsmouth's 'sinks of iniquity' and prepare them for a life in the services.[74] These boys were sent for training on the hulk *HMS Northampton* from 1894.[75] Osborne noted that 'it was impossible to realise that many of these smart, well-set-up young fellows had once been underfed and neglected lads whom Dolling had got hold of in former years and pulled up out of the social abyss'.[76] He praised those young soldiers and sailors who left his mission and 'went forth to shed their blood in order that the English flag might continue to proudly fly'.[77] Alternatively, for those boys unsuitable for naval training, Dolling encouraged emigration and spent over £1,000 of parish funds on the project. However, the greatest financial outlay was Dolling's parsonage, which cost over £4,000 and was designed to allow an informal relationship to develop between the missionaries and those seeking help.[78]

Dolling's St Agatha's parsonage seems to have been modelled on Jay's mission in Shoreditch. The Reverend Arthur Osborne Jay, a friend of Dolling (not to be confused with C.E. Osborne, Dolling's biographer), horrified contemporaries by sleeping in the Mission building, which was complete with a homeless shelter, gymnasium and boxing club.[79] Dolling's parsonage possessed a gymnasium, over twenty beds for his guests, a room for the Winchester boys and a room for himself. Living in such close quarters to both the working-class youths and the young visiting missionaries, Dolling and Jay rode roughshod over carefully constructed social boundaries and protocols of Victorian society. Indeed, Dolling recalled that he would often invite visiting Winchester boys to his room to talk. In addition, Dolling undoubtedly forged a close relationship with the boys he trained. Osborne observed that 'Dolling's sailor-boys abounded all over the globe, their photographs lined in part, the walls of the parsonage, and whenever they had leave and were in England, some of them were sure to be staying in the house'.[80] Indeed, Dolling wrote that 'all over the world at this moment there are my dear boys, who look to this place [the parsonage] as their home, from whence all the love they have ever known has reached them'.[81] However, Dolling's informal relationship with 'his boys' did raise questions over his conduct, since he would invite the 'slummiest' boys into his room and would often accompany boys to low music halls.[82] His biographers consistently noted both his feminine and masculine qualities. Clayton described Dolling as possessing 'the sympathy and tenderness of the women with the strength and courage of the man'; he was 'not so much non-sexual as bi-sexual'.[83] Likewise, Osborne noted Dolling's duel persona since he exhibited a 'masculine strength' with a 'feminine' character.[84] Like his missionary counterparts in the outposts of the British Empire, Dolling fashioned a homosocial society that was free from bourgeois domesticity. Gaining approval for its religious objectives, the mission afforded Dolling the opportunity for excitement and to forge relationships that were on the margins of respectability. Portsea's squalor and its militarised environs attracted Dolling since, as Osborne observed, 'excitement did not weary him, it stimulated his efforts; and Portsmouth, whatever its faults, is not dull'. Indeed, Osborne went on to portray a vivid image of Portsmouth in the 1890s:

The dashes of colour afforded by the uniforms of the soldiers and sailors who fill the streets; the constant music of the bands as the troops swing past from route-marching; the summer concourse of all sorts of odd people to the sea-front (just like the individuals who fill up so many of John Leech's drawings in the best days of *Punch*); the briny atmosphere, as it were, that pervades the whole place – suited him thoroughly. Dolling, would have died of ennui amid suburban villas. Landport, even when he employed his most lurid colours in the painting of it, was far more congenial to his mind as a place to live in than any region of prim decorum could ever have been.[85]

Osborne's insights into the seamy side of Portsmouth may explain why Dolling was one of many missionaries drawn to the town. However, Dolling's description of Portsmouth as the 'sink of iniquity' was too much for local councillors who were keen to uphold Portsmouth's good name. In 1894, Leon Emanuel, the Mayor of Portsmouth, complained that a 'serious stigma had been cast on the borough of Portsmouth by a reverend gentleman'. Emanuel criticised Dolling for living 'not five minutes or so' in Portsmouth and making 'wicked' allegations 'without a shadow of foundation in fact'. In contrast Emanuel had 'been born and bred in the ancient borough of Portsmouth, and he was proud beyond measure to stand there that evening as one of its sons'.[86] Portsmouth's unique position as a bastion of imperial naval strength ensured that it was the subject of many more missionaries than either Coventry or Leeds. Indeed, Portsmouth's juxtaposition within empire attracted men like Shutte and Dolling who brought with them the approach and methods of the East End's slum priests and ideals of the university settlements. Between 1870 and 1900, there were a host of soldier and sailor homes and retreats for 'fallen women', and between 1900 and 1914 there were no fewer than forty mission rooms set up in or around Portsea.[87]

In Coventry, the profile of the city's charities and missionaries differed markedly to that of Portsmouth. The trade directories between 1874 and 1940 reveal that most of the few charities that existed were long-established enterprises that specifically provided for the ailing watchmaking and weaving trades. The 'Coventry Watchmakers Widows and Orphans' charity, for example, was designed particularly to cater for the families of artisans, and typified the paternalistic dimension that had been integral to the town's late eighteenth- and early nineteenth-century trades.[88] No such charities developed with the bicycle and motor industries because of the speed of their growth and the widely held view that these semi-skilled workers earned a good wage.[89] However, the city's housing infrastructure was unable to cope with this rapid industrial development, and living conditions for those transient casual workers sharply deteriorated. Between 1874 and 1940, the number of philanthropic institutions fluctuated between six and eight charities or missions, with no provision made for 'fallen women'.[90] Whereas the number of missionaries who sought to tackle the slums in Coventry was substantially fewer than in Portsmouth, there was a strong conviction that certain areas in the city were becoming increasingly lost to uncivilising influences. Moreover, Coventry missionaries, like their counterparts in Portsmouth, were met with derision by local councillors keen to uphold the town's good name. Indeed, there were striking contrasts between the reception of London missionaries and those in the provinces since the weak civic leadership in London ensured that sensational claims from urban explorers were often left unchallenged. A vibrant local press and vigilant urban elite in the provinces meant that social explorers' publicity campaigns met with some opposition. Just as Dolling had been castigated by Portsmouth's urban elite for his publication of slum life, so too were Coventry religious missionaries for their claim that the city was 'the filthiest place in the Midlands – nay the world'. By the 1890s, the influx of labour working in the bicycle and car industries had placed an intolerable pressure on the city's housing stock which triggered a debate on the nature of the slums in the local press. The religious missions and socialist lantern shows were accused of sensationalism as some councillors either denied the existence of the slums or blamed the residences' low morality for perpetuating overcrowded and unsanitary conditions.[91] Along with the religious missionaries, the Medical Officers were some of the few members of the respectable classes to enter the slums. In 1899, the Coventry Medical Health Officer heightened fears of the slum by reporting that 'these insanitary houses, close filthy and evil smelling . . . are hot beds of corruption and crime and drunkenness and everything vicious in the city'.[92] Campaigners regaled readers with testimonies of squalid conditions in which the inhabitants were described in bestial terms citing the proliferation of public houses and slaughterhouses for their slippage into barbarity. Residents in these areas, it was reported, would think nothing of sitting down to a family meal with a corpse laid out in the same room.[93] Not only did the slum reduce families to bestial levels of existence, it could also change physical appearances. According to one missionary, these new urban conditions would foster a languid people, drink-obsessed and leading to oversized heads and water on the brain.[94] Influenced by leading councillors who held substantial business interests in the city's engineering industries, the debate in Coventry centred on the fear that the city was creating a workforce unfit for the new industrial challenges ahead.[95] However, despite the fact that slum housing was limited to a number of well-known streets and that the city had become known as a 'Klondike' town, there were few social investigations into urban poverty.[96] Unlike in Portsmouth, the fear that urban decay would impact upon matters of nation and empire was somewhat secondary to the fortunes of the bicycle and motor industries and the reputation of the city as an industrial powerhouse.

The population increase in Leeds during the nineteenth century, on the other hand, led a good many of the urban elite to worry about urban degeneration. Whereas Coventry slums were identified through notorious street names, whole districts circling the centre of Leeds were deemed to have fallen into urban decay. The districts were easily recognised, not only through the poor-quality housing but also through the 'heathen' people who resided there. After a body was discovered in an Elland canal in 1893, the coroner, on failing to locate a bible for use in the inquest, complained that 'I think you will find more bibles among the blacks where the missionaries go than here'. The *Yorkshire Evening Post* reported the apparent absence of Christianity in parts of Leeds under the headline 'In Darkest Elland'.[97] Furthermore, by 1914 the Leylands district had become the home for over fifteen thousand Eastern European Jews who had fled the Russian pogroms.[98] Taking a similar stance to the social explorers in the East End during the same period, Leeds social commentators wrote of a 'foreign colony at the heart of an English town' that had 'taken such complete possession' of the area that 75 per cent of the children were Jews.[99] Mr John Burnett, who was researching the Leeds sweating system for the Board of Trade in 1888, reported that

> The streets in the Leylands are beginning to assume distinctively foreign characteristics. The names above shops are foreign, and the notices in the windows are printed in Hebrew characters. The words spoken are unintelligible to English ears, and about the race of children in the streets and the people at the door there can be no mistake.[100]

However, it was an investigation into the Jewish quarter by a journalist from the *Lancet* that really inflamed local anxieties on the issue of 'alien' immigration. Presented as a scientific study on the conditions of the sweating industry, the *Lancet* report contained all the hallmarks of 'new journalism' and was condemned by one councillor as 'sensationalist'.[101] Commenting on the unsanitary conditions in Leylands, the reporter noted that 'it is only with regard to the foreign population that the nuisance has arisen'.[102] Indeed, the *Lancet*'s description of the Jewish manufacturer conformed to the East End stereotype Jew who would employ sharp practices to acquire maximum profit at the expense of the perilous conditions of his workforce. Indeed, the *Lancet* overtly associated Leylands with contagion since it was described as only a 'stone's throw' from a smallpox outbreak and 'only separated by one comparatively broad street from the district which suffered principally from the typhus epidemic'. However, it was in fact the English workers' district that been struck down by the smallpox and typhus epidemic. While inspecting the properties at the centre of the epidemic, the *Lancet* appeared surprised that the tenants were English and worked for the large established manufacturers as opposed to the Jewish sweat shops. In one visit to an English women's home it was noted that her dwelling was filthy 'though it is scarcely fair to complain of the condition of her home seeing the slender wages she is able to earn'. No such sympathies were extended to 'foreign Jews' who 'do not understand' the English sanitary standards. However, just as the Jewish community had confused Booth's researchers, the *Lancet* acknowledged that Jewish homes 'are particularly clean, and they are much more careful in respect to their food than their neighbours' and that 'they are a remarkable intelligent race'.[103] Thus, despite all of the evidence to the contrary, the thrust of the report identified the Jewish people, with their lust for profit and unclean personal habits, as the source of contagion. Moreover, for the middle-class reader, the fear that contagion might spread beyond Leylands through the products produced in the sweating shops heightened anxieties. The *Lancet's* reports were reprinted verbatim in the *Leeds Mercury* and caused considerable concern in the town. The scientific journal warned readers that 'we maintain that there is no guarantee whatever that clothes made in the privacy of these little cottages in back streets will not occasionally be contaminated by germs of diseases such as smallpox or scarlet fever'.[104] The *Lancet* had helped foster a climate of fear in Leeds with a 'scientific clarity' and authority that mere social commentators could not match. Indeed, in a response to the first of the *Lancet's* reports, the liberal *Leeds Mercury* informed its readers that 'We extend hospitality to the unfortunate Jews who are driven by the fanaticism from their own lands, but we are entitled to be protected against the dangers which may arise from their habits and defiance of the law'.[105] The *Lancet* reports sought to contrast the conditions of the East End Jews with their counterparts in the Leeds Leylands district. In doing so, this seemingly independent investigation confirmed pre-existing prejudices about Jewish health, customs and behaviour and marked out the community as requiring additional surveillance in the fear that, left unattended, the nation's stock and ultimately the imperial project might be undermined.[106]

These fears of urban decay and contagion led Dr William Hall, a local surgeon, to carry out an extensive study that intended to measure the development of both the 'Anglo Saxon and Jewish races'. His quest was supported by Sir John Gorst, a former Vice President of the Education Committee, who accompanied Hall on visits to Leeds elementary schools in 1904.[107] Drawing on evidence from the Physical Degeneration Committee, for which Hall had made a significant contribution, Gorst argued in the House of Commons the necessity for free or subsidised school meals. He asked 'how could they carry on this great Empire, if they allowed causes of this kind which affected the physical condition of the people to continue to operate, and thus prevent their having soldiers and sailors fit to serve for the protection of the Empire?'[108] Hall, who was a local factory surgeon, claimed to have measured over a hundred thousand children in the Yorkshire area and estimated in 1903 that over 50 per cent of the poorest class of Leeds child suffered from rickets.[109] His extensive research was called before the Inter-Departmental Committee on Physical Deterioration of 1904 which had been convened because of the poor physical condition of Boer War volunteers. To the astonishment of some of the committee, Hall's research demonstrated through statistical analysis and photographs that the 'alien Jew' was far superior physically to their English counterparts. Hall rejected the idea of hereditary degeneration and instead argued that the poorest Anglo-Saxon children's stunted development was due to 'increased neglect'.[110] He cited the nutritious food consumed in the Jewish household and the pivotal role of mothers who largely stayed at home 'to fulfil their duty'.[111] These findings were considered 'odd' by members of the committee as they seemed to contradict the received wisdom that, in the hierarchy of races, the Eastern European Jew was considerably below the Anglo-Saxon.[112] Hall's 'striking photographs' showing the physical superiority of the Jewish children drew derision from some members of the Committee. Some dismissed the images as unrepresentative 'selections' of children as the evidence 'quite differs from what has been found on the Continent, in Poland'.[113] Indeed, this scepticism of Hall's work was articulated by the witness the Reverend W.E. Rees, a member of the Salford Education Committee:

> I should be inclined to doubt Dr Hall's of Leeds results; and, so far as they are sound, there is one factor which I think he has omitted, namely, that the Jewish is a sub-tropical race and they mature more quickly. At thirteen you would expect a Jew boy to be more advanced than an English boy, just as you find the English boy relatively more advanced than the Norwegian boy.[114]

Despite Hall's findings, the discussion in the Leeds press during the early twentieth century dovetailed into the national and imperial anxieties over the pernicious influence of the 'alien invasion' that was so evident in the 1904 Inter-Departmental Committee. As Searle has noted, at this time 'journalists and politicians continued to discuss the problem of 'physical deterioration' in language which often bordered on panic'.[115] Furthermore, there can be little doubt that debates about the Jewish worker in the East End informed debates in Leeds. John Dyche, a Russian Jew who settled in Leeds during the 1890s, complained that 'politicians on the stump', 'sensational journalists seeking good copy' and 'responsible statesmen such as Chamberlain' propagated the view that the British workman was being ruined by the Russian Jew.[116] Entering into a discussion with Arnold White in the *Contemporary Review* in 1898, Dyche noted that the Jews had 'baffled' Charles Booth's researchers in the East End since they had started with *a priori* assumptions and judged other people 'by one's own standard'.[117] Complaints about the Jewish community in Leeds were acute during this period, particularly when they used public amenities outside of their 'prescribed area'. In a series of letters in the *Yorkshire Evening Post*, a lively discussion ensued, with the majority of correspondents taking an anti-Semitic stance. In one letter the author complained that

> we have no objection to the alien in the abstract but when a place of recreation is provided in a particular neighbourhood the inference is that it is intended to benefit primarily those who live in the immediate vicinity. We consider, therefore, that we have a legitimate grievance, when, on the only days we can use our park, we find it over-run with 'extraneous bodies.' On Saturday and Sunday last these aliens came 'not as single spies but in battalions' – roads, park and seats all crowded with them, and no place for a weary Gentile to rest.

Another letter criticised the Jewish community for their poor 'public cleanliness' and added that 'until the alien is prepared to conform to a higher standard he must not be surprised if respectable citizens complain'. A follow-up correspondent declared that he was 'not surprised that there is an anti-Semitic movement in Leeds'.[118] Although the civic authorities did not intervene to prohibit Jews from using the public parks, in 1908 a number of Leeds publicans barred Jews from using the main public bar. This was brought to the attention of the local magistrates, who sought advice from the Secretary of State, Winston Churchill. It was reported that, despite the Jews in question being 'perfectly respectable and well conducted':

> In Leeds recently, some of the large public houses have started to prevent Jews entering the main public rooms especially those in which music was being performed. The Jewish community brought the matter before

the Licensing Bench and asked the Justice to refuse the licence on the grounds of the house being badly constructed. The solicitors who represented the publican stated they would not allow Jews into these rooms but would provide for them in other rooms. The whole of the Jews in Leeds are very much upset about this attack upon them and Jews in other towns are talking the matter up. I do not know whether anything can be done in the matter but I am sure a race feeling in our larger towns is something to be avoided.[119]

These accounts illustrate the uneasy relationship that had developed between Eastern European Jews and the indigenous population in Leeds and the sense that the 'Other' ought not stray from a prescribed area of the city.

Conclusion

Social investigations into the city in the late nineteenth and early twentieth centuries were undoubtedly driven by the social and cultural anxieties that emanated from London. London was the heart of the empire and so social researchers ultimately linked urban decay and physical degeneration to imperial concerns. The East End became a playground for journalists, slum priests and university men and women who, through newspapers and memoirs, dramatised their efforts in civilisng the poor. Sensational reporting met with little opposition in an East End that lacked an urban elite with a substantial civic stake in the area. Towns experiencing similar social problems during this period proved irresistible to social observers. Thus, whereas Coventry's relative prosperity saw a more localised response to poverty, places such as Portsmouth and Leeds were visited by philanthropists and social observers who had developed their analysis of poverty and its consequences for empire in London. However, unlike in the East End, philanthropists like Dolling and journalists from the *Lancet* had to navigate their way through local civic elites anxious to protect their own and their town's reputation. Thus while the social research on provincial towns was certainly informed by imperial anxieties stemming from the 'East End crisis', social investigators' claims were tempered by an interested and active civic elite who placed their town's reputation before the welfare of the empire. While historians have rightly noted that the contemporary anxieties surrounding the city became acute with the poor health of recruits for the Boer War, the following chapter explores a rather different side of the conflict. It explores how, when viewed through a municipal perspective, civic identity became fused with an imperial adventure that fostered a genuine popular response to an imperial war.

Notes

1 C.F.G. Masterman, *The Heart of Empire. Discussions of Problems of Modern City Life in England* (London, Fisher Unwin, 1901), pp. viii–ix.

2 Masterman, *The Heart of Empire*, pp. 21–2.

3 A. Mayne, *The Imagined Slum: Newspaper Representations in Three Cities, 1870–1914* (Leicester, Leicester University Press, 1993); M. Valverde, 'The Dialect of the Familiar and Unfamiliar: "The Jungle" in Early Slum Travel Writing', *Sociology*, 30, 3, August 1996; J. Marriott, *The Other Empire. Metropolis, India and Progress in the Colonial Imagination* (Manchester, Manchester University Press, 2003); S. Koven, *Slumming. Sexual and Social Politics in Victorian England* (Princeton, Princeton University Press, 2004).

4 *Household Words*, 11 June 1853, p. 168.

5 *Household Words*, 31 August 1850, p. 551.

6 *Household Words*, 22 June 1850, p. 299.

7 F. Driver, *Geography Militant. Cultures of Exploration and Empire* (Oxford, Blackwell, 2001), p. 182.

8 Valverde, 'The Dialect of the Familiar and Unfamiliar', p. 496.

9 Marriott, *The Other Empire*, p. 160.

10 Marriott, *The Other Empire*, p. 160.

11 B. Luckin, 'Revisiting the Idea of Degeneration in Urban Britain, 1830–1900', *Urban History*, 33, 3, 2 (2006), p. 235.

12 P. Keating (ed.), *Into Unknown England, 1866–1913. Selections from the Social Explorers* (Glasgow, Fontana, 1976, 1981 edn), pp. 241–2.

13 Keating (ed.), *Into Unknown England*, p. 244.

14 Driver, *Geography Militant*, p. 198.

15 H.G. Wells, *The Time Machine* (London, Heinemann, 1895).

16 J.R. Walkowitz, *City of Dreadful Delight. Narratives of Sexual Danger in Late Victorian London* (London, Virago Press, 1992), p. 17.

17 Keating, *Into Unknown England*, pp. 65–6.

18 Koven, *Slumming*, p. 60.

19 W. Booth, *In Darkest England and the Way Out* (London, Salvation Army, 1890, 1970 edn), pp. 11–12.

20 T. Boone, *Youth in Darkest England. Working-Class Children at the Heart of Victorian Empire* (London, Routledge, 2005), p. 85.

21 Booth, *In Darkest England*, p. 191; Boone, *Youth in Darkest England*, p. 86.

22 Walkowitz, *The City of Dreadful Delight*, p. 31.

23 Driver, *Geography Militant*, p. 186.

24 Walkowitz, *The City of Dreadful Delight*, pp. 33–4.

25 D. Englander, 'Comparisons and Contrasts: Henry Mayhew and Charles Booth as Social Investigators', in D. Englander and R. O'Day (eds), *Retrieved Riches. Social Investigation in Britain, 1840–1914* (Aldershot, Scolar Press, 1995), p. 132.

26 LSE, Charles Booth on-line Archive, Police note books; http://booth.lse.ac.uk/notebooks/b357/jpg/23.html. Accessed 8 February 2011. For an account of the Dusthole district see D. Reeder, 'Representations of Metropolis: Descriptions of the Social Environment in *Life and Labour*', in D. Englander and R. O'Day (eds), *Retrieved Riches: Social Investigation in Britain, 1840–1914* (Aldershot: Scolar Press, 1995), p. 331.

27 Walkowitz, *The City of Dreadful Delight*, p. 35.

28 D. Englander, 'Booth's Jews: the Presentation of Jews and Judaism in *Life and Labour of the People in London*' in D. Englander and R. O'Day (eds), *Retrieved Riches: Social Investigation in Britain, 1840–1914* (Aldershot: Scolar Press, 1995), p. 290.

29 Quoted in W. Besant, *East London* (London, Chatto and Windus, 1899, 1903 edn), pp. 195–6.

30 Besant, *East London*, pp. 193–4.
31 Walkowitz, *The City of Dreadful Delight*, p. 35; Englander, 'Booth's Jews', p. 305.
32 J. Brown, 'Charles Booth and Labour Colonies', *Economic History Review*, 21, 2, August 1968, p. 357.
33 Driver, *Geography Militant*, p. 193.
34 J. McLaughlin, *Writing the Urban Jungle. Reading Empire in London from Doyle to Eliot*, (Charlottesville, University of Virginia, 2000), pp. 125–6.
35 J. London, *The People of the Abyss*, (London, Thomas Nelson and Sons, 1903, 1916 edn), p. 263.
36 McLaughlin, *Writing the Urban Jungle*, p. 105.
37 London, *The People of the Abyss*, pp. 126–7.
38 London, *The People of the Abyss*, p. 25.
39 London, *The People of the Abyss*, p. 324.
40 London, *The People of the Abyss*, pp. 324–5.
41 London, *The People of the Abyss*, pp. 167, 172.
42 London, *The People of the Abyss*, p. 171.
43 London, *The People of the Abyss*, p. 173.
44 Quoted in Walkowitz, *The City of Dreadful Delight*, p. 113.
45 Walkowitz, *The City of Dreadful Delight*, p. 113.
46 Koven, *Slumming*, p. 229.
47 Koven, *Slumming*, pp. 229, 255.
48 Koven, *Slumming*, pp. 265–6.
49 Koven, *Slumming*, p. 265.
50 Luckin, 'Revisiting the Idea of Urban Degeneration in Urban Britain', p. 241.
51 A. Day, 'A Spirit of Improvements: Improvement Commissioners, Boards of Health and Central-local Relations in Portsea', in R.J. Morris and R.H. Trainor (eds), *Urban Governance. Britain and Beyond 1750* (Aldershot, Ashgate, 2000), p. 112.
52 B. Doyle, 'Mapping Slums in a Historic City: Representing Working Class Communities in Edwardian Norwich', *Planning Perspectives*, 16, 2001, p. 52.
53 Doyle, 'Mapping Slums in a Historic City', pp. 57, 59–60.
54 S. Gunn, *The Public Culture of the Victorian Middle Class. Ritual and Authority in the English Industrial City, 1840–1914* (Manchester, Manchester University Press, 2000, 2007 edn), p. 60.
55 The term 'Devil's Acre' appears to be first used by Charles Dickens in the 1850s to describe a deprived area of Westminster, London. The term was adopted by Portsmouth's anti-drink campaigners in the mid-1890s. See *Household Words*, 22 June 1850; *Hampshire Telegraph*, 8 September 1894.
56 K. Richardson, *Twentieth Century Coventry* (Bungay, Chaucer Press, 1972), pp. 35, 221.
57 Gunn, *The Public Culture of the Victorian Middle Class*, p. 62.
58 C.E. Osborne, *The Life of Father Dolling* (London, Edward Arnold, 1903), p. 58.
59 For a more detailed analysis of Portsmouth 'outcasts' see R. Denyer, 'The Bitter Cry of Outcast Portsmouth: Poverty and Crime 1860–1900' (BA dissertation, University of Portsmouth, 2004).
60 *Hampshire Telegraph*, 15 October 1892.
61 Portsmouth City Record Office (hereafter PCRO), 11A/J/5, R.N. Shutte, 'Mission of the Good Shepherd, Portsea', 1870, p. 1.
62 PCRO, Shutte, 'Mission of the Good Shepherd', p. 2.
63 PCRO, Shutte, 'Mission of the Good Shepherd', pp. 2–3.
64 *Hampshire Telegraph*, 13 December 1876.
65 *Hampshire Telegraph*, 13 December 1876.
66 *Hampshire Telegraph*, 15 October 1892.
67 Osborne, *The Life of Father Dolling*, p. 55.
68 R.R. Dolling, *Ten Years in a Portsmouth Slum* (London, S.C. Brown, Langham & Co., 1896, 1903 edn), p. 18.

69 Osborne, *The Life of Father Dolling*, p. 126.
70 For example, *Leeds Mercury*, 8 July 1896; *London Quarterly Review*, 27 January 1896; *The Speaker*, 22 August 1896; J. Clayton, *Father Dolling. A Memoir* (London, Wells, Gardner, Darton & Co., 1902), p. 23.
71 Osborne, *The Life of Father Dolling*, p. 85.
72 Clayton, *Father Dolling*, p. 56.
73 Osborne, *The Life of Father Dolling*, p. 244.
74 *Hampshire Telegraph*, 24 February 1894. The 'sinks of iniquity' quote and description of Portsmouth's slum in his book caused outrage among Portsmouth's urban elite who feared that it would damage the town's national representation.
75 Dolling, *Ten Years in a Portsmouth Slum*, p. 112.
76 Osborne, *The Life of Father Dolling*, p. 89.
77 *Hampshire Telegraph*, 3 March 1894.
78 Dolling, *Ten Years in a Portsmouth Slum*, p. 185.
79 Koven, *Slumming*, p. 256.
80 Osborne, *The Life of Father Dolling*, p. 89.
81 Quoted in Clayton, *Father Dolling*, p. 42.
82 Koven, *Slumming*, p. 256; Clayton, *Father Dolling*, p. 42.
83 Clayton, *Father Dolling*, p. 134.
84 Osborne, *The Life of Father Dolling*, p. 178.
85 Osborne, *The Life of Father Dolling*, p. 67.
86 *Hampshire Telegraph*, 24 February 1894.
87 *Butcher and Co Borough of Portsmouth Directory, 1874–5* (London, 1875); *Chamberlain's Directory 1881–2* (Portsmouth, 1882); *Kellys Directory of Portsmouth 1892, 1900, 1909–10, 1913–14* (London). For a useful analysis of Agnes Weston's sailor's home see M. Conley, *From Jack Tar to Union Jack. Representing Naval Manhood in the British Empire, 1870–1918* (Manchester, Manchester University Press, 2009), ch. 2.
88 *Coventry Directory 1874* (Coventry, Curtis and Beamish).
89 B. Beaven and J. Griffiths, 'Urban Elites, Socialists and Notions of Citizenship in an Industrial Boomtown: Coventry *c.* 1870–1914', *Labour History Review*, 69, 1, April 2004, p. 13.
90 *Coventry Directory 1874, 1886, 1892, 1901* (Coventry, Curtis and Beamish); *Spennell's Annual Directory of Coventry and District 1912, 1919* (no publisher or location identified); *Coventry Directory 1932, 1940* (Surrey, Coomelands).
91 *Coventry Standard*, 3 March 1899; *Coventry Herald*, 10 March 1899.
92 *Midland Daily Telegraph*, 27 March 1906.
93 *Midland Daily Telegraph*, 18 July 1906.
94 *Coventry* Times, 18 March 1891.
95 B. Beaven, *Leisure, Citizenship and Working-Class Men in Britain, 1850–1945* (Manchester, Manchester University Press, 2005, 2009 edn), p. 104.
96 *Coventry Standard*, 3 March 1899.
97 *Yorkshire Evening Post*, 7 March 1893.
98 See Chapter 1.
99 *Leeds Mercury*, 21 August 1888.
100 *Leeds Mercury*, 21 August 1888.
101 *Leeds Mercury*, 11 June 1888.
102 *Leeds Mercury*, 9 June 1888.
103 *Leeds Mercury*, 16 June 1888.
104 *Leeds Mercury*, 16 June 1888.
105 *Leeds Mercury*, 11 June 1888.
106 See Chapter 5.
107 *Yorkshire Evening Post*, 5 September 1904.
108 Quoted in G.R. Searle, *The Quest for National Efficiency. A Study in British Politics and Political Thought, 1899–1914* (London, Ashfield Press, 1971, 1990 edn), p. 235.

109 Leeds City Archive, LC/ED/62/2 St Peter's Square School Board Log Book, March 1903; see also *Yorkshire Post*, 28 March 1903. Also see Dr Hall's obituary in *British Medical Journal*, 10 November 1923, p. 903.
110 Parliamentary Papers, *Inter-Departmental Committee on Physical Deterioration*, vol. II, 1904, p. 30.
111 *Inter-Departmental Committee on Physical Deterioration*, vol. II, 1904, p. 35.
112 *Inter-Departmental Committee on Physical Deterioration*, vol. II, 1904, p. 147.
113 *Inter-Departmental Committee on Physical Deterioration*, vol. II, 1904, p. 147.
114 *Inter-Departmental Committee on Physical Deterioration*, vol. II, 1904, p. 78.
115 Searle, *The Quest for National Efficiency*, p. 61.
116 J.A. Dyche, 'The Jewish Workman', *Contemporary Review*, 73, January 1898, pp. 35–6.
117 J.A. Dyche, 'The Jewish Immigrant', *Contemporary Review*, 75, March 1899, pp. 379–80; for Arnold White's reply to an earlier article see A. White, 'A Typical Alien Immigrant', *Contemporary Review*, 73, February 1898.
118 *Yorkshire Evening Post*, 9, 10 June 1904.
119 National Archives, HO 45/24551, 'File relating to Jews being refused entrance into public houses in Leeds', 20 February 1908.

CHAPTER THREE

Civic ceremony and the citizen-soldier during the Boer War, 1899–1902

Reminiscing about his homecoming after serving in the Naval Brigade following the Indian Mutiny in 1857, William Hopkins complained that their arrival back in Portsmouth provoked little interest from the town's inhabitants, no civic reception and minimal recognition from the Admiralty.[1] Hopkins's low-key return to Portsmouth was in stark contrast to the experience of his successors fifty years later who were fêted in the local press, celebrated after military successes and granted civic parades. While it must be acknowledged that the Indian Mutiny and Boer War were very different conflicts, it is clear that William Hopkins recognised a transformation in his own lifetime in how the civic authorities and population imagined and celebrated empire. This chapter explores how, by the end of the nineteenth century, the development of civic identity and a growth of a popular local patriotism became fused, at key moments, with grand imperial adventures. It challenges recent studies that suggest that working-class patriotism during the Boer War was simply the product of imperial values disseminated by a hegemonic state. This book adopts a more nuanced approach and argues that, while working-class patriotism characteristically prioritised local identity over the national, the two identities were not mutually exclusive. By the late nineteenth century, working-class males' identity in particular became increasingly linked with their immediate locality and manifested itself through a growing enthusiasm for, and pride in, local sporting teams and the factory, town or city they represented.[2] The deep-rooted male working-class attachment to the local, a local patriotism one might argue, became highly visible during imperial conflicts, particularly with the recruitment, departure and homecoming of local volunteers. The Boer War, which is the backdrop to this chapter, was both a very old and a very new conflict; it was largely fought in a traditional fashion, for instance through the use of cavalry, but its newness was epitomised by its impact on the media and the innovative interaction between the newspapers and those who fought in the war.[3] For the first time, citizen volunteers were sent to a theatre of war, prompting the provincial press to devote a significant portion of their war coverage to following the fortunes of their local heroes on an international imperial stage. This fusion between the local and empire was not constant and depended on a set of circumstances in which tangible local factors were framed within or alongside significant imperial events.

The extent and character of working-class patriotism, a live issue during the Boer War, continues to be of interest to historians today. Until the 1960s, it was a received wisdom that the recruitment of volunteers and the scenes of jubilation that followed the relief of Ladysmith and Mafeking were clear examples of a deep-rooted support for imperialism within the British working class.[4] Since then, the debate has largely steered down two opposing tracks of historiography. The first generation of historians to challenge the orthodox notion of deep-rooted working-class patriotism argued that the jingoism evident during the Boer War actually represented middle-class enthusiasm for empire. In his seminal study on the British working class and the Boer War, Richard Price argued that most working-class institutions were largely unaffected by the period of intense patriotism and that the jingoistic crowds that celebrated Mafeking were mostly led by young middle-class men. Price also contended that working-class recruitment to the army occurred not in intensely patriotic periods but during economic slumps.[5] This theme was developed by Hobsbawm, who maintained that working-class volunteers were motivated by an economic imperative rather than a lust for imperial glory and that 'the curve of volunteer recruitment of working-class soldiers in the imperialist South African War simply reflects the economic situation. It rose and fell with unemployment'.[6] This argument suggests that while the lower middle class were profoundly influenced by imperial propaganda, the working class were immune from such overtures. Hugh Cunningham's research on the volunteer movement also deprioritised patriotism as a motivation factor for enlisting and instead found that recruits volunteered primarily for recreational purposes.[7] Overall, he deduced that working people were not attracted to imperialism and that 'patriotism proved incapable of surmounting the barriers of class'.[8] More recently, Andrew August has played down imperialism's influence on the British domestic sphere and concluded that during the late nineteenth and early twentieth centuries jingoistic outbursts were 'short-lived and patchy, exerting little lasting influence on British politics or working-class attitudes'.[9] This strand of historiography is appealing for those historians who credit the working class with an ability to resist the seduction of imperialism and to carve out their own identity within their communities. However, no matter how sympathetic one is to this view, there remains the fact that across the country a substantial number of working-class men volunteered as citizen soldiers and thousands of working men and women lined the streets in civic ceremonies that celebrated their local volunteer forces. It is the reluctance of some historians to acknowledge the significance of working-class involvement in the Boer War that is the central bone of contention for those historians who have contributed to the second opposing strand of historiography.

Leading historians on Britain and empire, such as J.M. MacKenzie, are far from convinced that working-class communities were impervious to imperial propaganda. He argued that 'of all the systems of social discipline applied in the late nineteenth century, it was the imperial core ideology which worked best' and succeeded where factory discipline and the church had failed in influencing working-class opinion.[10] More recently, Stephen M. Miller has demonstrated that Price and Hobsbawm seriously underestimated popular patriotism by arguing that recruitment figures alone are not a satisfactory measure of working-class enthusiasm for the war. Miller rightly notes that historians must examine both those who were accepted for the volunteers and the 30 per cent who were deemed medically unfit for military service. Furthermore, he doubts whether the reductionist argument that identifies unemployment as a key causal factor for volunteering can be sustained given the mixed economic situation in Britain between 1899 and 1902. In addition, he notes that recruitment was 'ultimately a voluntary action' and that the unemployed were not obliged to enlist. Miller further undermines the economic incentive theory, pointing out that large numbers of the full-time employed temporarily left their work and volunteered for military service.[11] Miller's preferred explanation for volunteering is the existence of a genuine working-class patriotism that was nurtured by the state and associated cultural reference points of the late nineteenth century. He states that 'beginning at a young age, schoolchildren were inculcated with a strong sense of nationalism, a belief in racial ascendancy, and support for the imperial mission'. Furthermore, taking his cue from the contemporary J.A. Hobson, he argues that popular leisure institutions such as the music hall actively encouraged working men to enlist after Black Week when the British army suffered three significant defeats in December 1899. Finally Miller concludes that 'although a variety of economic and social factors determined one's course of action, the most widespread reason for enlistment in the Volunteers and Imperial Yeomanry during the South African War was the need for psychological fulfilment found in the expression of patriotism'.[12]

Miller is surely right in his criticism of the revisionist approach that prioritises economic incentives to explain working-class recruitment patterns. However, there are problems with Miller's approach. Most of his evidence is drawn from working-class autobiographies, a source that, by its very nature would tend to represent an atypical working-class perspective. In addition, more often than not, autobiographies will have gone through an editing process and been shaped by the publishers' desire to boost sales.[13] Secondly, Miller seems persuaded by the social control paradigm that attributes popular patriotism to the indoctrination of the working class by the state and other culturally imperial institutions. This approach is insensitive to the possibility that the imperial message could have been reinterpreted as it was filtered through local contexts, institutions and class and gendered identities. For example, Miller does not raise the possibility that recruits for the Imperial Yeomanry, who were principally drawn from the rural middle class, had motivations for enlisting different from those of the regular volunteers, who were largely composed of the urban working class. Urban working-class men clearly had social and cultural institutions and life experiences contrasting with those of their rural middle-class counterparts.[14] Indeed, Miller's focus on a range of autobiographies removes the individual from key localised agencies that may have influenced a citizen's decision to volunteer or attend a civic parade. In this scenario patriotism is monolithic and an uncomplicated phenomenon which does not allow for an individual's class, gender or local identity to coexist and itself influence national patriotism.[15] The following section, then, endeavours to explore patriotism at the provincial level and assess how local agencies such as municipal culture, the press and civic ceremony helped shaped identity during an imperial war.

Reporting the Boer War

As we have seen in Chapter 1, all three communities possessed a vibrant popular local press eager to capture a new mass readership. Furthermore, the Boer War was undoubtedly an enormous opportunity for provincial editors to tap into and nurture a popular interest in the conflict through supplying telegraphed and up-to-date news on their local soldiers' endeavours. Indeed, it was the first significant conflict in which the new provincial press examined a great imperial issue through a local lens. Never before had the reading public been so inundated with such sensational foreign news complete with associated maps and illustrations that, significantly, were inter-spliced with reports on the conflict from the local angle.

In Portsmouth, Coventry and Leeds, the popular press brought the Boer War home to the reading masses. Aside from producing khaki-coloured commemorative Boer War editions, the *Midland Daily Telegraph* took an active role in initiating street celebrations to celebrate military successes.[16] For example, the newspaper purchased a Coventry-made car, adorned it with patriotic colours and drove it through the city spreading news of the relief of Ladysmith. In trumpeting their innovation, the *Midland Daily Telegraph* pointed out that it was a Coventry-produced car that had brought the news to an expectant public, just as Coventry-made bicycles were helping the cause at the front.[17] In all three communities, reports from both the traditional and the daily press on the Boer War campaign were often linked with stories boasting local involvement in the conflict. For example, the *Hampshire Telegraph* announced that

> One thing is certain, namely that from all points of view Portsmouth's part in the war is one for every citizen of the town to be proud of. Indeed, when the strife is over, and matters assume their proper aspect it will undoubtedly be apparent that Portsmouth had a greater and more important bearing upon the war than any other town in England. Aldershot can claim the honour of having sent the greatest number of troops; London can boast of her City Volunteers, Southampton can declare that it was from her harbour that the ships which carried Thomas Atkins sailed away, but Portsmouth can say with pride that from the amongst her ships there went forth the Powerful and the Terrible, vessels from which were drawn the men and guns that saved the beleaguered Ladysmith from capture.[18]

This fusion of the local and imperial was amply demonstrated in the reports that focused on the heroics of the local regiments. In 1900 at the height of the Boer War, an editorial in the *Leeds Times* led with the phrase 'Bravo Yorkshire!' and gave a celebratory account of how a Yorkshire regiment engaged in hand-to-hand combat with the Boers:

> For once in a while our men met their foes face to face in the fight near Rensburg the other day, and with New Zealand and Yorkshire to the front, drove them back at the point of the bayonet, the use of which, I can thoroughly understand, was as discomforting to the Boers as it was satisfying to our men.[19]

Another device to bring the experience of battle home to an eager readership was the publication of letters by home-town soldiers. Most newspapers, both traditional and new, featured 'letters from the front' and only the liberal journals the *Leeds Mercury* and the *Leeds Times* from the newspapers surveyed refrained from adopting this innovation. There can be little doubt that a local soldier's first-hand account of battle heightened interest in the war and perhaps helped increase sales. Indeed, during the height of the Boer War, the *Evening News* began publishing letters on the front page of the newspaper at the expense of advertisements.[20] Furthermore, the tone and content of the letters that newspapers chose to publish differed according to the publication. Whereas the more traditional newspapers were content to publish morale-boosting letters that described the soldiers' conditions and optimism for the future, some new newspapers included rather sensational letters that graphically described soldiers in combat. For example, the *Leeds Daily News* printed a letter it entitled 'Gallant Leeds Lads'. It read 'We had a steep hill to climb, the enemy were on top. When we got near them the Colonel shouted "charge!" The enemy's sentry shouted "Halt! Who comes Dat?" Some of our men shouted "Britishers, you - - - - - - - !" and one of them shoved his bayonet through him.'[21] The *Yorkshire Evening Post* also published letters that cast the war as a sporting contest and presented in a style of writing that tapped into the football craze that was sweeping the nation.[22] One Leeds soldier wrote enthusiastically, 'British Empire 5, Transvaal and Orange Free State 0', and that 'the feature of the game was the splendid all round play by the visitors, who received a tremendous ovation'.[23] While these vividly portrayed adventures of County regiments brought a local and popular dimension to the Boer War, a sense of local patriotism was undoubtedly heightened with stories of how the ordinary 'citizen soldiers' had volunteered to leave their employment and join battle at the front. Moreover, in pursuit of increasing their circulation, newspapers did not refrain from reporting dramatic stories that had negative connotations for Britain's war effort. The *Coventry Times* printed a lengthy letter from Trooper Hornby, who explained how his troop had been ambushed by the enemy. Headlined as 'Coventry Soldier's Exciting Experiences', Hornby's account told how their troop had been confronted by Boers who came within 200 yards of them and that 'I do not reckon to miss a man at that distance. I can safely count on two of them.' However, he recalled that 'the Boers did let us have it; the branches and leaves were falling on us as the bullets swished through the trees. The worst sounding bullets were the explosive ones, which cracked like whips around us. It was the hottest fire I have been under since the Sanna Port affair.' After keeping them back for half an hour, Hornby 'was determined to chance it' but, owing to his horse stumbling, was captured by the enemy:

They came to us and took our rifles and ammunition, and then set about taking our clothes, pointing their guns at our heads and demanding that we take off our boots and socks and riding breeches, spurs, and some of us our hats. My hat was not good enough for them. Anyway, they took everything but our shirts and tunics. We had three wounded, one Lieutenant Todd, who was the worst shot. Lieut. Todd got a bullet through his chest. After a great deal of cheek and calling us filthy names, the Boers had the kindness to show us which direction to take in order to reach our camp.[24]

Hornby's letter is interesting as the early sections, when he and his troop initially held off the advancing Boers, are written in swashbuckling style that conformed to a *Boy's Own* vision of imperial adventurism. However, the main substance of the letter essentially described a defeat and serious casualties that were compounded by the humiliation of the Boers taking their clothes. Similarly, the *Midland Daily Telegraph* carried letters under the heading 'the horrors of war' in which one Coventry soldier, Private Robson, wrote:

It was awful those four days marching, drinking water the colour of coffee, and eating biscuits you couldn't break. They are dying like sheep with dysentery and enteric fever . . . I had ulcers in both eyes. I was put into an open wagon with about fifty or more men wounded, some with disease. As the men died in the wagon they were buried in the sand.[25]

Another solider, Gunner Frank White, wrote despairingly that 'the people at home can have no idea of the shocking sight presented to our views', and described 'shaking and skeletal men for want of food'.[26] Thus while the local press undoubtedly helped nurture an interest in the Boer War, the principal motivation for including soldiers' letters was the local dimension rather than a morale boost for the greater imperial cause. The popular daily newspapers had learned that exciting narratives of local soldiers sold papers. The local press lavished praise on these volunteers, though the new press was particularly keen to support the citizen soldiers with fund-raising schemes whether they had been successful in battle or not.[27] Even the *Leeds Mercury*, which opposed the war, gave remarkable support to the citizen soldiers.[28] In all three communities, the new press kept a watch on how the civic authorities played their part in celebrating and honouring the volunteers.

Volunteer or 'citizen soldiers' were derived from three core groups established especially to serve in the Boer War that raised men from inside and outside the Volunteer movement. First, units were formed in early 1900 of approximately 110 men drawn from the regional active-service battalions. The second, the City Imperial Volunteers (CIV), was formed as an integral fighting force of over a thousand men drawn largely from London and the Home Counties. Third was the regionally based Imperial Yeomanry, which drew men from both existing Yeomanry and volunteer regiments and those who had never been associated with the movement but had experience of riding and shooting.[29] In all three communities, the press and civic elite singled out the urban volunteer, who had temporarily given up his work to fight, for special attention. As opposed to the experienced solider or the rural-based Imperial Yeomanry, 'citizen soliders' embodied a local patriotism since they were perceived to carry the reputation of the town (rather than the nation) into battle. Furthermore, the local press and civic elite in Portsmouth, Coventry and Leeds eyed the formation of the CIV with some envy as the volunteer battalions formed in their own regions carried the county's rather than the town's name. For example, the *Evening News* lamented that the city did not possess its own Portsmouth Imperial Volunteers similar to the City of London. The editor believed that if local patriotism would take hold, 'with what enthusiasm would it be received. What a name, a glorious retrospect in years after for Portsmouth.'[30]

The press's and civic elites' neglect of the Imperial Yeomanry can largely be explained by the rural and social class composition of the battalions. As Table 1 shows, the attestation papers for the Imperial Yeomanry in all three communities indicate that most recruits were based in rural areas and drawn from the farming sector. Manufacturers and skilled working men appear the least enthusiastic volunteers. Furthermore, while there was a larger proportion of unskilled men, the vast majority of these recruits resided in the countryside and were occupied in rural labouring jobs such as farm hands, grooms and stable boys. The attestation papers also reveal that very few Imperial Yeomanry recruits resided in Portsmouth, Coventry and Leeds and instead were scattered through the rural districts. In addition, many of the recruits were experienced soldiers which perhaps reduced the novelty of their position in comparison to the inexperienced volunteers. While evidence for the Citizen Volunteers is rather patchy, press reports strongly suggest that these citizen soldiers were solidly working-class.[31] For example, the first set of Citizen Volunteers to depart from Leeds was entirely drawn from workers engaged in skilled and manual work such as bricklaying, engineering and carpentry.[32] Indeed, the vast majority of working-class volunteers lived and worked in a city, a situation which allowed these citizen soldiers to carry their city's identity and civic pride into an imperial battle. Furthermore, even while in

Table 1: Occupation of Volunteer Imperial Yeomanry for Hampshire, Yorkshire and Warwickshire, 1900–2 (%)

	Gentleman	Farmer	Prof.	Manufacturer	Shopkeeper	Clerk	Skilled working class	Labourer	Misc.
Hants	0.7	11.0	33.0	0.0	7.0	5.3	6.0	13.0	24.0
Yorks	1.0	12.0	19.0	1.5	10.5	12.0	12.0	14.0	18.0
Warks	3.0	30.0	19.0	3.0	6.0	10.0	5.0	14.0	10.0

Source: National Archives, WO 128/7; 128/2; 128/15–16; Imperial Yeomanry attestation papers 1900–2.

South Africa, first and foremost their thoughts seemed to have turned to civilian life at home rather than being part of a great imperial adventure. During a reception in Coventry to mark the volunteers' return to the city, Lieutenant Smith warned that no one should underestimate

> the great interest we took in Coventry when we were at the front. Gentlemen, if there was one thing we looked forward to it was our *Coventry Herald* or any other Coventry papers. I had the *Coventry Herald* and I read it through, even the advertisements, including the births and marriages. (Laughter.) Gentlemen of the Council, – I can assure you that we never before took such an interest in your doings and sayings. (Laughter.) . . . I am sure gentlemen, we never thought Coventry were such a lovely city before. When we returned, I personally – and I think I can speak for every other man in the Company – considered it was perfect. (Hear, hear.) The beautiful green fields, the houses, the old familiar shops, and even the electric trams seem splendid. (Laughter).[33]

Clearly, at some level, citizens were motivated to join the volunteers out of a desire to represent their town, city or workplace, a connection that was strengthened by the local press that was delivered to the front. This bond with their town grew stronger with the harsh conditions they encountered on the Veldt, conditions that many volunteers were unprepared for. One working-class volunteer from Leeds, Cecil Rhodes, noted in his diary the strange mood of exuberance among his fellow troops as they set sail to South Africa. He wrote: 'whilst I am writing this there is a gang of fellows singing "God be with us till we meet again". It does sound peculiar but they are giving it "jip" and seem as happy as could possibly be, in fact if it was not for our uniforms, you would think we were a large picnic party.'[34] However, the true horrors of the war, and the near starvation of the volunteers at some points of the conflict were recorded by John Mear, a diarist with the Hampshire Volunteers. He recorded that

> We did 25 miles on the first day, but as the country was so hard to travel, and we could not get the transport up (the mules and cattle dropping like rotten sheep) we only made 5 miles the next day: We are getting $\frac{1}{2}$ lb. Flour a day, no vegetables for weeks, men very hungry, with sore feet, were ached. Koomati Port, fairly 'done up' for want of food.[35]

Likewise, Sergeant Tinckler of the Warwickshire Volunteers complained that the Boers did not fight with honour and that the Warwickshires 'tried to be gentlemen in Khaki . . . We have been in the jaws of death and the mouth of hell.'[36] The reality of warfare, however, was initially masked for many of the citizen soldiers by the sheer enthusiasm of the civic and popular response to their decision to volunteer.

As we shall see, the huge wave of support given by family, friends and workers for their citizen-soldier colleagues ensured that a town's normal business was temporarily halted to celebrate the volunteers' departure parade. Further evidence of working-class support for the volunteers was the establishment of volunteer funds. In Coventry, the *Midland Daily Telegraph* established a Relief Fund for Coventry volunteers, publishing regularly the donations from the large engineering factories and whether they were derived from staff or employees. For example in January 1900, of the eleven factories cited, nine sent contributions solely from workers while the remaining two sent donations from both staff and workers. The subscription list clearly shows that in most cases it was the workers themselves who had organised funds for the *Midland Daily Telegraph*, further underlining their support for the Coventry citizen soldiers.[37]

Thus while the press, civic elite and public lavished praise on *their* volunteers with banquets and departure parades, the Imperial Yeomanry were largely left to their own devices. The *Leeds Daily News* reported that while the volunteers had left amidst scenes of great excitement, the Imperial Yeomanry departed under very different circumstances. The reporter noted 'there was no assembling in the city square, no standing around in uniform. Instead the men found their own way to the station with their little following of friends and relatives, and, for the most part passed unrecognised'.[38] A similar uncertainty about the city's relationship with the Imperial Yeomanry was played out in Coventry. In organising the volunteers' homecoming from South Africa, Coventry councillors had entirely focused their attention on the Coventry citizen soldiers and even queried whether the Imperial Yeomanry should be included in the elaborate civic parade and banquet.[39] The sense that the provincial press was attempting to capture a popular readership through emphasising the importance of local identity has shown that the dissemination of imperialism was a more complex and nuanced phenomenon than the social control paradigm would suggest. However, while imperialism was filtered through local contexts and institutions, there still remains the possibility that the press or civic institutions successfully inculcated the public in imperial sentiment, albeit at a local level. It is, then, perhaps worth exploring in some depth the civic ceremony and the public's response to volunteer events since the strength of civic culture and identity differed in the three towns. Thus, if civic culture was a successful conduit for imperialism greater public enthusiasm in Portsmouth and Leeds would be expected as these towns possessed a greater municipal presence than Coventry.

Town military parades and the people

The War Office did not offer official guidelines on how towns should organise military parades for their soldier citizens, and instead the decision of whether to mark the volunteers' departure was devolved to the local authorities. However, the striking similarity of the organised parades in Portsmouth and Leeds suggests that those organising and participating in the events had shared assumptions on how the volunteers should be celebrated. Such assumptions were often learned from Victorian popular culture and illustrate how cultural forms became appropriated into the civic and military realm. Moreover, the use of theatrical songs in ceremonies may also have engendered a sense of occasion for the viewing public. A case in point was the song 'Soldiers of the Queen' which seems to have been sung at recruiting rallies and farewell parades across the country. Originally written for the theatre in 1881, it became diffused into wider society and intrinsically linked to volunteer recruitment drives.[40] Thus the song both featured at organised events and was sung by crowds at informal gatherings that had formed to celebrate the volunteers. In Portsmouth, the naval base and dockyard ensured that the civic authority had long been practised in combining civic and military ceremony. There was a strong civic presence in Fleet Reviews or with the launch of ships from Portsmouth Dockyard. Furthermore from the 1890s, the navy spread its influence in civilian Portsmouth as during Fleet Reviews the Admiralty purchased huge quantities of flags and bunting for the streets and major thoroughfares of the town.[41] However, elaborate civic ceremony and mass public involvement in military events came very late in the nineteenth century. For example, commenting on a Fleet Review in 1878, the *Hampshire Telegraph* described a low-key affair in which 'no formal attempt was made by the town to celebrate the occasion'.[42] Indeed, whereas Fleet Reviews during the mid-nineteenth century were largely military affairs, by the 1880s the civic elite and employers had encouraged greater civic involvement by granting school and work holidays to celebrate the event.[43] The Boer War, however, took the fusion of the civic and military to another level that allowed the regional press and civic elite to celebrate local patriotism within the milieu of an imperial quest. Prior to leaving for the front, the Hampshire Volunteers were treated to a civic banquet hosted by the Mayor. The local press reported these events in detail, the *Hampshire Telegraph* proclaiming that such banquets caused 'a fresh wave of patriotism' to sweep over Portsmouth.[44] However, the volunteers' departure from the town in February 1900 allowed the civic authorities and the press to engineer a more spectacular public show of local patriotism. The Hampshire Volunteers symbolised the growing synthesis between the civic and military and thus a careful choreography was developed to celebrate their departure to the front. In a set routine for each departure, the volunteers marched from the Drill Hall into Commercial Road, the main thoroughfare of Portsmouth, where a crowd of between ten and twelve thousand lined their route. The troops then marched to the band's 'Soldiers of the Queen' to the station where they boarded the train. Despite the large numbers of spectators, the police successfully managed the crowd as only members of the Corps, friends and the civic elite were allowed on the station. The last ceremonial act was left to the Mayor and Aldermen, who passed down the carriage shaking hands with the officers and men. The ceremony was complete after the civic dignitaries left the train and the band sent them on their way with a rendition of 'Auld Lang Syne'.[45] Significantly, the civic elite rather than military personnel appear to have presided over the ceremony, reinforcing the sense that these men were essentially civilians which heightened the sense of local patriotism.

In Leeds, the city's departing volunteers participated in parades that were almost identical to the military and civic ritual that was customary in Portsmouth. The Yorkshire Volunteers were treated to an official civic banquet, complete with entertainment. In February 1900 the *Yorkshire Post* reported that the volunteers marched from their barracks to the music of 'Soldiers of the Queen' and were accompanied through the city's main thoroughfares to the station by an 'enthusiastic crowd of immense proportions'. On entering the station the soldiers met 'a mass of humanity, surging and swaying in an endeavour to get near the gallant young engineers'. As was the case in Portsmouth, the final act of the volunteers' farewell ceremony was left to the civic dignitaries who boarded the train to meet the men personally. It was noted that each man received a gift from the Mayor 'who took each of the men by the hand, and spoke a cheerful word to them'.[46] Both Leeds and Portsmouth possessed strong and vibrant municipal cultures so it is perhaps no surprise that the civic elite organised banquets and parades to send off their citizen soldiers. Indeed, the local pride in Leeds broke out into local civic rivalry since the *Yorkshire Post* published a letter complaining that Leeds City Council had not treated their men as well as Bradford, which had given each volunteer a life policy worth £250. Within days Leeds City Council had responded by insuring their own volunteers for similar sums.[47] The abundance of military ceremony within the civic realm and its extensive media coverage demonstrates that in both Portsmouth and Leeds the municipal authorities and the press looked for every opportunity to further their community's association with imperial successes. However, there were limits to civic involvement in military affairs. Thus, while the military authorities appear to have allowed the civic elite to perform a significant role in events linked to citizen soldiers, they sometimes objected to their presence and associated ceremony during purely military proceedings. On one occasion, Portsmouth's civic elite requested that the Admiralty allow a Mayoral delegation, complete with robes and ceremonial attire, to formally welcome *HMS Powerful* into Portsmouth after its successes during the Boer War. It was reported that

> the Commander-in-Chief replied that it was the wish of the authorities to limit as far as possible those on the jetty to the relatives of those on the *Powerful*. The Naval Officers would, he added, be in their working clothes, and the presence of the corporation in their robes would in some respects conflict with the privacy of the occasion, and give it an air of publicity and ceremony which he was anxious to avoid.[48]

Thus while the civic elite were keen to associate the town with *HMS Powerful*'s victorious homecoming, the Admiralty was concerned to limit this event to a private military affair.

As has been shown in Portsmouth and Leeds, both the press and the civic elite worked in tandem in initiating and disseminating a fusion of local patriotism and imperialism during the Boer War. Indeed, it would be tempting to suggest that the vast crowds that gathered to cheer the volunteers off to war were evidence that the press and urban elite through civic ceremony performed a powerful hegemonic influence over a newly literate working class. However, the events in Coventry during the Boer War reveal that the working class were far from mere passive actors and instead were participants in a form of local patriotism that emanated from their own realms of work and leisure.

Initially, the only civic recognition for Coventry Volunteers about to depart for the front was the pledge that a tablet listing the men be commissioned for the Civic Offices. In a speech supporting the commemorative tablet, Alderman Hill thought that 'they might thoroughly trust the men who had left the city for the front to uphold the traditions of the ancient city of Coventry'.[49] However, unlike in Portsmouth and Leeds, there was no civic banquet or parade to celebrate the volunteers' departure to the front. The *Midland Daily Telegraph* reported that before their departure the volunteers were 'entertained by, in most cases, their fellow-workmen at the places where they had been employed, and next by a number of the citizens. That there was no official send-off was much regretted by the citizens.'[50] The *Coventry Herald* complained that the corporation had not organised an official send-off and that 'there is already evidence that this tardy recognition will cause widespread displeasure'.[51] The failure of the civic elite to organise a civic celebration for the volunteers also provoked a number of letters to the local press. For example, one correspondent looked to the leading citizens to initiate 'a movement which would enable the people of Coventry to give tangible expression of their good will and admiration of the pluck and loyalty of those brave fellows who have volunteered for active service'.[52] Thus, the civic elite's misjudgement of the public mood meant that events for the volunteers were organised by either those connected with the Volunteer Army or local employees. Events organised by the Volunteer Army were poorly attended, as the *Coventry Herald* noted that, while the musical entertainment attracted senior military personnel and the local MP, 'the Coventry public certainly did not respond very heartily, or evince very much patriotism by their attendance'.[53] More successful and less formal 'farewell concerts' were held by local firms that entertained large audiences with a mixture of songs and comic music. Undoubtedly the music had an imperial emphasis, with Kipling's 'Absent Minded Beggar', 'Soldiers of the Queen' and the 'Death of Nelson' featuring in most concerts. Employers, such as Rudge-Whitworth, Humber and Singer, hired hotels and public houses, where, along with the musical entertainment, there were presentation of gifts to volunteer employees and the collection of relief funds for their families.[54]

While the crowded employers' concerts were testament to the enthusiasm and support by workmates of their volunteer colleagues, a rare insight into audience behaviour at a mainly working-class music hall sheds further light on popular attitudes to volunteers and the Boer War. William Bennett, proprietor of a Coventry music hall, invited the volunteers to a Saturday night performance prior to their departure to the front. However, it soon became clear that the presence of the volunteers excited the crowd, who

> took matters into their own hands, though every thing was done in good part, and there was no disorderly behaviour. If a song had a chorus, that chorus was shouted till the band became a mere tinkle; if there was no chorus then the song itself received most particular attention at the hands and voices of the volunteers. Miss Florrie Haydon introduced a verse specially composed for the occasion into her song 'Under the same old flag' and it was greeted with tremendous applause. Then Mr Smith (of the Humber works) sang 'Soldiers of the Queen' from one of the boxes. The audience ran away with the chorus, and if they did not sing it correctly, made up for want of musical knowledge by volume of sound. Throughout the performance the greatest enthusiasm prevailed, and the various items were thoroughly enjoyed.[55]

This celebration of the volunteers in a Coventry music hall reveals a number of important issues on the dynamic relationship between the performers and audience. There can be little doubt that the audience embraced the celebration of the Volunteers and their imperial adventure with great gusto. Indeed, much of the evening's entertainment appears to have been directed by the crowded auditorium, joining in with songs, changing choruses and, at one point, eliciting a song from a member of the audience. Significantly, the report suggests that the audience was, at times, less conversant with some of the imperial songs and rather more intent in giving the volunteers an enthusiastic send-off. The sense that the crowded auditorium took their cue less from an organised programme of events and more from their own learned traditions is borne out in the volunteers' farewell parades.

With no civic recognition of the volunteers' departure to the front, the scenes in Coventry differed markedly from those in Portsmouth and Leeds. The *Coventry Herald* reported that the city went 'wild with excitement', noting that while there was no civic involvement 'the Volunteers had no reason to complain of any shortcomings on the part of the public'. As with Portsmouth and Leeds, the volunteers were to march from their barracks through the main thoroughfare of Coventry to the railway station accompanied by the band playing 'Soldiers of the Queen'. The crowded streets were twenty-deep and filled with local factory workers intent on 'sending off' their colleagues; some of them were waving banners such as 'Another one from Humber'. Indeed, such was the interest among the Coventry workforce, employers had little option but to temporarily close their factories during the parade.[56] However, unlike the controlled and orderly street processions in Portsmouth and Leeds that, through civic planning, had clearly demarcated the roles of participants and spectators, the Coventry parade became engulfed by the crowd, which began to dictate events. The soldiers marched on from the barracks among the densely packed cheering crowds until

> the people grew beyond restraint. One wild rush, and they had broken up the serried ranks of the 'thirty', and hoisted them shoulder high. The band ceased playing 'Soldiers of the Queen,' and onward the men were carried to the strains of 'farewell!' slowly onward till the station was in full view . . . Nearly forty police, under the Chief Constable, were on duty at this particular point. They might as well been at the other end of the town. The crowd metaphorically and literally seized upon them, and pushed them hither and thither till they were as chaff before the wind. All the spectators wanted was to shake those thirty men by the hand.

[85]

Amidst chaotic scenes, the crowd poured into the station and neither the police nor railway staff were able to prevent people leaping on to the line in their enthusiasm and delaying the departure. As the *Coventry Herald* noted, 'the people were determined to have their own way for once' and the volunteers had to force their way through the crowd to board the train. In a contrast to Portsmouth and Leeds, there was no farewell from the city's civic leaders on the train and instead the volunteers left to a great roar from the crowd and 'one last universal waving of hand kerchiefs and hats and caps and sticks'.[57] The events in Coventry leading up to and including the volunteers' departure reveal that the absence of civic leadership did not discourage a popular response to Coventry's contribution to war. Indeed, the officially organised and heavily policed parades in Portsmouth and Leeds may well have *contained* a popular enthusiasm that was so evident in Coventry.

The citizen-soldier homecoming

The cheering crowds that greeted the citizen soldiers as they set off for the station to embark on their duties in South Africa were replaced by a more sombre mood in all three communities as the war dragged on. While the local press had celebrated the citizen soldiers' quest in taking the good name of their town into an imperial battle, the newspapers also responded to the public's appetite for news of their friends and family abroad. Indeed, as we have seen, journalists did not self-censor their material and included stories of local soldiers that did little to improve the public's morale. It is perhaps not surprising, then, that the arrangements for the return of the citizen soldiers approximately a year after they had left their communities were more commemorative than celebratory in character. The civic elite in Leeds and Portsmouth opted to arrange low-key formal greetings with the families and local dignitaries and limited military parades to the main thoroughfares. In Leeds, the volunteers were met at the station by the Lord Mayor and a military band, while in Portsmouth the reception of the soldiers at the station was described as 'very quiet'.[58] Despite the public's rather sombre reaction to the volunteers' return, the press was acutely interested in how the ravages of war had impacted upon the citizen soldiers. The *Hampshire Telegraph* reported that the Hampshire Volunteers had unfortunately not had the opportunity to engage in enemy combat and had been restricted to garrison duties. The men themselves were largely subdued since 'they carried themselves like a lot of smart regulars, and showed excellent discipline by abstaining from unnecessary cheering or demonstration of delight at having returned to English soil'. However, the journalist observed that the men were 'bronzed and burly' and that 'they looked remarkably fit . . . indeed some of the younger members of the Company had actually filled out'.[59] The civic elite, public and returning soldiers had temporarily lost their appetite for the grand civilian–military parade in both Leeds and Portsmouth.

In Coventry, however, where the municipal elite were slow to detect the mood of the community prior to the volunteers' departure, plans were made to commemorate their homecoming with a public parade and civic banquet.[60] The *Coventry Herald* noted the contrast between the volunteers' departure and homecoming, commenting that the latter was a much more orderly affair, with almost the entire police force on duty policing a crowd of about thirty thousand. Observers reported children, women and men shouting 'themselves hoarse' with the excitement of seeing their friends and relatives.[61] However, to some extent, the ceremony *itself* lacked the celebratory character of the troops' departure and instead the proceedings adopted a more sombre mood. In conducting the ceremony, the civic leaders had to address both the death of Warwickshire soldiers and a war-weary public. The Warwickshire soldiers had not fared so well on the Veld as their Hampshire counterparts. Indeed, despite the press's undoubted intention of celebrating the troops' heroic battles for the empire, reporters could not help commenting, with some concern, on the returning soldiers' condition. With an expectant crowd and a lavish civic reception planned, the popular clamour to see the heroic local soldiers had reached fever pitch. The *Coventry Herald* reported that 'the return of the Volunteers was eagerly and somewhat impatiently awaited. The streets in early morning were more crowded than usual, and Broadgate and the top of Hertford Street were in a state of congestion two hours before the train steamed into the station.'[62] In glimpsing the soldiers for the first time as they stepped off the train, the *Coventry Herald* reporter clearly had difficulty in reconciling the image of the heroic imperial adventurers with the men gathered on the platform:

> There was a good deal that was remarkable in their appearance. Spare and gaunt, and perhaps a little weary, they struck the spectator as a body of men who had gone through much privation, and to whom a substantial meal would be most welcome. There did not look to be an ounce of spare flesh among them. Bronzed, lithe, keen-eyed, and hollow cheeked, wearing uniforms which bore many evidences of much hard and rough usage, they presented a great contrast to their spic and span comrades in neat scarlet tunic, and the invalided trio who stood in the rear of the rank were, compared with them, of a complexion startling fair.[63]

In that one description, the mask of imperial strength and power slipped to reveal the horrors of an empire at war. Such was the shocking sight of their appearance that the reporter felt compelled to convey the troops' condition to his readers. To be sure, the thousands of people who lined the streets could not have failed to make similar comparisons between the soldiers' departure from Coventry and arrival twelve months later. Moreover, this sombre mood was to continue since both the civic elite and press confronted the uncomfortable fact that not all the soldiers had returned. Three 'Coventry men' died in the war and were eulogised for their patriotism for their city and empire. However, at least two of these men, Privates Robinson and Dobrowolski, were not Coventry-born and had resided in the city for approximately two years. Robinson was a Yorkshire man working as a machinist for the Premier Cycle Factory, while Dobrowolski had worked as a clerk for the Dunlop Pneumatic Tyre Company.[64] Thus to be born and bred in the city was not a measure of local patriotism – a more significant factor was their readiness to volunteer to serve 'their' city in an imperial conflict. For the civic leaders, this was the distinct difference from regular troops as volunteers were the exemplary citizens of their city or town. The *Coventry Standard* commented that 'Our Volunteers have proved themselves to be more than citizen-soldiers – they are citizens and soldiers in the fullest and best sense; and we are proud of them'.[65] In the civic reception for the returning soldiers, Alderman Gulson noted that while the city had entertained regiments stationed in Coventry in St Mary's Hall 'we have no precedent for such a gathering as is assembled here to-night. (applause.) Here we meet to welcome our own citizens – (hear, hear) – and friends and fellow-country men; men we have long known and loved; men of peace, men whom we should be not likely to part from'.[66]

Conclusion

This chapter has sought to examine the development of a local and imperial synergy that caught the popular imagination during the late nineteenth and early twentieth centuries. The celebration of empire was particularly acute when it became associated with tangible local factors such as civic parades and the honouring of citizen soldiers. The importance of local factors in creating a sense of empire may explain why the working class's apparent enthusiasm for empire appears uneven – swinging from apathy when a local dimension was absent, to untamed enthusiasm when civic pride was integral to the occasion. By the end of the Boer War, in all three communities the press and civic elite had forged a similarly structured narrative of their locality's contribution in the conflict. The manner in which the newspapers reported the conflict at home and abroad and the civic ceremony that developed around military events projected a sense of civic social occasion that fused both local and national patriotism. Undoubtedly for the press and civic authorities, who were the principal disseminators of the message, the volunteers had become the living embodiment of local patriotism, showcasing their civic loyalties within an imperial war. However, through contrasting newspaper reports and civic ceremony during the early stages of the volunteer involvement, it is clear that the desire to celebrate the citizen soldier was not led solely by the civic elite and press. The strong civic cultures in Portsmouth and Leeds meant that the careful choreography surrounding the civic celebration of volunteers may well have prevented further instances of the chaotic scenes in Coventry where the crowd seized control of events. Rather than view the press and civic elite as the sole architect of local patriotism, we should view the provincial press's intense interest in the citizen soldier as a *response* to working-class attitudes that articulated their own identity and locality in the late nineteenth and early twentieth centuries. Indeed, the provincial press was more likely than its national counterpart to publish letters and accounts of the conflict that did not complement the official narrative of the war. Thus, in the search for sensational stories, accounts from soldiers of their defeat and humiliation at the hands of the Boers found their way into the local press. Likewise, journalists could not withhold from the public the shocking appearance of the returning volunteer soldiers. This is reflected in a wider context with the shift in the type of newspaper from the traditional press oriented towards the national to the more popular new daily press that sought to attract a newly literate working class. These newspapers were quick to respond to the rise of mass commercial sport and the clear linkages that were to be made with civic pride. A social control paradigm that elevates the importance of official institutions in the dissemination of imperial propaganda will undoubtedly overlook important cultural contexts and identities that developed independently within communities during the late nineteenth and early twentieth centuries. Thus working men, in particular, had developed a growing pride and attachment to their locality which, by the late nineteenth century, had been nurtured and developed by the local press and civic elite. Viewed within this context, the great desire to celebrate the volunteers was not so much an example of successful state hegemony but more an amplification of local patriotism within an imperial setting. The public's appetite for the celebration of a city or town's contribution to an imperial war reached its zenith during the South African War. Although, as we shall see, local patriotism was an important feature of the First World War recruitment campaign, popular allegiance to the local began to wane while images of those bedraggled soldiers who had returned from the Boer War still lingered in popular memory.

Notes

1 *Hampshire Telegraph*, 2 June 1900.
2 J. Hill, 'Rite of Spring: Cup Finals and Community in the North of England', in J. Hill and J. Williams (eds), *Sport and Identity in the North of England* (Keele, Keele University Press, 1996).
3 K.O. Morgan, 'The Boer War and the Media (1899–1902)', *Twentieth Century British History*, 13, 1, 2002, pp. 1–2.
4 Henry Pelling was one of the first historians to question whether imperialism was deep-rooted in working-class communities. See H. Pelling, *Popular Politics in Late Victorian Society* (London, Macmillan, 1968), p. 87. For a review of this mostly contemporary material see S.M. Miller, 'In Support of the "Imperial Mission"? Volunteering for the South African War, 1899–1902', *Journal of Military History*, 69, 3, July 2005, pp. 695–6. For a more in-depth analysis see S.M. Miller, *Volunteers on the Veld. Britain's Citizen Soldiers and the South African War, 1899–1902* (Norman, Oklahoma Press, 2007).
5 R. Price, *An Imperial War and the British Working Class* (London, Routledge, 1971), p. 205.
6 E.J. Hobsbawm, *The Age of Empire, 1875–1914* (London, Abacus, 1997 edn), pp. 160–1.
7 H. Cunningham, *The Volunteer Force: A Social and Political History, 1859–1908* (London, Croom Helm, 1975), p. 104.
8 H. Cunningham, 'Jingoism and the Working Classes, 1877–78', *Bulletin of the Society for the Study of Labour History*, 19, 6–9, 1969, pp. 26–7.
9 A. August, *The British Working Class, 1832–1940* (Harlow, Pearson, 2007), p. 151.
10 J.M. MacKenzie, *Propaganda and Empire* (Manchester, Manchester University Press, 1984), p. 258.
11 Miller, 'In Support of the "Imperial Mission"?', p. 699.
12 Miller, 'In Support of the "Imperial Mission"?', pp. 701, 711.
13 See D. Vincent, *Testaments of Radicalism. Memoirs of Working Class Politicians 1790–1885* (London, Europa, 1977), intro. For an example of how a working-class autobiography was heavily influenced by its middle-class sponsors and publishers see B. Beaven and J. Griffiths, 'Urban Elites, Socialists and Notions of Citizenship in an Industrial Boomtown: Coventry c. 1870–1914', *Labour History Review*, 2004, 69, p. 1.
14 B. Beaven, *Leisure, Citizenship and Working-class Men in Britain, 1850–1945* (Manchester, Manchester University Press, 2005), intro.
15 J. Thompson, 'Modern Britain and the New Imperial History', *History Compass*, 5, 2, 2007.
16 *Midland Daily Telegraph*, 30 April 1901.
17 *Midland Daily Telegraph*, 9 February 1951.
18 *Hampshire Telegraph*, 7 April 1900.
19 *Leeds Times*, 13 January 1900.
20 For example see *Evening News*, 22 January and 9 February 1900.
21 *Leeds Daily News*, 1 January 1900.
22 Beaven, *Leisure, Citizenship and Working-Class Men*, ch. 2; the same reference to sporting contests was employed by letter writers in the First World War. See Chapter 4 below.
23 *Yorkshire Evening Post*, 13 April 1901.

24 *Coventry Times*, 1 May 1901.
25 *Midland Daily Telegraph*, 20 March 1900.
26 *Midland Daily Telegraph*, 10 April 1900.
27 See *Evening News*, 13 March 1900; *Midland Daily Telegraph*, 10 February 1941.
28 See *Leeds Mercury*, 18, 20, 21 December 1899.
29 Price, *An Imperial War and the British Working Class*, p. 180.
30 *Evening News*, 15 January 1900.
31 The attestation papers for the volunteers have either been lost or passed into private ownership. The attestation papers for the Imperial Yeomanry, on the other hand, are located in the National Archives WO 28. An attestation paper is the contract in which the recruit agrees to join the armed forces. The document outlines the recruit's age, residence, occupation and agreed length of service.
32 *Leeds Daily News*, 2 February 1900.
33 Coventry Local Studies Library, 'News cuttings from the *Coventry Herald* 1900–1', p. 226; The *Hampshire Telegraph* also noted that the Hampshire Volunteers enthusiastically read the local press; see *Hampshire Telegraph*, 18 May 1901.
34 Leeds City Archive, WYL 707/1813, 'Diaries of Cecil Rhodes', 14 May 1900.
35 Portsmouth City Record Office, 1350A/1, 'John Mear's War Diary', p. 14.
36 CLSL, 'News cuttings from the *Coventry Herald*', p. 225.
37 *Midland Daily Telegraph*, 1 January 1900.
38 *Leeds Daily News*, 8 January 1900.
39 Coventry Local Studies Library, 'News cuttings from the *Coventry Herald* 1900–1', p. 223. The Imperial Yeomanry were, however, celebrated in the Shires. See *Leeds Daily News*, 30 January 1900, for an account of Leamington and Warwick sending off the Warwickshire Imperial Yeomanry.
40 S. Attridge, *Nationalism, Imperialism and Identity in Late Victorian Culture* (Basingstoke, Palgrave, 2003), p. 32.
41 K. Lunn and R. Thomas, 'Naval Imperialism in Portsmouth, 1905–1914', *Southern History*, 10, 1988.
42 *Hampshire Telegraph*, 14 August 1878.
43 *Hampshire Telegraph*, 16 August 1890.
44 *Hampshire Telegraph*, 27 January 1900.
45 *Evening News*, 12 February 1900; *Hampshire Telegraph*, 17 February 1900.
46 *Yorkshire Post*, 3 February 1900.
47 *Yorkshire Post*, 3 February 1900.
48 *Hampshire Telegraph*, 14 April 1900.
49 *Coventry Herald*, 16 January 1900.
50 *Midland Daily Telegraph*, 30 April 1901.
51 *Coventry Herald*, 2 February 1900.
52 *Midland Daily Telegraph*, 13 January 1900; *Coventry Herald*, 2 February 1900; for more complaints about the lethargy of the civic elite in organising celebrations during the Boer War see *Midland Daily Telegraph*, 2 March; 17 May 1900.
53 *Coventry Herald*, 2 February 1900.
54 *Coventry Herald*, 26 January 1900.
55 *Coventry Herald*, 26 January 1900.
56 *Coventry Herald*, 26 January 1900.
57 *Coventry Herald*, 26 January 1900.
58 *Yorkshire Evening Post*, 3 May 1901; *Hampshire Telegraph*, 18 May, 25 May 1901.
59 *Hampshire Telegraph*, 18 May 1901.
60 CLSL, 'News cuttings from the *Coventry Herald*', p. 223.
61 CLSL, 'News cuttings from the *Coventry Herald*', p. 223.
62 CLSL, 'News cuttings from the *Coventry Herald*', p. 223.
63 CLSL, 'News cuttings from the *Coventry Herald*', p. 223.
64 *Midland Daily Telegraph*, 30 April 1901.
65 *Coventry Standard*, 3 May 1901.
66 CLSL, 'News cuttings from the *Coventry Herald*', p. 225.

CHAPTER FOUR

Fragmenting communities: patriotism, empire and the First World War

Assessing his own contribution to the imperial project, Lord Meath proudly boasted that Empire Day had instilled a sense of patriotism in the English population that had paved the way for the 'rush to colours' at the outbreak of war in August 1914. While Meath may well have overstated his case, the belief that Edwardian society had inculcated the volunteers with imperial and patriotic messages has been consistently endorsed by a number of historians. Indeed, traditionally, historians viewed the working class's enthusiasm for combat as an indication that the war instilled a sense of patriotism for nation and empire and helped lessen the social tensions of Edwardian society.[1] However, labour historians, in particular, have taken a rather sceptical view on the working class's conversion to imperialism and have instead questioned the effectiveness of propaganda and the volunteers' motivation for enlisting.[2] This chapter, while investigating this historiographical discourse, explores the issue of working-class and middle-class patriotism during the war from a rather different perspective. It is argued here that both standard accounts of war enthusiasm fail to focus sufficiently on the important local contexts that shaped the dissemination of war and imperial propaganda.

The contention that the First World War had an extraordinary impact on social relations in England continues to influence current historiography. For example, George Robb has recently argued that a stratified and class-conflicted Edwardian society became transformed on the outbreak of war. Despite the continuing relevance of class identity, he claims that there was a shared notion of struggle and a desire to save the nation. He added that 'ultimately working-class support for war proved as enthusiastic and enduring as that of the elite. Words like "duty" and "honour" occurred almost as often in working-class diaries and letters during the war years as in those from the middle class.'[3] Likewise, Andrew August points to long-established working-class patriotism that predated the outbreak of the First World War as an explanation for the 'rush to colours' in August 1914.[4] Significantly, both Robb and August cite the working class's national patriotism as an important influence for war enthusiasm, leaving aside the issue of empire. Indeed, Bernard Porter dismisses out of hand the possibility that working-class men were fighting for the empire. For Porter, working-class men were fighting for 'freedom, fairness and anti-Prussian militarism'.[5] Other historians, however, view working-class volunteering in 1914 as evidence of both national and imperial patriotism. Alexander Watson and Patrick Porter argue that the cult of sacrifice and duty was embedded in Edwardian society, cutting across the political spectrum. The celebration of sacrifice and martyrdom could be found in propaganda literature relating to imperialism, suffragettes, Irish Republicanism and working-class movements. They argue that, through literacy, schooling and other forms of sociability, the cult of sacrifice was so familiar to working men that they naturally projected it upon defending their nation and empire.[6] It has also been argued that propaganda not only was successful in persuading volunteers of the glamour of battle but also convinced civilians of both the idealised nature of battle and the atrocities carried out by the enemy. Censorship prevented citizens from grasping the hardship endured by soldiers while consistent propaganda whipped up a vicious hatred to the German enemy. This belief, that the civilian population was alienated from the realities of war, rests upon the assumption that the state operated both a highly efficient censorship regime and a successful propaganda campaign. The national press also plays a significant role in the civilian 'alienation thesis' since it projected patriotic messages of nation and empire to a new working-class readership.[7] This theme is pursued by David Silbey in his impressive analysis of working-class war enthusiasm, arguing that the Edwardian working-class man was perhaps unprecedented in exhibiting a conscious attachment to nation and empire. According to Silbey, this global view was fostered by the national press, popular literature, education and working-class organisations. Thus through the national press:

> Workers, especially urban workers, had daily contact with the larger world of politics, culture, society and empire. The working-class generation of 1914 grew up in a world in which information was much more widely accessible than ever before. Their horizon extended beyond the neighbourhood, village, or city.

Silbey asserts that, by 1914, the British working class would not have volunteered for war without having an erudite knowledge of the world outside of their own neighbourhood, and their motivation 'lay in a single and supporting factor: their increased awareness and sophistication and their belief in a larger empire and nation'.[8] He argues that some historians rob the working class of the responsibility of their actions and this is both 'inaccurate and demeaning'. In short, they had made a choice and it was to go to war.[9] Silbey offers a powerful argument that places the working class's attachment to nation and empire at the heart of the explanation for military enlistment in the first few years of the war. However, Silbey's emphasis on the importance of the national press has perhaps led to an underestimation of the importance of localism, a phenomenon that is afforded only a short paragraph in his monograph.[10] The revolutionary design, production and circulation of a new regional press that targeted a working-class readership towards the end of the nineteenth century ensured that imperial issues were filtered through a local perspective. To be sure, working-class men were aware of their nation and empire, but it was filtered through the local and their worldview may not have mirrored the vision of empire found in national newspaper coverage. Pierre Purseigle's recent research on local communities in the First World War found that a town's civic elite and press were, to an extent, local transmitters of national institutions. However, his cases studies of Northampton and Béziers in France revealed that urban elites were not merely conduits for state propaganda. Instead, 'the local elites were especially concerned and aware of the constraints that hampered their public expression. In many cases, they demonstrated civil society's willingness to assert a distance from distortions of information, whether originating in the societies themselves or in agencies of the state'.[11] Local elites knew the limitations of state propaganda, filtering out or distancing themselves from some government initiatives while framing the war and empire in terms that would likely appeal to their locality. Working-class engagement with the war and empire, then, was less the product of state inculcation through the national press and education systems but instead rested more upon a synergistic relationship between a town's citizens and the local press and urban elite. Similarly, Bonnie White's and Helen McCartney's research on volunteer armies in the First World War revealed that people's experiences were determined by local issues since the central state exercised little influence over the lives of the general public. White has recently noted that 'there is still very little understanding of the impact of the recruitment campaigns at a local level' and that 'early strategies such as posters, badgering, threats, and fear mongering were poorly received and largely ineffectual in Devon's rural areas'.[12] In a clear contrast to Silbey's assumption that citizens were developing global perspectives,

McCartney's analysis of middle-class volunteers revealed that 'their aspirations, expectations and connections were limited to the local and their loyalties were tied to village, town and county'.[13]

This chapter advances the case that local contexts were significant in shaping the recruitment strategies that called men to fight for their nation and empire. However, while working-class citizens continued to view the wider world through their own communities, in a contrast to the Boer War, the Great War's deeper impact on society and ongoing festering social tensions meant that this was not a shared vision of empire.

Local elites at the outbreak of war: 'practical patriotism'

From the outbreak of war, the government delegated the recruitment of soldiers to local bodies. While the War Office oversaw national policy and the later stages of training, local civic bodies produced recruitment campaign literature, held mass recruitment meetings and organised the men who had successfully volunteered.[14] The local elites performed a pivotal role from the onset of war and would have been the first official body to frame the political, cultural and economic significance of war to their local populations. The autonomy granted to local elites ensured that recruitment campaigns were often tailored to local contexts and disseminated intensively through a supportive local press.[15] However when left to their own devices, local elites sometimes made appeals to the public that were at some odds with War Office propaganda. Whereas leading national figures in recruitment such as Kitchener and Lord Meath emphasised the importance of nation and empire, local elites disseminated patriotic messages that were somewhat closer to home. Given Portsmouth's military significance, one might have expected the local press and civic elite to have presented patriotism in the War Office's terms which saw the conflict as a battle to save nation and empire. Portsmouth's urban elite largely comprised small shopkeepers and local businesses. Thus, just after war was declared, the Mayor and *Evening News* began a campaign of 'practical patriotism' that was designed to encourage the general public to continue purchasing goods from local suppliers. According to the newspaper, the commercial situation in Portsmouth 'is bad' and it was 'the duty of the public to make it better'. The outbreak of war had seen the cancellation of excursions and holidays to Southsea which had hit the local small businesses reliant on this seasonal trade. The editor asserted that those who abstained from purchasing goods in Portsmouth were

[95]

Without intending it, acting selfishly and unpatriotically, and we now make an earnest appeal to all classes of the community to revert as far as possible to the conditions which prevailed a fortnight ago. Let us show that we are not afraid by going about our business as usual . . . Let practical patriotism on these lines be our present aim and the adversities now threatening Portsmouth will disappear like chaff before the wind.[16]

The *Evening News*'s appeal was followed up by the Mayor of Portsmouth who urged 'the public of Portsmouth, not to postpone the giving of their accustomed orders to tradesmen' adding that the Prince of Wales appealed for people to 'stand by one another'.[17] Likewise in Leeds, the civic authorities' first concerns when war broke-out was for the impact it would have on the local economy. Reports of rising food prices, profiteering and a rise in poor-house admissions prompted the local press to encourage readers not to panic and that despite war 'it was business as usual'.[18] It was feared that the war would induce a prolonged recession which led to consumers purchasing only essential commodities. An initial slump in textile orders threw large numbers of workers into unemployment.[19] However, by 1915, Leeds manufacturers had successfully converted from the production of civilian to military clothing. The Jewish Leylands district particularly benefited from the 'khaki boom', a point not lost on the *Yorkshire Evening Post*:

In the Jewish quarter of Leeds khaki is quite the vogue nowadays, chiefly because so many men and women have been and are still engaged on the production of uniforms for our Armies. It is no uncommon sight to see men trundling handcarts – and women perambulators – containing loads of Government over-coats and tunics from one workshop to another.[20]

Government munitions contracts were also instrumental in providing a boost to the Leeds economy. The Leeds civic authorities were quick to seize the opportunity of exploiting government investment and formed the Leeds Munitions Committee in August 1914. Indeed, in 1915 the first national shell factory was constructed on the outskirts of Leeds: it covered over 400 acres and employed sixteen thousand workers.[21]

Thus, the immediate concern on the outbreak of war for the civic elites in both Leeds and Portsmouth was how their respective economies would fare under the strain of international conflict. Indeed, after war was declared the people of Portsmouth and Leeds were being advised to continue consuming and behaving as if in peacetime conditions. During the first few weeks of war the national government might have expected the local authorities to impress upon their citizens the extraordinary nature of the crisis, yet the municipal elite appear to have initially prioritised local commercial interests.

Similarly in Coventry, at the outbreak of the conflict the local elites reverted to a period of introspection to solve an unexpected civic crisis that war had ushered in. On 14 August 1914, the Mayor of Coventry outlined the city's arrangements to launch the Prince of Wales' Distress and Relief Fund for the war. In this town meeting, the Mayor's speech opened not with details of the fund but with an impassioned defence of his own patriotism.

> I am sure there is no man in Coventry, be he a British citizen by the circumstances of his birth or by the force of the law and his connections, who will not do his duty. (Hear, hear.) I am rather, you will agree, in a peculiar position – a unique position (Hear, hear) – but those citizens who know me will bear me out that I shall – that I intend to do my duty. (Hear, hear and applause) . . . But if my heart is bleeding for all the innocent victims of war – (hear, hear) – I can say that, in the first place, it is bleeding for the noble sons of this country . . . I look forward to the support of every citizen. (Hear, hear). I want to gain your respect and obtain your love.[22]

This unusual appeal to the Coventry public can be explained by the Mayor's country of origin. Siegfried Bettmann was a German-Jewish businessman who had settled in Coventry in 1890, founding Triumph bicycles in the same year. Bettmann became a naturalised British subject in 1895, allowing him to enter into civic politics for the Liberals and eventually become Coventry Mayor in 1913. He was the first foreign-born councillor to become a mayor in Britain, and was initially received with enthusiasm across the political divide. The Conservative weekly paper, the *Coventry Standard*, praised Bettmann's qualities and commitment to Britain, while local councillors heaped praise on his contribution to the city's civic life and business community.[23] On his election to Mayor, Vernon Pugh, a fellow councillor, praised Bettmann as 'he has become the perfect John Bull, and in short, had acquired a genuine English spirit'.[24] However, the outbreak of war changed everything. According to Bettmann, when war was declared 'it broke many lives, and amongst these was my life as far as public action was concerned'.[25] The traditional two-year Mayoral office was ruthlessly cut short by an anti-German resentment that was particularly acute within the civic elite and business community. Bettmann had been a successful Chairman of the Maudslay motor company, but when war broke out Maudslay and his colleagues were 'different men'. Bettmann recalled that his colleagues 'looked upon me as an enemy, and treated me as such. They would not speak to me, and would not

1 Siegfried Bettmann (1863–1951) Mayor of Coventry 1913–1914.
By kind permission of the Coventry Transport Museum

reply to questions I put to them, it was their firm resolve to get rid of me.' Coventry's industrialists feared that any association with Germany would damage their trade and business networks. John Budge, a former colleague of Bettmann, told him that 'you do not know how they talk at the Club about you and the Company. A bl . . . Company presided over by a bl. . . . Hun.' Budge thought his position was untenable and added, 'you need not fret; perhaps the Germans will soon be over here, and then you will have the time of your life!!!'[26] Bettmann's exclusion from the Coventry business community was complete with his expulsion from the Masonic lodge he had helped establish at the turn of the century. It led Bettmann to believe that the depth of hatred of Germans permeated all social classes but 'especially the higher and middle classes of English life'.[27] His public appearances as Mayor during the outbreak of war had led him to believe that most working people did not share the anti-German anxieties of the business community. It was with some trepidation that Bettmann stepped on the stage to chair the first public meeting after war had broken out in September 1914. To his relief he recalled that 'my entrance into the hall, however, was greeted with such demonstrative cheers that the would-be interrupters were frightened' and remained silent throughout the evening. After the meeting, a fellow speaker informed him that 'you ought to be a proud man to-night. The way in which you were received by the people should be a proof to you of the high esteem in which you are held.'[28] Despite the absence of a deep-seated anti-German hostility in public meetings, the business community's treatment of Bettmann led him to have some foreboding of how the war would affect his Mayoral office. Indeed, Coventry's civic elite drew heavily from the locality's industrialists. Moreover, Bettmann was faced with anti-German agitation from both the national and the local press. Horatio Bottomley used his *Daily Mail* column to pronounce that all Germans were vermin who should be exterminated and demanded that Bettmann resign from public office. His campaign was joined by the once supportive conservative *Coventry Standard* that began to echo the concerns of Tory councillors who believed that expressions of mass patriotism would founder in a city with a German Mayor. The pressure became unbearable and Bettmann resigned from office prior to the city's first 'Grand Patriotic Demonstration' organised to enlist soldiers for Kitchener's army.[29]

It was perhaps significant that Bettmann submitted his resignation prior to the 'Grand Patriotic Demonstration' since his place of birth had triggered a discourse on the relationship between race, nation and empire among Coventry's civic elite. How, they argued, could a German Mayor passionately convey the spirit of English patriotism that would convince Coventry's young men to enlist? This belief was compounded by Coventry's mediocre recruitment totals. By early September, Captain Key, the recruiting officer, complained that recruiting was 'quiet' and reminded young men 'there is no excuse for the vigorous and healthy youth with no encumbrances, who fail to prove themselves loyal to his King and Country by not enlisting in some branch of the service'.[30] The editor of the *Midland Daily Telegraph* was not surprised by the decision, believing that the war was a 'racial conflict' and that, in the best interests of city, nation and empire, an Englishman should assume the responsibilities of Mayor.[31] Likewise, the *Coventry Times* agreed that Bettmann's 'loyalty to the city and loyalty to the Empire' was best demonstrated through his resignation. An election of a new Mayor was swiftly implemented and in the accompanying speeches it was emphasised that the replacement, Councillor Pridmore, was 'a member of an old Coventry family'. In addressing the perceived absence of civic patriotic zeal, the new Mayor demanded that the corporation must take an interest in recruiting soldiers, adding that 'Public influence must make itself felt with those who can go, but do not go: the football youths, who think nothing about was has happened in Belgium, who fail to realise that was has happened there may happen here'. For Pridmore, Britain's victory would be intrinsically linked to 'the destiny of our race', an assumption that clearly excluded non-Anglo-Saxons from leading a municipality in a time of war.[32]

The local press made clear connections between the appointment of an English Mayor and the recruitment campaign, with the *Coventry Times* welcoming the new Mayor as, hitherto, the problem of slackers had not been tackled. Indeed, the newspaper made the rather dubious claim that recruitment had improved markedly immediately after the appointment of Pridmore. Indeed, in November 1914, the *Coventry Times* noted that speeches in the Town Council had 'passed beyond the narrow limits of locality into the wider sphere of national patriotism'.[33] The removal of a German Mayor in Coventry propelled the issues of race, local patriotism, nation and empire centre-stage in debates about lacklustre recruitment during the early days of the war. The Mayoral crisis had provided City councillors and the business community with a convenient explanation for the uninspiring recruitment rates in the city. An English Mayor, and more especially one born in Coventry, could use the rhetoric of patriotism to forge a symbolic imperial chain from city to nation to empire in a fashion that Bettmann could never have hoped to achieve. During the initial stages of the First World War, Portsmouth, Leeds and Coventry all appear to have been consumed with their own particular civic issues that appeared to take precedence over initial recruitment campaigns. The civic elites' immediate concerns were, in Portsmouth's and Leeds's case, for the local economy, while Coventry's civic crisis overshadowed the initial recruitment campaigns during the first three months of the war. However, despite this rather stuttering start to the war, the civic bodies and the local press were destined to play a key role in the promotion and recruitment of men for the regular and City battalions.

Local elites, the press and working-class recruitment campaigns

From the day that Kitchener called for men across the country to enlist for a new army of half a million men, the provincial newspapers and the civic elite scrutinised recruitment figures on a daily basis. Initially, local elites focused on Kitchener's Army and measured their own town's recruitment drive on the success or otherwise of this new army. However, by early September, the Pals or City battalions became centre-stage and the local elites' time, energy and, significantly, perception of how recruitment was faring began to rest with these local companies. As a result, it is difficult to obtain an accurate account from the local press of whether a town was successful in recruiting men across the board. Furthermore, civic leaders had little guidance in what constituted a good recruitment profile and were left to look anxiously over their shoulders at competing towns' enlistment figures and recruitment campaigns for some comparison.

While all three communities wrestled with differing social contexts at the outbreak of war, the local press and civic elite adopted similar strategies in their recruitment campaigns. The local press, as it had done in the Boer War, published letters from the front that attempted to capture both the excitement and the dangers of war. The provincial popular papers continued to play a duel role of increasing their circulation through sensational letters depicting life on the front and encouraging patriotism among men to enlist.[34] These objectives were not always compatible, as the local press tended not to practise self-censorship. One journalist in Leeds noted that publication of letters from the front and interviews with wounded soldiers 'brings home to us all the horrible reality of war', adding that the working class were 'fully acquainted' with facts of the war.[35] The press, on the other hand, was the main publicity platform for recruitment rallies. Advertisements placed in newspapers, venues staging recruitment meetings, and interviews and editorials in the local press were all honed carefully to the sensitivities of social class. Organised leisure and the workplace were identified as potentially useful recruiting grounds and accordingly the patriotic message was responsive to these class exclusive activities. For example, a striking similarity across the three communities was the importance that football played in propaganda targeted at working-class men. During the first few months of the war, newspapers received a significant number of letters criticising working-class men for showing more interest in football than the war effort. In Coventry, the new Mayor began his term in office with an attack on the 'football youths who think nothing of what has happened in Belgium', while a correspondent to the *Yorkshire Evening Post* complained that youths were anxiously scanning the *Football Post* for the latest results.[36] He added that he had seen a crowd of spectators who would have been ideal material for Kitchener's Army, 'active, well built young fellows, eagerly discussing not Belgium's sorrow but the merits of their favourite players'.[37] Meanwhile, F.G. Foster, Chairman of the Naval Disasters Fund in Portsmouth was appalled at the level of football enthusiasm in the town. At a time when the British Empire was in peril, Foster recalled that

> I was in Commercial Road, thinking seriously of the National crisis and of the future, when I saw some newsboys running and heard them shouting in a most exciting manner. I, like many others from the war, hurried to obtain a copy, and found to my disgust all the excitement and fuss was about Pompey half-time or full-time, I know not which.[38]

Professional footballers were also the target for much criticism since they performed an important role model for young men. One *Evening News* correspondent complained that 'these plucky devils propose to use their manhood in propelling a leather sphere up and down a less muddy pitch, instead of "charging the Germans home"'.[39]

This hostility to the popularity of football during the early stages of war was replicated in the national press with *The Times* leading the condemnation.[40] At both a local and a national level, football's record of soldier recruitment was considered unfavourably against rugby union, cricket and rowing. The Football League which met in September 1914 to discuss the crisis, however, insisted the programme should continue 'in the interests of the people of this country'.[41] The football authorities and clubs were accused of placing their commercial interests ahead of patriotism by persevering with football fixtures. Indeed, Matthew Taylor has argued that the eventual suspension of regular football schedules from the start of the 1915–16 season was based on economic considerations rather than external patriotic pressures. Taylor adds that football's perceived lack of patriotism, along with a number of financial scandals during this period, triggered a middle-class and upper-class desertion from the sport. From 1914, public and grammar schools shunned football in favour of rugby union, which had a patriotic war record and purportedly instilled 'true manhood and leadership'.[42]

Despite the criticism heaped upon football, the working class's attachment to the sport remained strong. Indeed, the local press's attempts to draw working people away from the game and focus on the war failed miserably and had a damaging impact upon newspaper circulation. The owners of the local press had little option but to follow public demand as described by one journalist in Leeds:

> The local evening newspapers have quickly recanted their decision not to publish any football editions during the war. After holding out for a week against the invasion of rival papers who were quick to see the opening they now announce that the football specials will be resumed to-morrow as usual, but the further information is vouchsafed that 'the football editions will also contain the latest war news' – in case, no

doubt, the football enthusiast should forget the game of cannon ball which is being played on the continent by teams including the reserves of about twenty million men.[43]

With firm popular support for football, along with the football authorities' determination to continue through the early part of the war, the newspapers and civic elites had little option but to target supporters with patriotic messages. For example, military battles were sometimes reported in sporting terms to catch the eye of the male working-class reader. In September 1914, the *Midland Daily Telegraph* printed a letter from a sailor sent to his brother in the midlands describing the battle in the style of football report:

> We sank five ships and ran a few off last Friday about six in the morning, and we won five-nil. Not bad, considering we are playing 'away.' Their goalkeepers could not hold us, we were so hot. Our forwards shot beautifully, and our defence was sound. We agreed to play extra time if we had not finished, but we had done it in time . . . We are all getting ready for the big match of the season now when their battle fleet chooses to come out.[44]

From October 1914, recruitment rallies were held at football grounds with the full approval of the local press and civic elite. In October 1914, the *Evening News* announced that the whole of the new Portsmouth battalion along with the war-wounded would attend the home match with Luton. It was reported that the Portsmouth battalion would then make an appeal to the crowd for volunteers who could enlist 'then and there'.[45] The attempt to militarise football was given a further impetus when the *Evening News* printed an adaptation of the popular 'Play up Pompey' song, entitled 'Pompey Boys'. The newspaper urged supporters to sing:

> God bless the lads of Pompey,
> The Boys in red and blue
> Who one and all rose to the call
> To see Old England through,
> We're proud of every Briton,
> From near, or far away,
> But we're extra pound of the little crowd
> Of Pompey boys to-day
>
> Chorus – Hallo ! Hallo!
> Play up Pompey
> Kaiser must go,
> 'Off-side' is he.[46]

In Leeds, the Mayor and the President of Leeds City football club joined forces and organised a recruitment rally after a match. The

President of the Leeds club addressed the crowd with 'you have been loyal to the colours of your club in days gone by, I ask you to respond now with the same loyalty to the call of your country in her time of need.'[47] It was also notable that, in the first recruitment rally in Portsmouth, Lord Beresford appealed to the 'crowd who are interested in football but do not always play' to instead show support for their countrymen and enlist forthwith.[48] Interestingly, these appeals to the crowd did not cite the importance of, or threat to, the Empire. Instead public oratory to football crowds and songs issued through the press identified war as a threat to 'Old England' and urged workers to demonstrate their loyalty to their locality and nation. Such propaganda was designed to use football to stoke a civic or local pride that would transcend into national and imperial patriotism once the uniform was donned.

Perhaps the most spectacular recruiting rallies were the large civic organised events that launched the appeal for men to enlist in early September 1914. Each locality adopted a similar set of proceedings, with the Mayor chairing a number of patriotic speeches from dignitaries with connections to the area. Each event was publicised extensively in the local press and extremely well attended. Significantly, appeals to men began with a reminder of what was at stake. Nation and empire figured noticeably in the 'stirring speeches' and editorials that surrounded these rallies. However, the readership of newspapers and the audiences in public meetings were first and foremost invited to consider how they themselves could match the heroism, patriotism and traditions of their forefathers who had established their own town's distinctive and celebrated reputation. The *Evening News* claimed that the 'spirit of Portsmouth – a spirit nurtured in war and tempest and sacrifice through the centuries past – will stir young men to emulate the deeds of their fathers to offer their all to country and King and, if need be to die'.[49] The former Liberal MP for Coventry, A.E.W. Mason, echoed these sentiments in an early recruitment rally, stating that 'Coventry in the past has always been on the side of freedom and always to the front when fighting for their own rights'. Likewise, Pridmore, the Coventry Mayor, thought that the city 'would be true to its traditions and would find more and more men until they came out top dog'.[50] In Leeds, civic rivalry over the numbers of men recruited energised much of the local press's coverage of enlistment. After Brigadier-General Wright expressed disappointment with the recruitment in Yorkshire, the *Yorkshire Evening Post* believed that Leeds ought to be exempt from such criticism since the city's daily enlistment figures doubled that of their near neighbours of Bradford, Halifax and Huddersfield.[51] Inter-civic rivalry was particularly strong between Leeds, Liverpool and Manchester, with the *Yorkshire Evening Post* publishing monthly recruitment data in these areas.[52]

An important stage for working-class recruitment was the workplace. All three communities suffered economic downturns during the early stages of the war owing to the problems encountered by manufacturers converting production from civilian goods to military products. As a consequence, the manufacturers were initially only too pleased to encourage recruitment rallies in their workplace since enlistment would help ease the over-supply of labour. For example in Coventry, almost four hundred Humber employees had enlisted by early September after mass recruitment rallies were held in the firm's grounds. In one meeting the Chairman, Edward Powell, explained to the crowd that it was his intention to keep the works open as long as possible during the war. However, in order to achieve this he would have to reduce the number of employees and hours worked. He announced that, following the example set by other firms, preference for employment would be given to married men and urged single men to join the army. It appears that most factories in Coventry held these meetings and, by arrangement with the local recruitment officer, sent batches of men to enlist at set times as not to overwhelm the recruitment office. Significantly, in all of the factory meetings, employers appealed to their workers to demonstrate their pride in their workplace, city and nation.[53] Commenting on the slack trade in the Leeds textile trade, the editor of the *Yorkshire Evening Post* believed that men 'are realising that joining the colours and preparing to fight the nation's battle is far better than waiting for the distress of little or no employment'.[54] When one reporter interviewed a group of men waiting to enlist outside a recruitment office, he reported that 'the clothing trade was slack and they said they wanted work'.[55] In Portsmouth, recruiting rallies were held in various parts of the town in a bid to capture the attention of both 'well trained men from the workshop and men with ability from the office'. Significantly, in working-class areas of Portsmouth Labour councillors addressed the crowd along with recruits who were 'allowed to mount the platform and tell the audience how they were faring in the ranks. "We are getting 3s a day each one of them declared, "and they put chums together in one squad".'[56] Thus, the recruitment drives in factories and working-class areas mixed a local patriotism with the practicalities of employment and income. Undoubtedly the opportunity of employment and the possibility to serve with work colleagues combined to persuade some workers to enlist. It was the attraction of enlisting with work colleagues that was the key feature of the Pals or City battalions.

Middle-class recruitment campaigns: the Pals

Whereas working-class recruits were expected to join Kitchener's New Army, new exclusive local Pals or City battalions were formed to attract middle-class volunteers. With a promise that recruits would serve with people of their own class and take the name of their town or county into battle, Pals battalions sprang up across the country. The idea has been credited to Lord Derby, though the experience of the citizen volunteers during the Boer War undoubtedly signalled advantages of exploiting civic pride and loyalty.[57] Initially the formation of Pals battalions was left entirely to the discretion of local government, but, with uneven recruitment patterns across the country, the War Office assumed control. From mid-September 1914, local councils were required to request permission to raise a battalion, while, in some cases, the War Office intervened and appealed to a town to form local contingents if recruitment had deteriorated in an area.[58]

In all three communities, recruitment for City battalions dominated the local press's recruitment coverage, overshadowing the general enlistment campaigns for Kitchener's New Army. The local press and civic elite prioritised the middle-class battalions over Kitchener's New Army since the former were an expression of civic culture and a tangible manifestation of a city's contribution to the war effort. In Leeds the popular local newspaper, the *North Leeds News*, declared that, while it was commendable that between six and seven thousand men had joined the regular army, 'it is to the City battalion that the citizen will look as the special custodians of the honour and fame of the city, and we have no hesitation in saying that the battalion will prove worthy of the great part they have been called to play'.[59] In Portsmouth, the Mayor declared that soldiers in City battalions were different from regular troops since they 'have claims upon the patriotism of the manhood of town and country'.[60] During patriotic rallies in Portsmouth, potential recruits were reminded that they were fighting for the Empire. However, speakers emphasised that intrinsically tied to the defence of empire was the preservation of their locality. The Labour MP Will Crooks asked the men of Portsmouth 'to remember their own homes and hopes and desires and to carry their minds to Belgium and reflect for a moment upon their obligations'.[61] Equally, the Mayor of Leeds warned of the war's impact on the Empire by reminding his audience of the atrocities that would ensue should the Germans reach Leeds. He declared that 'we shall have to come forward to defend the Empire or the Germans will be over here "bossing" us. They would do exactly what they have done at Louvain and Bruges. They would smash up our mills and would ruin Leeds for a century.'[62] Moreover, inter-city rivalry also spurred on the civic authorities to embark on a Leeds Pals battalion. The *Yorkshire Evening Post* noted that

> In one hour to-day a full battalion of commercial men was enrolled in Liverpool. Another battalion is to be enrolled forthwith. Birmingham is following Liverpool's example. Cannot Leeds do what Liverpool has done and Birmingham is preparing to do? There is a vast recruiting ground in Leeds at present untapped. It consists of the middle-class population . . . In these days when the cult of the open air flourishes, and men spend their leisure in the cricket and football fields, the golf course and tennis courts and the weekend camp, office work has not debilitating effect worth speaking of.[63]

By early September, the Leeds City battalion had begun recruiting volunteers from 'all walks of professional and commercial life'. As a symbol of its civic importance, the Town Hall was designated as the City battalion recruitment office, a clear contrast to the anonymous building in a Leeds side-street used for enlisting Kitchener's Army. A reporter from the *Yorkshire Evening Post* visited the Town Hall and noted that it was 'quite a common sight to see three or four men from one office walk into Victoria Hall together', having been given permission by their employer to leave their desks. Some employers were even more enthusiastic to see their worker enlist: as one volunteer explained, 'our boss told us to get out of the office and put our names down at once, or he would kick us out!'[64] However, it seems that a man's profession was not sufficient in itself to enlist since recruitment sergeants demanded he come from a middle-class family. Mr E. Robinson from Leeds attempted to join the Leeds Pals and recalled that

> I was asked what my father did for a living, much to my surprise, and I suggested I wanted to join not my father. I said I was a clerk, but they insisted I should say what my father did. It was curiouser and curiouser, but eventually I said he was a farm worker. Very politely, very firmly it was told to me that only professional men's sons or whose fathers had businesses, could join . . . it was exclusive.[65]

In Coventry, a proposed company of non-manual workers was launched for commercial and professional young men of the Coventry and Warwickshire region. The *Midland Daily Telegraph* announced that 'young men of the city and county who belong to office staffs and fill other positions of a similar kind will thus have an opportunity, if they desire it, of doing their soldiering among their own friends and acquaintances and people of their own ways'.[66] As with the propaganda directed at working-class recruits, local sport characterised enlistment campaigns directed at the middle class. For the middle class, however, the sports of rugby union and athletics were targeted in particular. A greater emphasis was placed on the players of rugby union rather than, as with football, the spectators. For instance, chairmen of local teams in Coventry appealed to the local press for all players in the area to join up, with one chairman confidently proclaiming that 'seventeen of our members will respond to our country's call and offer themselves immediately for enlistment'.[67] In Portsmouth, middle classes were invited to 'come and join your pals in khaki and take part in THE GREAT RACE to the recruiting office next Saturday. Join the 2nd Portsmouth battalion.' The 'Sporting Recruitment Rally' attracted over ten thousand spectators to witness a race of men from Portsmouth's 2nd battalion, though, more importantly, the event's core aim was to persuade male spectators to sign up for the town's 3rd battalion.[68] In Leeds, the *Yorkshire Evening Post* called for those fit men who at weekends flourished on the tennis court, cricket field and golf course to demonstrate their athleticism in the theatre of war and enlist.[69] Clearly, a company that maintained class exclusivity was deemed an attractive proposition to middle-class professionals pondering whether to enlist. However, the local press's celebration of local battalions, and by association their favouritism of the professional and commercial classes, did not go unnoticed by working-class readers:

> When our lads enlist on their own without fuss or bribery, they have to go where and with whom they are sent. May I suggest that when the Lord Mayor equips his Feather Bed Battalion that he be sure and not forget dressing gowns, slippers, eider downs, whiskies and sodas, and if he can manage it, to throw in a few billiard tables. I have no doubt that the Battalion will greatly distinguish itself.[70]

This criticism of the Leeds battalion reveals simmering class tensions within the community. As we have seen, the civic authorities and the local press disseminated a call for men that appealed to a commitment to their immediate locality and empire. The tangible surroundings of their community were projected on a greater call to save the Empire. With a successful recruitment campaign that targeted both working- and middle-class men, each town could proudly take its place in representing the community in the imperial struggle. Thus at stake in all three recruitment campaigns was the reputation of the town within the broader context of the British Empire.

Monthly and daily recruitment levels in Portsmouth, Coventry and Leeds

Recruitment figures published in the local press are notoriously difficult to evaluate as the local recruiting bodies and newspapers wished to avoid revealing a consistently set of poor statistics for fear of engendering poor morale and defeatism. Furthermore, the press would merge daily figures to produce more impressive results, rendering it difficult to identify whether certain events or rallies had triggered an increase in recruits. However, through drawing evidence from daily official statistics generated for the War Office, we can gain an insight into the important local contexts that influenced both working- and middle-class men to enlist.[71] The entrenched social divisions of generation, race and class were sufficient to undermine the civic elites' rallying call for volunteers that placed their town at the centre of the imperial project. As we have seen, the Boer War volunteerism occurred as towns and cities were developing distinct civic and sporting identities that fused, for that moment in time, both popular and civic enthusiasm for an imperial war. Although civic elites in all three communities adopted similar recruitment strategies as in the Boer War in emphasising local patriotism, the stakes, and accordingly the social tensions, were far greater in the First World War. This view is borne out in the recruitment figures for the period August 1914 to May 1915, particularly with regard to working-class volunteerism.[72]

Table 2 reveals that, viewed in monthly totals, Portsmouth, Coventry and Leeds experienced similar of peaks and troughs in recruitment patterns. All three communities recorded the highest numbers volunteering in September and then, apart from a couple of spikes in levels of recruitment in Leeds, volunteers gradually fell away as war

Table 2: Monthly figures of men enlisted in Portsmouth, Coventry and Leeds, August 1914–May 1915

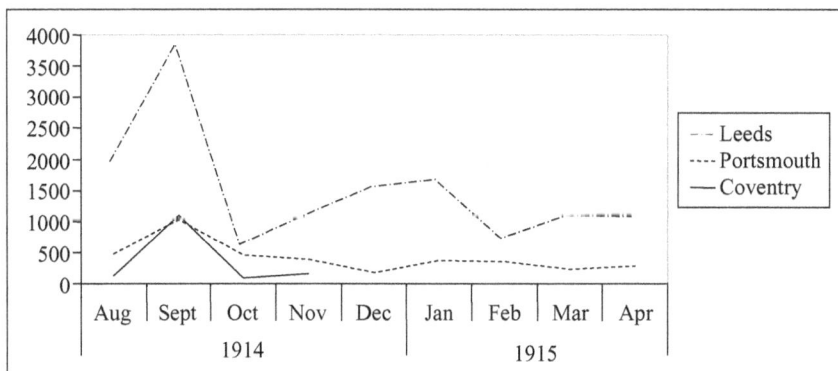

Source: National Archives, NATS 1/398, 'Approximate number of recruits raised daily'. By mid-November 1914 the collection of data from Coventry was discontinued presumably owing to the low levels of daily recruitment

progressed; a scenario that conforms to the view that there was a popular 'rush to colours' amidst a nationalistic and imperial frenzy. However, although these figures reveal general trends, the daily figures provide a more detailed and subtle picture of recruitment in which the impact of civic, sporting, workplace and Pals rallies can be measured.

Table 3 identifies the key dates for recruitment and the numbers of men raised on the day of the event. The civic authorities invested a great time and energy in staging recruiting events in the town centres or the football matches, and there is some indication that the results were disappointing. All three communities launched a call for men to join Kitchener's Army through 'grand patriotic rallies' presided over by the Mayor and civic dignitaries. As we have seen, the monthly figures seemed to confirm their success. However, the daily figures reveal a very different story that questions their impact on the men attending the event and those who read about it in the local press. The Coventry rally enlisted only 37 men on the day and then 32, 16 and none in the following three days, while the Leeds rally in September could only persuade 36 men to enlist on the day, with 27, 21 and 16 on the subsequent days. The Leeds Mayor was determined to take the message of recruitment to the public and organised an illuminated tram car to travel through the city encouraging men to enlist. Despite much publicity and fanfare, the illuminated tram did not excite potential recruits, with only 27 men enlisting, followed by 16 and none on the following two days.

Portsmouth's 'Call of the Empire Rally' failed to convince any men to enlist at the event or on the following day and only 27 and 43 on the subsequent days. The *Evening News* acknowledged that after a patriotic rally 'it seldom happens in cases of this kind that there is a rush to the recruiting office'.[73] Follow-up recruitment rallies in October and November failed to encourage men to enlist at events, as only 5 signed up in Coventry and none in Portsmouth. Football matches fared no better, with only 26 and 8 men enlisting on the days the Mayor and recruiting sergeants addressed football recruit crowds in Portsmouth. Likewise, the *North Leeds News* recorded a spectacular failure to recruit after a football match. The sports reporter wrote, 'who said footballers were cowards? At the Headingly match on Saturday speeches were made at half-time from the recruiting platforms. There were eight thousand spectators present and how many recruits do you think presented themselves? . . . 0.'[74] The *North Leeds News* lamented that while patriotic songs and speeches were celebrated with great gusto at rallies, football matches and music halls, as soon as the event was over 'the patriotic feeling seems to subside'.[75] If rallies in the Town

Table 3: Key dates and men enlisted in Portsmouth, Coventry and Leeds, September 1914–May 1915

Date	Event	Men enlisted
1 September 1914	Portsmouth	97 (largest single day recruitment)
2 September	Portsmouth 'Call of the Empire' rally	0
6 September	Leeds Pals battalion launched	367 (largest single day recruitment)
4 September	Coventry Humber employees laid off	182 (largest single day recruitment)
10 September	Coventry patriotic rally	37
22 September	Leeds recruitment rally	36
26 September	Portsmouth recruitment rally	18
28 September	Leeds football crowd recruitment rally	0
5 October	Portsmouth football crowd recruitment rally	26
10 October	Warwickshire Pals launched	5
15 October	Portsmouth Town Hall rally	0
31 October	Portsmouth football crowd recruitment rally	8
13 November	Coventry recruitment rally	5
27 November	Leeds illuminated tram car recruitment drive	23
4 January 1915	Leeds Pals parade and recruitment Rally	140
5 January	Leeds Pals parade and recruitment Rally	146
31 January	Portsmouth recruitment rally	0
26 April	Portsmouth Second battalion rally	23
1 May	May Day recruitment rally	10

Source: *North Leeds News; Yorkshire Evening Post; Coventry Herald; Midland Daily Telegraph; Hampshire Telegraph; Evening News,* National Archives, NATS 1/398, 'Approximate number of recruits raised daily'

2   The Leeds Pals recruiting Tram in 1915.
By kind permission of Leeds Library and Information Services www.leodis.net

Hall and football matches targeted at the working class were largely ineffectual, how can we account for the relatively high levels of recruitment in September and the spike in enlisters in Leeds during January 1915? Coventry's daily recruitment figures in September reveal a clear correlation between employers laying off workers and men enlisting. The city's highest recruitment level for a single day was 4 September 1914, when 182 men enlisted at the same time that the Humber works had encouraged their staff to sign up because of the lack of work. Indeed, during August and September 1914, Coventry's engineering industries experienced severe short-term problems in converting their machine tools from peace-time production to military hardware and munitions. The *Midland Daily Telegraph* reported 'a long queue of men outside the Labour Exchange' and the effect of war was to bring 'business practically to a standstill'.[76] However, by mid-October, the newspaper reported that the city's engineering industries had successfully converted from domestic to war goods, a development that saw a fall in enlistment from 1,108 in September to only 87 recruits in the whole of October.[77] In Portsmouth and Leeds the 'rush to colours' in September coincided with Pals recruitment rallies that targeted the middle class. In the three days following the launch of the Leeds Pals battalion 902 men enlisted, while Portsmouth's largest single day of recruitment of 134 coincided with appeals to join the Portsmouth Battalion. Most of these men, the *Evening News* noted were drawn from the 'county districts', a trend that was also noted in Warwickshire's Pals recruitment drive.[78] The spike in Leeds recruitment in January 1915 was also related to the city's Pals parade and recruitment rallies held 4 and 5 January. Enlistment rose dramatically from zero on 3 January to 140 and 146 during the parades, then falling to 76, 86 and 49 on the subsequent days of the parades. Another increase occurred in March when the Leeds civic authorities were so concerned that the numbers raised were inferior to cities such as Liverpool and Birmingham that members of the recruitment committee organised personal visits to men yet to enlist. The *Yorkshire Evening Post* reported that 'a member or members of the committee call personally at the address and have a quiet talk to the man or men named. The visitors urge the necessity of the case, and the man has the opportunity of explaining the difficulties in the way of enlistment.'[79] This strategy appears to have worked in the short term as recruitment levels rose from 659 in February to 1,004 in March, dropping slightly in April to 981. However, this rather intimidating approach to enlisting men raises the question of whether those who received visits can really be described a 'volunteers'.[80] A similar approach was adopted in Portsmouth in 1915 in which men would be randomly stopped and questioned as to why they had failed to enlist. Recruiting officers were encouraged to identify a likely recruit in the thoroughfares of Portsmouth where he would 'be firmly tackled and a few pointed questions put to him'.[81] The *Evening News* calculated that in October 1915 there were between five and six thousand able-bodied men of fighting age in Portsmouth who were unstarred, in other words, not working in essential industries. It warned these men to expect canvassers at their door 'who will point out to them "plainly and politely" the need of the country'. However, with this rather confrontational approach, allegations that recruits were coerced into joining surfaced, prompting an investigation into the matter by the Mayor.[82]

The daily recruitment figures tend to reinforce the notion that the spectacular civic rallies or parades failed to ignite a popular enthusiasm for enlisting to fight. While working-class citizens still took pride in their locality, a local, national and imperial patriotism could be exhibited through means other than Kitchener's Army such as pride in their work. This work, be it in the Portsmouth dockyard or

Coventry's and Leeds's engineering industries, was closely associated with the town's own narrative of its role in the war effort. However, while factories produced war goods which were a clear manifestation of the workforces' patriotism, middle-class professions such as clerks or managers had perhaps a more difficult task in exhibiting an outward show of patriotism. Others enlisted for the excitement, as one Leeds clerk recounted: 'Belgium atrocities didn't cut much ice, but I was feeling sick of a humdrum life that led nowhere and promised nothing.'[83] This may go some way in explaining why middle-class volunteers appeared to have responded more keenly to the rallies encouraging Pals recruitment in all three communities. Furthermore, the daily enlistment figures reveal that the Great War had a far from unifying impact on society and instead increased anxieties that specific social groups were reluctant to pull together for the national and imperial cause.

Fearing for the Empire: social tensions on the home front

The relatively modest recruitment figures in Portsmouth, Coventry and to some extent Leeds strained social relations in all three communities. Prewar social tensions were seized upon by commentators who utilised the platform of the local press to identify the causes of slow recruitment. The widespread notion that the war would galvanise a sense of social cohesion was perhaps more a product of postwar nostalgia rather than of wartime experience. In a souvenir book to commemorative the Great War, William Gates, the editor of the *Evening News*, pronounced in 1919 that

> Portsmouth can look back upon this period of sacrifice and suffering with satisfaction and pride. In nothing essential did it fail; in all things asked of it in the national cause the response was immediate and full; it gave its best; it poured out its treasures unstintingly; it submitted to restrictions and bore privations with a smile.[84]

Similar assessments on how local populations responded to the call to war were made in countless commemorations across the country. Their sentiments fit neatly in the popular vision of the Great War which saw social tensions temporarily resolved in the face of a common enemy. However, these commemorative books were less an audit of a town's war record and more a memorial to those who had fallen. The social tensions within society during the war were, in effect, airbrushed out of local histories. It may explain why, in 1919, William Gates chose to forget his earlier criticisms of the recruitment campaign aired in his *Evening News* leader columns during the war. In

1914 he wrote, 'in urging the young men of Portsmouth to join the local battalion of Kitchener's Army, it is perhaps necessary as well as just to say that the town itself has not risen to the occasion . . . Portsmouth as a whole has, to its great shame, shown a great lack of interest.'[85] As editor of the *Evening News*, William Gates reflected the town's concern that Portsmouth men were failing to respond to the call of empire in the midst of an international crisis.[86] Indeed, only days after the declaration of war, William Gates warned readers that the people of Portsmouth had been slow to address Kitchener's call for men. He noted that 'judging by the appearance of the streets by day and night' eligible men in the town 'numbered many hundreds' adding 'what are they waiting for?'[87] Other correspondents to the *Evening News* were more specific and critical of the fashionable young males who 'loafed' around Southsea seafront. According to one observer these men, or 'nuts' as they liked to be called, 'are to be seen careering around Southsea – and other places – on motor cycles and side-cars, mostly carrying "flappers" and with machines bedecked with Union Jacks'.[88] At the heart of this criticism was the belief that a new generation of young men's apparent reluctance to enlist and save the Empire stemmed from the degenerative influence of modern society. In short, the male stock of Britain had become emasculated. Leonard Ashby of St Paul's Vicarage in Southsea encapsulated this unease when he complained about the young men on the seafront:

> What are they doing? They are hanging about the pier with their hands in their pockets and their feet encased in marvellous and wonderfully coloured socks. They are smoking cigarettes, throwing stones into the water, and mooning about in chairs with girls! This is the manhood of England, which has been left for us to contemplate at this time. Meanwhile in Belgium there are REAL men, lying behind their rifles and facing death in order these over-socked emasculated specimens of femininity may lounge about the seaside and feel 'immense.'

Clearly Ashby, who was not a man to mince his words, called for someone to 'whip them with scorn into some semblance of manhood', and 'make men of them'.[89] Ashby was not a lone voice since the *Evening News* reported that they had received 'many letters' complaining about the young men's reluctance to enlist.[90] The perceived low level of recruitment in Portsmouth was, then, blamed on an effeminate generation of youths that crossed social class boundaries. Indeed, concerns deepened when it was revealed that the first patriotic rally for the Portsmouth Battalion in September fell significantly short of the five hundred men were expected to enlist. Despite patriotic rallies and the *Evening News*'s constant urging for men to enlist, the view taken by the urban elite was that the recruitment campaigns had largely failed.[91]

In Leeds, long-standing social tensions erupted almost immediately after war was declared. As we have seen, from the late nineteenth century, the concentration of Eastern European Jewish communities of the Leylands district of Leeds raised considerable anxieties for the city's urban elite. The civic authorities had implemented an intensive programme educating Jewish children on the importance of the British Empire that predated Meath's Empire Day. Both headmasters of the Jewish elementary schools, Leylands and Darley, had embraced Empire Day with great gusto, inviting key Anglo-Jews such as Lord Rothschild to present Union Jack flags to the schools.[92] The First World War, then, would prove the first patriotic test for the Eastern European Jew. A Jewish boy born in the 1890s would have undergone considerable imperial teaching during his schooling and, by 1914, would be in a position to enlist. This fact was not missed by the local press and civic authorities, who scrutinised the Jewish community for their response to the war effort. Shortly after war broke out, the Reverend Mr Abrahams organised a patriotic meeting at the 'Great Synagogue' in Leeds. Abrahams, who had been a key figure in the early Empire Day movement in Leeds, appealed to the Jewish community 'to show their love for the throne and country by volunteering sacrificing their best efforts and even their lives for the Empire's cause'.[93] However, only four days after Britain declared war on Germany, the *Yorkshire Evening Post* published a letter from a Leeds resident who wrote:

> I was in Leeds on Thursday night and was struck with the enormous number of Jewish young men walking and standing about Briggate and Boar Lane, the great majority of strong and healthy appearance. In view of the hospitality that Russian and Polish Jews enjoy in this country, it seems to me that these able-bodied men owe the sacred duty to the country of joining the English colours in this now urgent need.[94]

The letter sparked a furious response from Jews, most of whom pledged loyalty and support to the Empire, with one describing the letter as 'nothing short of effrontery upon the patriotism of my co-religionists'.[95] The *Yorkshire Post*'s decision to publish letters complaining of young Jewish men shirking their military duty may have helped legitimise a growing feeling of anti-Semitism in the city. The letters continued into September, prompting one Jewish correspondent to complain of overhearing a meeting of men in a Leeds Park in which it was said that 'after the war we will drive every Jew out of this country'.[96] The same correspondent pointed out to the readers of the *Yorkshire Evening Post* that by September approximately four hundred

Jews had enlisted.[97] However, even when Eastern European Jews did volunteer, they were treated with suspicion and their inclusion raised fears that racial deficiencies would inhibit the efficiency of Britain's fighting force. One reporter who mingled with a crowd of volunteers gathered to enlist noted that in 'this motley crowd' he found six or seven Jews. Indeed, he was surprised to find that they were 'thick-set fellows with good teeth'.[98]

By 1915, however, the local press had decided that the Leeds recruitment campaigns had been undermined by the city's Jewish community. The *Yorkshire Evening Post* posed the question 'shirkers, who are they' and then proceeded to identify the young Jewish man as the chief culprit. The editor complained that only approximately 550 Jews had enlisted from a Jewish population of 25,000. While the editor had exaggerated the Jewish population in Leeds – it stood closer to 15,000 – there was certainly no Jewish 'rush to colours in 1914'.[99] There were perhaps two reasons for this. First, the Jewish quarter of Leeds became the chief district for the manufacture of army uniforms. This war work did not require the skilled tailoring of traditional Leeds firms but instead employed the semi-skilled labour of machinists to mass produce government clothing supplies. It was reported that six Jewish firms had government contracts, with many others gaining sub-contract work employing well over two thousand people.[100] Clearly, then, the clothing manufacturers in the Leylands district were drawing from a pool of labour engaged in vital war work, prohibiting a significant number of young Jewish men from enlisting. However, another, and perhaps more likely, explanation is their antipathy towards the imperial cause. The Jewish community in Leeds appear fairly independent and autonomous, despite the attempt by the civic and educational authorities to instil a sense of local, national and imperial patriotism.[101] Their apparent apathy towards civic and national causes, however, masked an enthusiasm to participate actively in their own Jewish institutions and networks. It was reported that

> The average Leeds Jew has an exceptional sense of personal responsibility for the preservation and up-keep of the charitable and communal organisations that matter. If you were to call on a Sunday morning on even the poorest working-class Jewish home in Leeds, you would find on the mantelpiece a handful of coppers and a number of multi-coloured pamphlets on institutions such as the Board of Guardians, the Talmud Torah, the Jewish Hospital, the Kosher Kitchen . . .

The Leeds Jewry were contrasted favourably with their counterparts in London who had 'not the slightest sense of responsibility for the maintenance of communal institutions'.[102] These strong communal ties rendered the imperial teaching of the Edwardian period largely ineffectual. Meath's vision of an Empire Day inculcating the values of imperial duty and sacrifice did not appear to have taken root in the Jewish district of Leeds. It was a problem that the conservative local press and civic elite saw as an obstacle to the impressive recruitment levels witnessed in other large cities such as Liverpool and Manchester.[103]

The numbers of men recruited to Kitchener's Army and the local battalion in Coventry were comparatively modest compared to Leeds and Portsmouth. However, unlike in the other two communities, the civic elite and local press did not find the recruitment statistics overly troubling. Furthermore, despite Coventry's large preponderance of young single working-class men who had migrated to the city in search of work, there was a notable absence of letters criticising 'young knuts' and 'swells' so common in other areas. Indeed, readers of the *Midland Daily Telegraph* had to wait for over three months after the declaration of war for a letter claiming it 'a perfect disgrace' for fit young men 'to walk about with a free and easy attitude'.[104] On the whole, however, the local press and civic elite saw the city's contribution to the war effort in terms of munitions and engineering rather than men for the forces. The editor of the *Midland Daily Telegraph* thought recruitment in Coventry had been 'steady' and satisfactory. He observed that 'especially when one takes into account the fact that there are many young fellows engaged in factories where War Office work is being undertaken, and, as it has been pointed out, such service is equally important as that of joining the colours'.[105] The newspaper's belief that Coventry's greater contribution to the war effort lay in the supply of munitions and military hardware was also shared by some significant councillors who owned engineering firms. After an initial difficult conversion period, manufacturers experienced a boom in productivity that rendered labour a scarce commodity.[106] The civic elite had staked the city's civic pride and patriotism on the provision of essential military equipment to the war effort. Given Coventry's rather turbulent industrial relations prior to the war, this was a brave ambition of intent which ultimately unravelled as war developed. The main grouping of Coventry's socialists belonged to a reformist tradition and from the onset of war joined a Liberal and Conservative consensus and urged workers to support the war effort. Furthermore, the core of Coventry socialists who had entered public life since the 1890s were firmly entrenched within a Fabian tradition that saw bureaucratic collectivism as a means of resolving social and economic problems.[107] These early socialists were also from skilled craft backgrounds and, like their urban elite peers, were at odds with the new Coventry factory worker.[108]

[118]

Leading members of the prewar socialist movement either held firm religious convictions or played a key role in Coventry's small but vocal temperance movement.[109] The civic elites' mistrust of the Coventry semi-skilled worker, along with weak unionisation, created a political vacuum in Coventry factories that was fully exploited by the emergence of the shop stewards, movement during the war. Indeed, militant shop stewards were successful in harnessing popular resentment towards key employers and extended their influence from the factory shop floor to the municipal sphere.[110] Thus reformist Labour councillors aligned themselves with the other municipal parties and avoided campaigning on key issues that might have disrupted the war effort such as high food and rent prices and general housing provision. As a consequence, newly formed radical movements took up these popular issues and became the standard bearer for the opponents of war.[111] The shop stewards' movement, along with other emerging strands of socialist thought such as Guild Socialism, rejected the traditional Fabien emphasis upon bureaucratic collectivism, preferring to see the workplace as the key area for democracy and control in society.[112] The shop stewards' movement had begun in Clydeside in 1914, and spread to key engineering centres such as Sheffield and Coventry where it led a successful wartime strike involving fifty thousand workers in 1917.[113] Indeed, the public's dissatisfaction with municipal activities enabled a new breed of socialist, more committed to direct action than working within official structures, to make important connections with Coventry's industrial working class. These socialists caught the tide of popular feeling by providing the rallying point for significant industrial and rent strikes in Coventry in 1915, 1917 and 1918.[114] Much to the local elites' embarrassment, the national press condemned the Coventry worker as treacherous shirkers costing the lives of troops in the trenches. *Punch* ran a series of cartoons on the strikes that contrasted the slouching, money-grubbing, unpatriotic Coventry worker with the up-standing, patriotic and loyal Tommy. In 1918, a *Punch* cartoon depicted a Coventry worker, with a remarkable resemblance to Lenin, raising a dagger to plunge into the back of a Tommy in the trenches.[115] A correspondent in *The Times* thought that that 'I know no other word for this but murder', adding that 'let the strikers weigh these facts in the balance against their grievances, real or imagined'. Moreover, strikers had not only abandoned their support of the troops on the continent but also risked the lives of civilians at home. One correspondent asked what 'if to-night we had a visit from German aeroplanes over London and a number of women and children were killed' owing to the strike's impact on military hardware?[116] However, the most damning criticism came from the *Aeroplane* journal, which contrived to suggest that

Coventry workers were inherently self-centred and unpatriotic. It thundered:

> Coventry is to-day the Centre of the contempt of the British Empire, because its aircraft shirkers went on strike at one of the most critical moments of the war . . . Something over twenty years ago I worked in Coventry. It does not seem that the people of Coventry have altered much since. In those days the aborigines of Coventry were the most self-satisfied, self-opinionated, self-conceited, self-centred, pig-headed, and muddle-headed people of even Saxon England . . . If shooting was good enough for the Irish rebels, why is it not good enough for the English traitors?[117]

With national vitriolic condemnation such as this, civic elites' attempts to demonstrate the city's patriotic contribution to country and empire through the industry of the Coventry worker lay in ruins. Far from fostering social unity in Coventry, the war had, in fact, exasperated prewar tensions that a call to unite behind country and empire could not diffuse. But what of the striking men themselves? Can the social conflict so evident in the workplace be interpreted as a strike against an imperial war? These questions are obviously more difficult to answer, though one should be cautious in assuming shop steward militancy embraced a political critique of the British Empire. At the heart of the dispute was recognition of the shop stewards' movement and workplace democracy. A government intelligence officer reported to the Cabinet Office that Coventry workers did not regard their strike as 'anti-war' as they exhibited real patriotism and pride in their work. He observed that 'the men appear to have been indignant at the reflections cast on their patriotism in certain papers, and the hints that their leaders had been seduced by German gold which appeared in others'.[118] Striking workers, then, forged patriotism within their own terms that drew pride in the knowledge that their workmates, workplace and city were contributing to a greater imperial cause. While this was clearly a fusion between locality and empire, it contrasted with the civic elites' vision of a socially cohesive city united behind the imperial cause.

Conclusion

If Lord Meath had monitored the local organisation and local reactions to the recruitment of men in our three case study communities, he surely would not have been so robust in his belief that Empire Day had inculcated an unadulterated imperial spirit in the people. From 3 August 1914, all three communities were consumed with local economic and civic problems provoked by the onset of wartime conditions. The civic authorities' introspective vision of the war and their initial disappointment at the levels of recruitment in the first few months of the conflict belie the claim that working-class men in these communities enthusiastically enlisted. In all three communities, the War Office's desired central message – that men should enlist to save the nation and empire – was somewhat lost beneath perceived localised crises. Charged with the responsibility of raising men for Kitchener's Army and City battalions, civic elites placed local patriotism at the heart of their call for men to defend their nation and empire. Certainly, some working- and middle-class men embraced this message of a local patriotism and imperial pride working in concert. The recruitment figures and press reports reveal mixed motivations for volunteers that range from employment, the quest for excitement and local pride. However, the strong fusion of local patriotism and empire, so apparent in the Boer War, had been weakened in the intervening years by social crises that had alienated certain groups from the civic project. As we shall see in the following chapter, the perceived social crises in our respective communities also had an important impact on the form and intensity that imperial messages took in the provision of education between 1870 and 1939.

Notes

1 A. Marwick, *The Deluge. British Society in the First World War* (London, Bodley Head, 1965).
2 B. Waites, *A Class Society at War. England 1914–1918* (Leamington Spa, Berg, 1987).
3 G. Robb, *British Culture and the First World War* (Basingstoke, Palgrave, 2002), pp. 67, 70.
4 A. August, *The British Working-Class 1832–1940* (Harlow, Longman, 2007), p. 170.
5 B. Porter, *The Absent-minded Imperialists. Empire, Society and Culture in Britain* (Oxford, Oxford University Press, 2004, 2006 edn), p. 257.
6 A. Watson and P. Porter, 'Bereaved and Aggrieved: Combat Motivation and the Ideology of Sacrifice in the First World War', *Historical Research*, 83, February 2010, pp. 150, 154; for earlier works on the impact of Victorian and Edwardian imperialism on the nature of patriotism see J.M. Osborne, 'Defining Their Own Patriotism: British Volunteer Training Corps in the First World War', *Journal of Contemporary History*, 23, 1988, p. 71.
7 See for example G. Messinger, *British Propaganda and the State in the First World War* (Manchester, Manchester University Press, 1992); J. Hartigan, 'Volunteering in the First World War: the Birmingham Experience, August 1914–May 1915', *Midland History*, 24, 1999.
8 D. Silbey, *The British Working Class and Enthusiasm for War 1914–16* (London, Frank Cass, 2005), p. 66.
9 Silbey, *The British Working Class*, pp. 49, 68.
10 Silbey, *The British Working Class*, p. 112.
11 P. Purseigle, 'Beyond and Below the Nations: Towards a Comparative History of Local Communities at War', in J. Macleod and P. Purseigle (eds), *Uncovered Fields: Perspectives in First World War Studies* (Leiden, Brill, 2003), pp. 97–8.

12 B.J. White, 'Volunteerism and Early Recruitment Efforts in Devonshire, August 1914–December 1915', *Historical Journal*, 52, 3, 2009, pp. 641, 666.

13 H.B. McCartney, *Citizen Soldiers: The Liverpool Territorials in the First World War* (Cambridge, Cambridge University Press, 2005), p. 57.

14 Silbey, *The British Working Class*, p. 28.

15 Purseigle, 'Beyond and Below the Nations', pp. 97–8.

16 *Evening News*, 15 August 1914.

17 *Evening News*, 22 August; see also 20 August.

18 *North Leeds News*, 14 August 1914.

19 *Yorkshire Evening Post*, 14 August 1914.

20 *Yorkshire Evening Post*, 29 March 1915.

21 M. Meadowcroft, 'The Years of Political Transition', in D. Fraser (ed.), *A History of Modern Leeds* (Manchester, Manchester University Press, 1980), p. 411.

22 *Midland Daily Telegraph*, 14 August 1914.

23 *Coventry Standard*, 10 November 1913.

24 CRO (hereafter Coventry Record Office), Acc 1417/1/1, S. Bettmann, 'Struggling' (unpublished autobiography, no date), vol. II, p. 490.

25 Bettmann, 'Struggling', p. 2.

26 Bettmann, 'Struggling', pp. 478–9.

27 Bettmann, 'Struggling', pp. 607–8.

28 Bettmann, 'Struggling', p. 572.

29 Bettmann, 'Struggling', pp. 497, 572.

30 *Coventry Times*, 9 September 1914.

31 *Midland Daily Telegraph*, 9 September 1914.

32 *Coventry Times*, 11 November 1914.

33 *Coventry Times*, 11 November 1914.

34 See Chapter 3.

35 *North Leeds News*, 6 November; 30 October 1914. Similar examples were found by White, 'Volunteerism and Early Recruitment', p. 641.

36 *Coventry Times*, 11 November 1914.

37 *Yorkshire Evening Post*, 12, 20 October 1914; for a discussion of whether football should be played during war in Leeds see *Yorkshire Evening Post*, 31 August 1914, and *North Leeds News*, 4 August 1914.

38 *Evening News*, 8 September 1914.

39 *Evening News*, 21 August 1914; for a defence of footballers see 22 August 1914.

40 M. Taylor, *The Association Game. A History of British Football* (Harlow, Longman, 2007), p. 120.

41 *Evening News*, 8 September 1914.

42 Taylor, *Association Game*, p. 121. For an example of how football was contrasted unfavourably with 'patriotic' rugby union see *Midland Daily Telegraph*, 2 September 1914.

43 *North Leeds News*, 11 September 1914.

44 *Midland Daily Telegraph*, 4 September 1914.

45 *Evening News*, 5, 30 October 1914.

46 *Evening News*, 11 November 1914.

47 *Yorkshire Evening Post*, 28 September 1914.

48 *Evening News*, 3 September 1914.

49 *Evening News*, 2 September 1914.

50 *Coventry Times*, 16 September; *Midland Daily Telegraph*, 13 November 1914.

51 *Yorkshire Evening Post*, 22 August 1914.

52 *Yorkshire Evening Post*, 10 September 1914; 19 April 1915.

53 *Evening News*, 4 September 1914.

54 *Yorkshire Evening Post*, 22 August 1914.

55 *Yorkshire Evening Post*, 31 August 1914.

56 *Evening News*, 28 September 1914.

57 Hartigan, 'Volunteering in the First World War', pp. 176–7.

58 Hartigan, 'Volunteering in the First World War', p. 176.

59 *North Leeds News*, 18 September 1914.
60 *Evening News*, 26 April 1915.
61 *Evening News*, 16 October 1914.
62 *North Leeds News*, 27 November 1914.
63 *Yorkshire Evening Post*, 31 August 1914.
64 *Yorkshire Evening Post*, 3 September 1914.
65 Quoted in L. Milner, *Leeds Pals. A History of the 15th (Service) Battalion (1st Leeds). The Prince of Wales Own (Yorkshire Regiment), 1914–18* (London, Leo Cooper, 1991), p. 22.
66 *Midland Daily Telegraph*, 8 October 1914.
67 *Midland Daily Telegraph*, 2 September 1914.
68 *Evening News*, 8, 13 September 1915.
69 *Yorkshire Evening Post*, 31 August 1915.
70 *Yorkshire Evening Post*, 8 September 1914.
71 National Archives, NATS 1/398, 'Approximate number of recruits raised daily'.
72 Coventry's daily recruitment figures cease to be compiled after November presumably owing to the very low numbers of men raised.
73 *Evening News*, 3 May 1915; *Yorkshire Evening Post*, 2 October 1915; *Midland Daily Telegraph*, 3 November 1914.
74 *North Leeds News*, 27 November 1914.
75 *North Leeds News*, 4 December 1914.
76 *Midland Daily Telegraph*, 28 August 1914.
77 *Midland Daily Telegraph*, 14 October 1914.
78 *Evening News*, 11 September 1914; *Midland Daily Telegraph*, 30 September 1914.
79 *Yorkshire Evening Post*, 3 March 1915.
80 National Archives, NATS 1/398, 'Approximate number of recruits raised daily'.
81 *Evening News*, 12 May 1915.
82 *Evening News*, 20 October; 11 September 1915.
83 Quoted in Milner, *Leeds Pals*, p. 22.
84 W. Gates, *Portsmouth and the Great War* (Portsmouth, Evening News, 1919), foreword.
85 *Evening News*, 7 November 1914.
86 See Chapter 5.
87 *Evening News*, 24 May 1914.
88 *Evening News*, 26 August 1914.
89 *Evening News*, 27 August 1914.
90 *Evening News*, 31 August 1914.
91 *Evening News*, 5 September; 4 November 1914.
92 See Chapter 5.
93 *Yorkshire Evening Post*, 10 August 1914.
94 *Yorkshire Evening Post*, 8 August 1914.
95 *Yorkshire Evening Post*, 10, 18 August 1914.
96 *Yorkshire Evening Post*, 7, 8 September 1914.
97 *Yorkshire Evening Post*, 9 September 1914.
98 *Yorkshire Evening Post*, 31 August 1914.
99 *Yorkshire Evening Post*, 19 April 1914.
100 *Yorkshire Evening Post*, 29 March 1915.
101 A.J. Taylor, 'Victorian Leeds: an overview', in D. Fraser (ed.), *A History of Modern Leeds* (Manchester, Manchester University Press, 1980, p. 390.
102 Modern Record Centre (hereafter MRC), MSS 240/R/3/71, A.R. Rollins Collection, 'Leeds Jewry'.
103 *Yorkshire Evening Post*, 10 September 1914; 19 April 1915.
104 *Midland Daily Telegraph*, 30 November 1914.
105 *Midland Daily Telegraph*, 28 November 1914.
106 D. Thoms and T. Donnelly, *The Motor Car Industry in Coventry since the 1890s* (Chatham, Croom Helm, 1985), p. 70.

107 J.A. Yates, *Pioneers to Power: The Story of the Ordinary People of Coventry* (Coventry, Coventry Labour Party, 1950), pp. 25, 27, 42; K. Richardson, *Twentieth Century Coventry* (Bungay, Chaucer Press, 1972), p. 192; Coventry Record Office (CRO), Acc 135, R. Barrett, 'socialism made plain', *c.* 1911.

108 Yates, *Pioneers to Power*, p. 29.

109 CRO, Acc 135, Roland Barrett, 'Socialism made plain; Acc 835/2, Hugh Farren, newspaper cuttings, p. 24; Yates, *Pioneers to Power*, pp. 37–8, 31. For further details on early Coventry socialists see B. Beaven and J. Griffiths 'Urban Elites, Socialists and Notions of Citizenship in an Industrial Boomtown: Coventry *c.* 1870–1914', *Labour History Review*, 69, 1, 2004, p. 12; *Midland Daily Telegraph*, 25 July 1924.

110 For an analysis of shop-floor culture and workers' attempting to exercise a degree of autonomy over the work process during this period see B. Beaven, 'Shop-floor Culture in the Coventry Motor Industry', in D. Thoms, L. Holden and T. Cladydon (eds), *The Motor Car and Popular Culture in the Twentieth Century* (Aldershot, Ashgate, 1998).

111 F. Carr, 'Municipal Socialism: Labour's Rise to Power', in B. Lancaster and T. Mason (eds), *Life and Labour in a 20th Century City. The Experience of Coventry* (Coventry, Cryfield Press, 1986), p. 183.

112 A.W. Wright, *G.D.H. Cole and Socialist Democracy* (Oxford, Clarendon Press, 1979), 63–5; R. Price, *Labour in British Society* (London, Croom Helm, 1986), p. 156.

113 National Archives, MUN 5/53/300/99, The shop steward movement. Intelligence Division, Ministry of Labour, February 1920; also see NA, Kew, Mun 5/55/300/47, Intelligence and statistics section weekly labour notes, 20 September 1918.

114 B. Beaven, 'Challenges to Civic Governance in Post-war England: the Peace Day Disturbances of 1919', *Urban History*, 33, 3, 2006, pp. 385–92.

115 *Punch*, 31 July, 2 October 1918.

116 *The Times*, 30 November 1917.

117 *Aeroplane*, 5 December 1917.

118 National Archives, CAB/24/34, 'The Labour Situation', 5 December 1917, p. 344.

CHAPTER FIVE

Educating the future citizens of empire: working-class schooling, 1870–1939

For over forty years historians have identified nineteenth- and early twentieth-century education as a powerful tool in conditioning working-class lives for the new challenges of a modern industrial society.[1] Whereas a regimented school day would prepare scholars for the factory system and regularised working week, a celebration of empire in the curriculum would help inculcate a sense of duty, discipline and patriotism – qualities that could be called upon in the event of an international crisis. The view that schooling acted as a powerful vehicle for disseminating the imperial message has, however, been vigorously challenged by Bernard Porter, who asserts that for most of the nineteenth century the school authorities saw no reason to share the empire with the vast majority of the population.[2] What follows is an investigation into the schooling experience of working-class children in Portsmouth, Coventry and Leeds from the late nineteenth century to 1939. At least three schools in each community were selected and, in each case, the area catchments were solidly working-class. This chapter focues on the three activities that dominated a pupil's daily experience of school. For most scholars their school day would consist of class time and the engagement with the curriculum, physical exercise, and extra-curricular activities. All three areas of the school day were fertile ground for planting the seeds of imperial fervour but, then again, the school curriculum could also foster the virtues of industrial discipline. These communities embedded in differing industrial contexts may offer an indication to where this balance lay. Thus, by drawing upon the contrasts and similarities experienced by pupils in these communities, the chapter endeavours to provide an insight into the changing nature of the imperial message, how it fared with other pressing virtues, and if and how it was delivered and received.

The 1870 Education Act has often been presented as legislation that imposed educational uniformity to equip Britain for an era of increasing international competition.[3] In reality it was perhaps a staging post to uniformity since the Act was in many ways a compromise to appease existing educational establishments. The Act did not establish a new national system; education was neither free nor compulsory and it accommodated the extant voluntary school system. The key breakthrough was the establishment of School Boards in areas deemed inadequately served by existing educational institutions.[4] While the School Boards appeared on an *ad hoc* basis, it was the growing industrial centres that were the chief beneficiaries of the Act, with Portsmouth, Coventry and Leeds being among them. A major change in the administration of state schools occurred with the 1902 Education Act in which 2,568 School Boards were replaced with 328 local education authorities. Councils now managed education as they did other public utilities, assisting both former Board Schools and voluntary schools through the rates. Although publicly funded schools in England moved from Board to local council control in 1902, these schools were also known as elementary schools throughout the period 1870 to 1939. Elementary schools provided a basic education for working-class pupils from the ages of five to fourteen.[5] The schools analysed here are Board, Council or Voluntary Church of England controlled schools and all sited in the heart of their cities serving predominantly working-class districts. As one might expect, a community's industrial background often shaped local educational structures, with the leading industrialists holding an influence on the provision of elementary education in Coventry and Leeds in particular. In Coventry, industrialists such as Alfred Herbert and Alfred White would regularly visit schools or invite school trips around their factories throughout the late nineteenth and early twentieth centuries.[6] Indeed, according to Coventry's Official Guide of 1909, one of the prime functions of the city's elementary schools was to train children for industrial work:

> The Educational Committee of the city Council have fully recognised that the educational facilities of the city must be adapted to its commercial requirements, and that a supply of skilful artisans is essential to the continued prosperity of the industries of the town; consequently stress is everywhere laid upon the value of hand and eye training. Schemes of work aiming at the cultivation of manual dexterity are being carried out in most schools . . .[7]

In Leeds, the large influx of Jewish immigrants had effectively created Jewish Council Schools, a development that caused disquiet among industrialists and the civic leaders. In line with most schools in the Leeds, both Leylands and Darley Street Board Schools situated in the heart of the Jewish quarter of Leeds were visited regularly by the civic elite and industrialists.[8] However, children in these schools were undoubtedly monitored more closely for 'degenerative traits' and for their commitment to the civic, nation and empire. In the absence of an influential industrial sector in Portsmouth, it was the navy that played a prominent role in the town's education. There was a large contingency of naval and military personnel on School Boards and, by the First World War, the navy had begun to influence the curriculum in Portsmouth schools.[9] The three communities shared a similar student-to-school ratio that averaged between 500 and 600 per school. In 1909, Leeds possessed 113 publicly funded schools catering for 64,157 scholars; Portsmouth had 36 schools and 24,908 children, while Coventry Council administered 25 elementary schools and 12,244 pupils.[10]

The elementary school curriculum

Any attempt to reconstruct the pupil's experience of the nineteenth-century curriculum is fraught with difficulties. The scarcity of nineteenth-century working-class biographies, the lack of oral history and the rather haphazard and unsystematic record keeping of daily school matters are obstacles in penetrating the opacity of the nineteenth-century classroom.[11] However we can, using the little primary source material available from the 1870s, gain snap shots of classroom subject matter, the tone of lessons and how the ethos began to change during the late nineteenth century as education became enmeshed with imperial anxieties. School log books, while rather sketchy in content, do reveal the day-to-day running of a school and provide a glimpse on how classes were taught and reasons for curriculum change. Moreover, the school textbooks, songs, physical exercise routines and extra-curricula-activities all indicate the ethos the school was attempting to project to the children and wider community in general.

In all three communities from the 1860s to late 1880s, Board Schools and schools in the voluntary sector appear to have followed curricula relatively free from imperial propaganda. For example, a close examination of the school log books reveals that the songs and poetry selected either carried a religious dimension or focused on the seasons and natural phenomena. Furthermore, a sprinkling of songs or hymns would also emphasise the importance of social hierarchy. For example, in Coventry's St Michael's Church of England School the following songs sung until the mid-1890s could fall into all of these categories: 'The World Rejoices', 'May Is Here' and 'I Am Not a Wealthy Man'. Only by 1897 is there the first foretaste of patriotism as the songs 'Hail Britannia' and 'England's Queen' are listed among the usual musical fare.[12] Similarly, the log book of Wheatley Street, a Coventry Board

School, did not list any songs, literature or poetry connected with empire until 1895. It was only in July of this year that the headmaster began reading children extracts from Stanley's *In Darkest Africa*, a full five years after the book had been published.[13] In Portsmouth's St Luke's School, songs and poems focused on the changing seasons such as 'Autumn Winds' and 'One Flake at a Time', while it was notable that there were no special celebrations to mark the Naval Reviews of 1867 and 1886. However, by the late 1880s new, more patriotic songs were introduced such as 'Hurrah for England' and 'The Fatherland', though even then material on the seasons dominated the musical curriculum.[14] In All Saints' Church of England School in Leeds, a similar curriculum was adopted in which pupils learned about 'animals, birds and natural phenomena' throughout the 1870s, 1880s and early 1890s.[15] The most striking feature in the school log books surveyed in all three communities is the very simple and narrow curriculum adopted by both voluntary and Board Schools until the late 1880s. The previous absence of a schooling culture in urban areas and inexperienced teachers confined teaching to the '3R's with inspectors recommending domestic classes for girls only in the mid-1870s. Indeed, log books reveal that sewing classes were the only specifically gendered provision in the curriculum.[16] Certainly, of the literature, songs or poetry listed in the log books, none appears to outline the duties and expectations of the exemplary male citizen. The experience of pupils in Portsmouth, Coventry and Leeds would appear similar to national trends in the classroom. Porter has noted that teaching in most working-class elementary schools were restricted to reading, arithmetic and Bible morality, with a view to teaching the rigidity of the social structure and in turn producing compliant and disciplined workers. The main problem facing schools was the payment by results system that was introduced in 1862 and not discarded until 1898. The government had placed an emphasis on the 3Rs and religious education, leaving little scope for other subjects. The teaching of history, geography and English literature, key vehicles for imperial dissemination, were missing from most elementary timetables.[17] Thus, in 1889, only one-fifth of the elementary schools reported teaching history.[18] According to one report in 1890, Educational Inspectors noted that the attempt to use history as a platform for patriotism had failed as in most elementary schools 'history has died a natural death'.[19]

The labour demands of local employers also placed pressure on the elementary school curriculum. Often elected on to School Boards (later Town Councils) or making official visits to the local schools, employers had a keen interest in the type of scholar that would emerge from the system. Both Wheatley Street School and Frederick Bird School in

Coventry were regularly visited by local industrialists from the city's motor and allied trades.[20] Likewise in Portsmouth, Portsea Infants' School and All Saints' School were the recipient of numerous members of the Admiralty, since the dockyard was the town's largest employer.[21] In 1889, St Luke's School established a commercial class that taught handicraft class work in woodwork with a view of establishing work routines and practices that would be useful in the Royal Dockyard.[22]

The adoption of a varied curriculum was also hampered by the practicalities of teaching working-class communities that did not prioritise formal education and treated schooling with some suspicion. In Portsea Infants' School, while the inspectors praised the extensive teaching of scripture in the curriculum, they later found that in scripture tests the 'vast majority failed to answer well'.[23] Likewise, an Inspector's report on St Luke's Church of England School in Portsmouth encapsulated the difficulty for teachers in the 1870s since even the most basic classes seem to have taught the pupils little. The Inspector noted that 'on grammar and geography a few boys in each class answer well but the great majority are perfectly ignorant of the subjects'.[24] This poor educational experience was compounded by absenteeism that was rife in Board, Council and voluntary controlled schools.[25] In Leeds, the St Peter's Square Board School reported persistent truancy in the 1890s, identifying the families' inexperience of formal education and the children's chaotic home life. At the start of the new school year in 1894, there were on average of 22 per cent of pupils missing for the entire month of September. The headmaster reported that 'they come from the poorest homes; father in prison, or father and mother just separated and a migration to the low parts of the city has become a necessity'.[26] The industrial and social life of a city would also regularly impinge upon school attendance, affecting not only those who lived in the 'lowest' parts of the city but also the children of the more 'respectable' working class. In Portsmouth, school attendance would dramatically fall when the Royal Dockyard closed for the day to allow workers to attend events such as ship launches, regattas or visits from dignitaries.[27] In Portsmouth, Coventry and Leeds, headmasters complained that the arrival of fairs and circuses in their respective towns would also significantly lower school attendances.[28] Finally, in cities like Coventry that experienced rapid growths in population from the late nineteenth century through to the interwar period, classroom overcrowding was a significant obstacle to pupil learning. For example in 1893, the height of an industrial boom in the city, Wheatley School girls' department was forced to admit 550 pupils to occupy classrooms meant for 420.[29]

This fairly basic curriculum that focused primarily on the 3Rs and drew from literature, poetry and song from the religious and natural worlds began to change with different levels of intensity in all three communities from the late 1880s. International competition and anxieties over the security of the empire brought the teaching of patriotism to national attention. In a Nation Union of Teachers Conference in 1890, a speaker complained that, whereas in other countries such as France and Germany schools were the nurseries of patriotism, Britain lagged behind with civic training. The new popular newspapers such as the *Pall Mall Gazette* amplified these concerns, suggesting remedies such as teaching history to disseminate 'a kind of domestic worship', and the production of a patriotic song book and use of civic handbooks.[30] From the late 1880s, the curriculum took on a distinctly imperial edge as military drill and imperial ceremony were introduced and extra-curricular activities with an imperial theme became more widespread. Masculinity, character, patriotism and imperialism became fused and reinforced in school textbooks and guidance notes for teachers. The *Citizen Reader*, authored by Arnold Forster and prefaced by W.E. Forster, became the adopted text of the elementary school after it was published in 1886.[31] According to Heathorn, this text 'highlighted the socio-cultural as opposed to the political relationship of the individual to the national collectivity'. Through espousing the virtues of men in the armed forces, the text was designed to instil patriotism and promote the idea of the imperial destiny of the Anglo-Saxon race.[32] The *Citizen Reader* informed pupils that 'the time will come for every man, who was strong enough to carry a rifle, to join the navy or the army, and to give up his time and his money, and, if necessary, his life, in order that the enemy might be defeated'.[33] By 1909, the *Practical Teacher* journal had outlined a four-week lesson plan on how the central ideas of manliness, courage, heroism and patriotism could be transmitted to the boy scholar. Both the army and navy figured heavily in conveying these core values, stressing that self-sacrifice was the ultimate test of courage and patriotism.[34]

However, evidence drawn from the log books suggests that, while all schools surveyed began to employ imperialistic teaching material, the intensity and dissemination of a rabid imperial doctrine was by no means uniform. While historians have generally agreed that the school curriculum became increasingly imperialised by the 1890s, the form it took and the degree to which schools immersed pupils in imperial propaganda depended upon the socio-cultural circumstances of their communities. Thus, in Coventry, it is clear that while after the 1890s the school log books record a sprinkling of imperial literature and songs, the school year was rarely troubled by matters of empire. While drill featured a little more in the Wheatley daily log book, there is little indication that it had taken on imperial overtones, but it continued to stress the importance of discipline and obedience – qualities useful in the industrial workforce. Local industrialists persisted in regularly visiting schools and organising engineering exhibitions for pupils to visit during school time in a bid to demonstrate the city's industrial progress.[35] Moreover, the growing importance of the Coventry Trades Council appears to have influenced the classroom. For example, in 1898, Board Schools were encouraged to donate money to an appeal for striking miners' children in South Wales, a cause that raised £2 in Wheatley Street School.[36] The Queen's Diamond Jubilee in 1897, however, signalled the incorporation of the first patriotic songs recorded in both Wheatley and St Michael's school log books. A two-day holiday was granted to the School Board children, while the Church schools enjoyed a full week. This reflected a pattern that was to continue into the twentieth century. While the Diamond Jubilee established a custom that a monarch's anniversary (birthday, death or coronation) would afford a holiday in Coventry schools, it was the religious schools that celebrated the monarch and empire more enthusiastically. The Boer War, a conflict that amplified the imperial message to an unprecedented level, triggered different responses from the Board and voluntary school sectors. The Coventry School Board does not appear to have granted a holiday to celebrate the homecoming of the Warwickshire Volunteers, which resulted in the Wheatley Headmaster having to cancel lessons as over one-third of his pupils failed to attend. St Michael's, on the other hand, signalled to pupils the importance of the event by granting them a half-day holiday.[37] The Coventry school log books, then, reveal that the 1890s witnessed a growing acknowledgement of the significance of empire, particularly in the voluntary school sector. While some historians have confidently argued that English schools were saturated with imperial rhetoric by 1900, it would be difficult to apply this argument to Coventry, where the day-to-day schooling did not markedly differ from the two previous decades. The industrialists' primary concern that the school should help foster an obedient and morally compliant workforce remained a chief characteristic of Coventry schooling throughout the 1890s and even into the Boer War.

Very different scenarios, however, developed in both Portsmouth and Leeds during the 1890s and early twentieth century. In Portsmouth, the balance of teaching shifted from fostering a compliant and disciplined workforce to more ambitious imperial-inspired objectives. One of the key reasons behind this shift was the significant transformation of how the navy projected itself to wider society. As

Jan Rüger has shown, from the 1880s the naval authorities developed a 'cult of the navy' in which rituals were invented to celebrate Fleet Reviews, launches of warships and a whole range of additional naval activities. Thus, while Fleet Reviews had begun in the late eighteenth century, it was only in the late Victorian and Edwardian period that they became professionally staged events designed to evoke patriotism and demonstrate the nation's immense naval power.[38] Portsmouth, of course, was at the centre of this naval cult, and its schools, particularly those in close proximity to the dockyard, became important conduits for the navy's patriotic message. Prior to the 1870s, naval reviews were largely ignored, failing to merit a mention in school log books or afford a school holiday. However, in all Portsmouth schools surveyed, the 1873 Fleet Review was celebrated with a holiday, and gradually naval influence in school life began to become more significant. Royal visits to the dockyard, Fleet Reviews and warship launches became accepted closure days for schools. This was in addition to the standard school closures in Coventry and Leeds that commemorated a monarch's birthday, death or coronation. The launch of warships and their home-coming during the Boer War also helped to strengthen ties between

3   St Luke's School was invited on to the *HMS Terrible* in 1900.
By kind permission of the Portsmouth History Centre

the navy and local schools. In 1900, senior boys of St Luke's were invited on *HMS Terrible* for tea and were provided with entertainment arranged by the officers and men.[39]

Other activities that Portsmouth schools engaged in included raising money for Boer War relief funds, celebrating the return of the Naval Brigade after the siege of Ladysmith and entertaining sailors who had returned from the conflict. In all Portsmouth Board Schools, holidays were granted for the relief of Ladysmith, Mafeking and the homecoming of the ships.[40] In contrast, Coventry Board School log books reveal that the relief of Ladysmith and Mafeking and the return of Coventry soldiers were not considered special occasions to merit half-day holidays. Likewise, in Leeds, only Mafeking and the return of soldiers were celebrated with school holidays in the school log books surveyed.[41] The Boer War helped establish firm links between the navy and Portsmouth schools that flourished through into the First World War. For example, the 1905 Trafalgar Day Centenary provided another opportunity to cultivate naval culture in schools. Over thirty senior pupils from All Saints' Portsea School were among a large number of Portsmouth schoolchildren who attended the rehearsals of the Trafalgar Tournament at the navy barracks. The schools' participation in this spectacular event helped entrench Trafalgar Day into the Portsmouth school calendar.[42]

The close ties between the navy and Portsmouth schools inevitably ensured that naval ritual and the town's importance to the military became embedded in the town's schooling. Naval and military bases, barracks and drill halls encircled the town centre and encroached into a child's schooling and leisure time, normalising the militarisation of civilian life.[43] For example, one Portsmouth man's childhood memories of the interwar period recalled how he joined groups of children following military bands around the town:

> A typical bit of fun was following the military bands across the town. They used to march around the town and finish up at the Garrison Church in Old Portsmouth. There were dozens of regiments then, it was a garrison town with Victoria, Cambridge, Milldam and Eastney and Hill sea barracks with different regiments.

Marching military bands proved an attractive spectacle for groups of boys, though having 'a bit of fun' trailing marching bands across the town undoubtedly proved a nuisance to the marching soldiers.[44] Thus, while Portsmouth's urban environment normalised military activities, military parades provided additional opportunities for street 'horseplay', and were perhaps not the most effective conduit for the imperial message.

National anxieties over youth street behaviour in the early twentieth century were perhaps even more pronounced in Portsmouth given
its prominent position as the 'gateway to the empire'.[45] Indeed, leading
Portsmouth teachers were often consumed with an underlying fear of
the consequences if boys were not instructed in patriotism, duty and
above all manliness. Thus imperial dissemination came from a position not of strength but of weakness since readers feared that modern
life in the poorest areas was creating an effeminate and apathetic boy.
Headmasters, who immersed their staff and pupils in the imperial
ethos, became increasingly vigilant for perceived inadequacies in the
boys' masculinity, a scenario all too apparent in St Luke's school.
Without doubt, St Luke's in Portsmouth was the most prominent
advocate for the celebration of empire and the militarisation of school
activities. Led by the headmaster, Mr Grimes, since 1886, the ethos of
the school projected through assemblies noticeably changed during the
1890s.[46] St Luke's, which prior to 1896 had not overtly disseminated
either a militarised or imperialised culture, introduced a drum and fife
band and incorporated celebrations of military heroes into assembly.
These celebrations were not confined to the great military figures but
also featured 'Portsmouth heroes'. Thus men who served in the armed
forces and who had children at St Luke's were given special praise
during assemblies.[47]

The move towards an imperialised and militarised ethos meant that
school activities became increasingly gendered. The fear that modern
urban life was initiating a crisis in masculinity became a recurrent
theme in a series of assemblies given by the headmaster. In June 1898,
Grimes dealt with the issue of manliness and work. While there was
no mention of the importance of masculinity when the commercial
department was opened in the school in 1889, Grimes appeared to have
viewed the intervening ten years with some distain since there had
been a growth of white-collared occupations that required little physical exercise. The headmaster warned pupils: 'don't think the ideal
existence is to suck the knob of a stick, wear a fathom of stiff collar
around your neck, and dangle your legs under a desk; don't ape the
contemptible "dude" – the "masher." Manual work is equally ennobling as any other.'[48] The message was clear; for the working-class
children in areas such as Portsea, their station in life dictated that they
were destined for manual labour, as any other form of employment
would compromise the only assets they could realistically exploit –
their masculinity and discipline. Significantly, while these concepts
remained central to the boys' work-related education, under Grimes's
leadership during the 1890s masculinity and discipline increasingly
became associated with empire. Thus in a speech on 'manliness' he

asserted that 'we like the word "manly". Who is there that isn't proud of "manliness" that made an Englishman the envy of the civilised world? Where is the country that can boast of so many heroes as old England can? And we are anxious, that St Lukes' boys shall grow up manly, courageous fellows.'[49] The Headmaster's preoccupation with the decline of masculinity in the urban areas was taken to new levels during the Boer War. In February 1900, at the height of the war, Grimes gave a speech to pupils entitled 'the Makings of a Man'. It is worth quoting in some length since it not only warned that Britain was in the midst of an imperial crisis, but declared that St Luke's boys had a duty to serve and save the empire. Grimes identified the 'stirring events now taking place in South Africa' for the inspiration for his monthly chat:

> Never was there a time in our history when true Britons were more urgently needed and never was a call to arms to defend our rights and manfully to prove to all the world that Britons would never be slaves, more promptly and patriotically responded to. From North, South, East and West, from the North Pole to the Southern Cross our countrymen are leaving hearth and home to give battle for the cause of freedom, the heritage of every Englishman. And now boys it will be your duty some day to assist in maintaining, and if necessary to fight for the great Empire, to build up which has cost us many precious lives, and darkened many, many homes.[50]

Speeches in assemblies, then, no longer talked about the ennobling qualities of manual labour but instead stressed the importance of duty and sacrifice for the empire. The integration of empire into the school curriculum found support across Portsmouth's political spectrum. Even the liberal *Hampshire Telegraph* declared that 'the time is apropos to think of devising further means for the education of the British race in the meaning of the word "Empire"', adding that it was 'vital' to teach 'the children of this country what the British Empire means, and the work it is doing in world'.[51] Indeed, in 1900, Portsmouth schools, civic leaders and the local press were at the forefront of an attempt to militarise the school day and create a direct line of recruitment from the playground to the volunteer movement. In order to establish how Portsmouth schools were leading a national campaign to militarise the school day, we shall now turn to the origins of drill and its implantation in the three communities under study.

The strong desire to incorporate the teaching of drill in elementary schools was reflected in the 1870 Education Act that recommended that scholars should attend drill for not less than two hours a week, and twenty weeks per year. However, despite pressure from some MPs, the government baulked at making drill compulsory. Although, drill was enshrined in the Act, in practice few schools had either the time or space to establish the teaching of drill as a significant component in the curriculum. A little after the 1870 Education Act, one HM Inspector of Schools, the Reverend H.W. Bellairs, lamented that 'the drill in our schools is generally bad', adding that he 'would like to see a regular system of military drill introduced, with marching tunes and, where practicable, with drum and fife bands'.[52] Bellairs would have remained frustrated for the next two decades, for his vision of school military bands across the country did not materialise until the 1890s. Until this period, the school log books in Portsmouth, Coventry and Leeds reveal that, while the teaching of drill was adhered to, it fell into the category of 'usual school drill' rather than the military type. For most schools, non-military drill was perceived as fit for purpose as it was deemed effective in inculcating and maintaining good standards of discipline. The dearth of suitably qualified instructors in military drill also limited its uptake in schools.[53]

However, in conjunction with the growing imperial ethos in schools already described, there was undoubtedly a move from the 'usual school drill' to military drill exercises in some schools during the 1890s. The teaching of military drill was not evenly taken up in the three communities, and its intensity and application reflected a school's specific local contemporary anxieties. From 1888, Leeds School Board employed a military drill sergeant and established an annual drill competition between board schools held at the Leeds Rifles' parade ground. The Leeds School Board's Chief Inspector reported that 'of the great value of the drill no one can have a doubt who has been present on one of the annual field days, when schools assemble and go through their evolutions. It is pleasing to observe the firm tread, the upright carriage of the boys as they march past, and the precision with which they perform their exercises.'[54] The view that military drill was improving the boys' physique was significant. An underlying concern for the Leeds authorities from the late nineteenth to the early twentieth centuries was the fear that poor environmental conditions and substantial immigration had physically weakened the working-class stock in the city.

In 1903, the Leeds School Board invited a medical researcher to examine one hundred children between the ages of ten and twelve to explore the physical differences between those residing in working- and middle-class households. Dr Hall gathered his evidence as part of a wider study that intended to investigate the perceived decline of the Anglo-Saxon race. He found that 30 of the 50 working-class children had rickets compared to 10 out of 50 children from the more affluent areas of Leeds. He also investigated the child's 'home life' and found deficiencies in morality and nourishment in working-class homes. He reported that over twenty years '100,000 children have been examined by me as to their fitness for factory labour: upward of 30,000 were rickety. We are no longer a straight limbed race.'[55] For the Leeds educational authorities, then, public drill displays would not only physically improve children but also reveal the extent to which working-class pupils suffered from physical deficiencies. The Leeds authorities were also anxious that Jewish immigration would have a detrimental impact on the health and civic culture of the city. Alongside its physical benefits, military drill was adjudged to be an effective method in instilling patriotism within Jewish scholars and help foster a commitment to both city and nation. For example, in a bid to demonstrate how military drill could improve physical health and cultivate a loyalty to their locality and nation, the Leeds Council invited the Inspector of Schools from London to a large Jewish Council School for a drill event. In June 1904, all Darley Street School's six hundred pupils performed a military drill, prompting the Inspector to note that drill helped introduce scholars to 'the subject of "duty"' in 'aspects of school life, the home life and citizenship'.[56] Indeed, it appears that the Jewish children were subjected to regular scrutiny by the authorities, who were keen to detect any signs of degeneracy. Later in 1904, Darley Street School was visited by the MP, and former Vice President of the Education Committee, Sir John Gorst and his daughter to inspect the health and well-being of the pupils.[57] It was reported that the school 'is attended by several hundred Jewish children, whom Sir John was interested to see in the light of recent comments as to the physique of the races as compared with Christian children'. After his inspection, Gorst commented 'upon the beautiful heads of hair possessed by many of the girls, and upon the good physique of the children'.[58] Thus, for the Leeds School Board, fear of physical degeneration was a major driving force behind the adoption of the military drill in their elementary schools.[59]

In Portsmouth, while undoubtedly there were concerns about urban degeneration, those calling the loudest for military drill were those who were attempting to forge close alliances between schools and the volunteers.[60] Thus, amidst the military anxieties that engulfed the Boer War, Portsmouth schools were at the forefront of a national campaign to bring military drill into schools. Prior to the Boer War, there had been some opposition to the incorporation of military drill into the school curriculum, particularly from those on the political left. In 1885, fearing that military drill was the first step to conscription, the Trade Union Congress (TUC) passed a resolution condemning schools that had increasingly militarised their physical exercises:

Seeing that military drill was introduced into Board Schools professedly for its physical advantages, and that it is now being followed up by the formation of cadet corps, the boys comprising which are to be dressed as soldiers, and supplied with rifles by the War Office, the Congress enters its emphatic protest against the cunningly devised scheme by which military authorities and a number of Board Schools have been, step by step, preparing the way for the pernicious continental system of conscription.[61]

Similarly J.A. Hobson, a renowned critic of new imperialism, argued that there was a 'persistent attempt to seize the school system for Imperialism masquerading as patriotism'. According to Hobson, imperial zealots were attempting 'to capture the childhood of the country, to mechanise its free play into the routine of military drill, to cultivate the savage survivals of combativeness, [and] to poison its early understanding of history by false ideals and pseudo-heroes'.[62] Such criticisms were, however, overwhelmed by the vociferous advocates of school military drill whose case was given an added credence by the perceived frailties of the British army during the Boer War. By 1903, influential research by George Shee had concluded that there was a serious deterioration of the national physique. Quoting Lord Rosebery, he lamented that 'it is no use having an Empire without an Imperial race'. Shee's research led him to believe that cramped and squalid conditions were fostering an inferior race that compared poorly to the competing European nations. The solution was compulsory military and naval training for schoolboys that would improve the physical health of the nation and maintain Britain's commercial supremacy. Significantly, military drill would also stimulate a loyalty to both mother country and empire and so 'bring about that Imperial Federation which is the dream of so many of us wish to see realised'.[63]

The Lads' Drill Association, established in 1899 under the presidency of the Earl of Meath, was at the forefront of the movement to militarise school life. Meath used his position in the Lords to call for compulsory military drill for boys to awaken a sense of patriotism and duty so that in times of international crisis young men would rush to the ranks, making compulsion unnecessary. Meath also believed it would instil a committed form of patriotism unlike the frivolous and vacuous 'pseudo-patriotism' which in his opinion emanated from the music halls.[64] Significantly, in its campaign to cultivate a healthy and patriotic youth, the Lads' Drill Association identified Portsmouth schools as exemplar in integrating military exercises into the curriculum.[65] Reporting on Portsmouth for the Board of Education in 1899, the Reverend C.C. Du Port noted 'in all boys' schools military drill with and without arms, always accompanied by instrumental music is the rule', adding that 'boys on leaving Portsmouth schools have attained to such proficiency in military drill that a large cadet corps might be formed if local funds and local energy were available'. He discovered that all large schools in Portsmouth possessed school bands using drum and fife which had been often funded by voluntary contributions.[66] Such was Portsmouth schools' enthusiasm for military drill that the Royal Commission on drill in elementary schools visited the town. A total of five schools took part, ranging from the town's Grammar School, which had its own cadet corps, to the Board and voluntary schools that had established drum and fife bands. Most of the pupils had arrived in full military dress and were praised by Lord de Montmorency for their attire and enthusiasm for drill which would be welcomed in the army and navy 'in to which many of them might later go'. The pupils performed a variety of military drills including dumb-bell exhibitions, trooping the colour, royal salutes and firing and bayonet exercises. While both boys and girls participated, most of the programme was devoted to the boys' military exercises since the girls were confined to dumb-bell displays towards the end of the day.[67] The display prompted one witness who reported that 'I cannot praise too highly the smartness and precision' of the military drills and wondered, 'could not other schools through out England and Scotland follow the example set by Portsmouth?'[68] The Royal Commission was clearly impressed with their visit to Portsmouth since the HM Inspector of Schools, E. Burrows, spoke of his admiration for the town's civic and educational leaders' attempts at linking military drill with the volunteer movement:

> By training schoolboys during their school life to know enough of physical and military drill to fit them to enter cadet corps after they leave school, and afterwards the local volunteer corps, they were made efficient and inured to military life . . . In Portsmouth they hold the lead so far as the practice of physical and military drill was carried out in schools and as a result of the drill display given by boys representing the Board and voluntary schools in Portsmouth before the high authorities a few months ago, a committee was now sitting in Whitehall to consider the whole question of physical and military drill in the elementary schools throughout the country.[69]

The *Hampshire Telegraph* joined in praise of the town's School Board in promoting military drill in the curriculum but wondered if this 'excellent training' would be lost if the boys were allowed to leave school without further military instruction. The editor suggested that 'a Cadet Corps should be formed which would act as a connecting link between the school and the Volunteer Corps. Hundreds of lads would readily join such a corps, the expense of which might be defrayed by public subscription, while its value to the country would be inestimable.'[70] The most prominent Portsmouth school in the military drill movement was St Luke's, as the band did not only form the guard of honour for the visiting commissioners but also performed at a Town Hall banquet for the crew of *HMS Terrible* on their return from South Africa.[71] St Luke's School had been somewhat of a role model for Portsmouth schools since its drum and fife band was fêted in the local press and was regularly invited to play at civic and military events in the town. Until the outbreak of the First World War, the band frequently marched through the main thoroughfares of Portsmouth on Empire Day and other national occasions. Formed in 1896 by a former army volunteer, the drum and fife band numbered over fifty performers and was presented with new patriotic colours by the Mayor in 1900.[72] Indeed in the same year, St Luke's' drum and fife band inspired the Mayor to call a public meeting and appoint a committee to establish a scheme for the formation of a cadet corps in other Portsmouth schools.[73]

The military drill and the proliferation of drum and fife bands has led historians to conclude that the imperial message was successfully inculcated into the nation's youth.[74] Certainly contemporaries who campaigned for military drill were convinced that children were committed volunteers for the imperial cause. In one letter to *The Times*, the Vice-Chairman of the Lads' Drill Association dismissed the idea that military drill was unpopular with schoolboys. After interviewing Portsmouth's Chairman of the School Board, he was assured that drill and the associated drum and fife band were the most popular subjects taught.[75] While it is clearly difficult to ascertain an Edwardian scholar's perspective, the school log books do allow insight into the complexities behind a child joining a drum and fife band. In St Luke's, joining the drum and fife band was consistently presented in the press as a purely voluntary action and one which demonstrated the pupil's commitment, duty and love of Britain and its empire. However, the log book reveals an element of compulsion in all but name. In May 1901, the Headmaster announced that

> there are a few boys who are either too lazy or maybe it is indifference to join our brigade. It seems a strange way to show interest in a school and its doings by standing aside from such a movement . . . The apathetic boy is not one to command respect of his teachers or fellows, and is likely to be forgotten and set aside in the race for life by his more enthusiastic school fellows. Mr Young would like to see all these defaulters come under his banner at once.[76]

Clearly at St Luke's, there was no opportunity to opt out of military activities without incurring the wrath of the headmaster. This, then, does suggest that recruitment figures to drum and fife should be treated with caution when assessing pupils' enthusiasm and commitment to the venture.

The First World War saw the militarisation of school life reach new levels in all three communities. In Leeds and Coventry, school log books reveal that the usual weekly activities were sporadically interrupted by visits from soldiers or day trips to military events. For example, from 1915, Leylands School in Leeds received visits from 'old boys' who had returned from the front while, in assembly, the headmaster read aloud letters from former pupils in the trenches.[77] Coventry schools also invited soldiers into the classroom and celebrated 'Tank Week' in 1918 by closing schools to allow children to visit a tank in Coventry's city centre. However, a survey of the log books for both Leeds and Coventry reveals a surprising continuity from prewar routines. The outbreak or war, for example, did not merit any special mention in the log books or any indication that headmasters addressed the school with the necessity of war and implications for the empire. Leeds and Coventry's industrial context may well account for the insularity of school life since the importance of the textile and engineering industries was essential in the war economy. Certainly, in the case of Coventry's protected engineering industries, conscription did not have the impact that it had upon other urban areas. By contrast in Portsmouth, the Edwardian preoccupation with schooling children for military service was only a prelude to a more sustained militarisation of the curriculum. In 1915, the *Evening News* viewed the war as the ideal time to accelerate the push for further militarisation of state schools. It noted that Portsmouth had gained high praise for its 'forward educational policy, notably in connection with its manual and physical training' and its incorporation of the military drill in schools. The editor argued that School Cadet Corps should be formed without delay as, ultimately, these young soldiers could eventually help in the war effort.[78] Two years later and boosted by the success of its drum and fife band, St Luke's formed its own School Cadet Corps.[79] Furthermore, while this was an obvious extension to the military drill, the curriculum and classroom routines took on a distinctly military flavour. By 1917, the Navy League had begun influencing the school curriculum by encouraging schools to enter naval essay competitions. To celebrate Trafalgar Day, children were taught about the importance of the navy and empire and set questions that assessed the British navy and its contribution in the Great War.[80] In addition, all Portsmouth schools closed on days when, towards the end of the war, the navy began to parade captured guns and submarines around the town.[81] Significantly, while children were taught the successes of the navy and empire, teachers did not shy away from citing the casualties of war to illustrate the importance of self-sacrifice. From the outbreak of war, All Saints' School in Portsmouth regularly announced the 'old boy' roll of honour of those who had fallen, praising their service, commitment and duty to the empire. Against the backdrop of the increasing rolls of honour, the headmaster gave addresses to the school on the responsibility of empire and the duty of self-sacrifice. Such eulogies provided a link between the school and empire and a clear indication of what was expected from those who would eventually join the forces.

Local role models were reinforced by national campaigns designed to capture the imagination of the young and instil pride in their armed forces and empire. For example, the death of a young sailor in the Battle of Jutland became a national symbol of sacrifice in 1916. Jack Travers Cornwell was a sixteen-year-old sight-setter in a gunnery crew aboard the *HMS Chester* who, despite suffering what were to prove fatal shrapnel injuries, continued to stand by his gun and engage with the enemy. Cornwell's age and heroism became a rallying point, and the national memorialisation of his death served both individuals' desire to mourn collectively and the state's call for duty and self-sacrifice.[82] The national media and organisations such as the Navy League focused on his age and noble actions to provide an example of the exemplar citizen for the nation's youth. As Mary Conley has noted, 'the commemoration of Jack Cornwell served many different ends, but one common goal was to elevate the sailor boy as a model to inspire the youth of the Empire for generations to come'.[83] While the Coventry and Leeds log books do not indicate that schools participated in any Cornwell memorials, the Navy League was successful in gaining access to Portsmouth schools and promoting its Jack Cornwell memorial fund.[84] Thus the navy's and Navy League's influence in Portsmouth ensured that the town's schoolchildren were presented with heroic local and national role models from the armed forces in a more consistent fashion than their counterparts in Coventry and Leeds.

The creeping militarisation of the school curriculum, which had gained momentum during the Boer War and Edwardian period, was arrested after the horrors of the First World War seeped into public consciousness. Within schools, the enthusiasm for preparing boys for military service declined and instead efforts were made to educate children in the virtues of empire that made full use of the new technological breakthroughs in communication of the early twentieth century. In Portsmouth, Coventry and Leeds, during the mid-1920s schools became increasingly innovative, with new media forms such as the wireless, record player and cinema. In 1925, Coventry's

Wheatley Street School began using a wireless for lessons in music and history and linked the radio to oversized speakers so large numbers of pupils could hear national events and royal speeches.[85] In 1923, St Peter's School in Leeds purchased a gramophone specifically to play records containing messages from the King and Queen.[86] Such was the success of this experiment that in 1925 the Leeds Educational Committee voted to purchase gramophones and records to play a range of music in the classroom that included vocal, piano, chamber and military music. Children were also taken to local cinemas for educational films.[87] In Portsmouth during the 1920s, the Portsmouth Welfare Association (PWA) began running cinema and lecture entertainment for the town's elementary schoolchildren. The Association, which was largely run by schoolteachers, was independent from Portsmouth's civic bodies and established to police the moral content of the town's leisure institutions. The PWA would stage magic lantern displays, films and lectures, charging 1d a child and attracting audiences of approximately a thousand children over a three-lecture series. The themes covered in the programme included Shakespeare, Dickens, local history and scenery, and empire. Indeed, empire seemed to figure prominently, with features such as 'scenes of India' and 'a tour of the British Empire'. An *Evening News* reporter who visited one event applauded the children's knowledge of Shakespeare and 'their enthusiasm for the Empire and its ruler, and for Nelson, Dickens, and Portsmouth's other heroes of the past'. However, while undoubtedly the pupils were willing participants, we must tread cautiously when assessing the effectiveness of this imperial propaganda. The *Evening News* reporter noted that the most popular films were of the comic variety, shown as a 'make weight' for the more serious material. Indeed, it was noted that at times the massed ranks of children did not behave as the PWA would have wished. The reporter observed that 'now and again their sense of massed freedom out of school hours bade fair to develop in rowdiness, but here the teacher element in the workers on the committee quickly came to the rescue'.[88] Clearly, Portsmouth's naval tradition and links with the empire ensured that the town's children were almost certainly exposed to more regular acclamation of empire in their extra-curricular activities than their counterparts in Coventry and Leeds.

However, the new technologies of radio and cinema were by the mid-1920s transporting great national and imperial events directly into the nation's classroom.[89] Moreover, greater efficiency and cheaper transport links also allowed schoolchildren to visit events celebrating empire in unprecedented numbers. For example, all three educational committees afforded some funding to allow children to visit the

Wembley Empire Exhibition of 1924. In Coventry, all children in the city were rewarded with a day's holiday to allow schools to take groups of children to the exhibition, while Portsmouth schools organised similar day trips to the capital.[90] Even the 400-mile return journey to the Empire Exhibition did not perturb the Leeds Educational Committee. Leeds school children journeyed by train and spent three days at the exhibition, staying at a children's campsite in Willesden. However, while the Educational Authority had negotiated reduced rail fares, the cost of the hostel, exhibition and transport would have prohibited poorer working-class families from sending their children.[91]

Perhaps one of the most ambitious educational trips planned by any Educational Committee in the country was organised by the Coventry branch of the Head Teachers Association in 1933. Approximately seven thousand schoolchildren boarded ten special trains from Coventry to Portsmouth to spend a day in the city's naval base and dockyard. The 'Navy Day', as it was dubbed, intended to educate land-locked Coventry children about the importance of the Royal Navy and its role in the empire. Each child was given a souvenir programme that introduced Portsmouth as 'the chief Naval Port of the Empire' and then described the specifications of over ten warships, armoury and historic battles. The children were shown round the historic Nelson's *HMS Victory* and the modern battleships:

> The boys were shown how to open the breeches of the naval guns, and were allowed to look up the riffled barrels as obliging sailors removed the muzzle caps from these oily weapons. They were allowed to turn the periscopes round and round, examine wonderful anti-aircraft guns on the *Courageous* and see how the aeroplanes are hoisted on to the great landing deck. They saluted the quarter deck as they boarded each ship.

Clearly, the souvenir programme and tour around the historic sections of the dockyard and their hands-on activities on the modern ships were intended to imbue a sense of Britain's naval power and its role in creating and defending the empire. This message was instilled further when Admiral K. Waistrell, Portsmouth's Commander and Chief, addressed a speech to the entire seven thousand children via a microphone and large loudspeakers in the naval gymnasium. Outlining the importance of the *HMS Victory*, he proclaimed:

> The ship was a great memorial not only to Lord Nelson, but also to that Navy which did so much to found the great British Empire to which the children should be so proud to belong. Our wonderful Empire . . . was made by men who went to the ends of the earth imbued by a spirit of loyalty to their King and country, and by an unselfish devotion to duty without thought of themselves.

He finished by suggesting that their visit to Portsmouth and the naval base should be a constant reminder of the loyalty and duty that had made the British Empire 'the finest in the world'.[92] The event attracted the attention of British Movietone News, who saw an opportunity to report on a mass school outing and, more importantly, celebrate the power of the British navy and empire. The company invested heavily in the occasion, recording on expensive sound film, rigging lighting in Coventry railway station and deploying cameramen on the train and in Portsmouth for the naval base tour. The news reel's focus on the heritage of the navy and its critical role in defending the empire was a message targeted at both the domestic and foreign markets since the film was distributed across the Empire, on the continent and in America.[93] Indeed, in a period of international tension and against the backdrop of the Geneva Disarmament Conference (1932–34), Movietone and other film makers were eager to present the British navy as a force to be reckoned with.[94]

The day trip to Portsmouth, then, exploited the improved transport links and advances in film technology to the full in a bid to ground children and the wider world in Britain's determination to defend the Empire through its celebrated naval strength. The tour of the naval base, presentations made to pupils and the message embedded in the film would have truly influenced the children if it was an integral part of their school curriculum and had the full commitment of the teachers concerned. However, a rare account of the trip captured in a student teacher's essay sheds light on how the imperial message was sometimes diluted when filtered through the teaching profession. Miss Steel, a student teacher, was required to write a detailed essay of the trip evaluating the educational worth of the excursion. Scoring a moderately impressive B+, she described some of the activities that the children seemed to enjoy such as the tour round *HMS Nelson*, and *Victory* and inspection of the ships' weaponry. Significantly, Steel did not see fit to record the speeches made by the dignitaries extolling the virtues of the navy and empire, despite its detailed coverage in *The Times* and *Midland Daily Telegraph*. Indeed, Steel was concerned that 'this visit aroused their admiration of the navy, and it may lead the boys to a love of war, though no doubt their interests could be guided into the right channels. The "giants of the ocean" seemed to place armament congresses right in the background.'[95] One is left to wonder whether there was a tension between the teacher's stress on international disarmament and the outing's emphasis on Britain's naval power and duty and loyalty to the empire. Thus the strength and emphasis of the imperial message may well have been far from uniform and heavily dependent on an individual teacher's perception of empire.

[145]

Furthermore, Steel also noted that, while the children later saw the film, there were no follow-up classes on the navy and empire that would have reinforced the purpose of the excursion.

Conclusion

Through investigating educational provision in three communities it has become clear that the imperial message did not infiltrate schools in a uniform fashion. To be sure, schools in all three communities followed similar patterns of engagement with empire and militarisation which began surprisingly slowly from the late 1880s. The rigid school curriculum left little space for teaching empire as the government demanded that the 3Rs should be prioritised over subjects such as history or geography that could have disseminated imperial sentiment. Furthermore, it is clear that no school or town rejected the imperial ethos, and all three communities engaged with the empire and militarisation during periods of intense imperial crisis such as the Boer and First World Wars. Where the differences lay between the towns was when civic leaders or headmasters identified local factors that could possibly undermine the British Empire. Thus while, Coventry's socio-economic context did not immediately trigger such concerns, in Leeds the urban elites' anxieties over immigration and urban poverty produced a raised a consciousness of empire. In the case of Portsmouth, its location as 'home' of the British navy meant that the town's space and architecture were dominated by militarised overtones throughout the nineteenth century. However, concerns over the future of masculinity led schools such as St Luke's to enthusiastically adopt overtly imperial propaganda into the curriculum. Incongruously, then, during an era in which the British Empire was at its largest, the most enthusiastic imperial propaganda in schools were from those anxious that their local problems would undermine the social fabric of their community and ultimately the wider imperial project. The following chapter pursues this theme further by investigating the pressing social concerns in all the three communities that shaped the civic leaders' adoption of Empire Day and their engagement with the largest imperial exhibition ever held at Wembley in 1924.

Notes

1 B. Simon, *Education and the Labour Movement, 1870–1920* (London, Lawrence and Wishart, 1965), pp. 166–75; P. A. Dunae, 'Boys' Literature and the Idea of Empire, 1870–1914', *Victorian Studies*, 24, 1980, pp. 105–21; for a critique of this perspective see J. Rose, *The Intellectual Life of the British Working Classes* (New Haven, Yale University Press, 2001), pp. 321–64.

2 B. Porter, *The Absent-minded Imperialists. Empire, Society and Culture in Britain*, (Oxford, Oxford University Press, 2004, 2006 edn), p. 115.
3 Not until the 1890 International Congress of Berlin did Britain realise that it was lagging behind other European nations. See H. Cunningham, *The Children of the Poor. Representations of Childhood since the Seventeenth Century* (Oxford, Blackwell, 1991), p. 176.
4 A. Penn, *Targeting Schools. Drill, Militarism and Imperialism* (London, Woburn Press, 1999), p. 10.
5 W.H.G. Armytage, *Four Hundred Years of English Education* (Cambridge, Cambridge University Press, 1964), p. 186; S.G. Checkland, *The Rise of Industrial Society in England 1815–1885* (London, Longman, 1964), pp. 257–8.
6 Coventry Record Office (CRO), CEE/log/20/1, 'Wheatley Street School log book 2', 30 May 1913; 23 March 1934.
7 *Coventry Official Guide 1909* (Coventry, 1909), preface.
8 *Hampshire Telegraph*, 20 April 1907; PCA, SA/CC/DS/39/3/A/1, 'St Luke's School log book', 22 September 1922.
9 *Hampshire Telegraph* 20 April 1907; PCA, SA/CC/DS/39/3/A/1, 'St Luke's School log book', 22 September 1922.
10 British Parliamentary Papers, *Board of Education. Report on the Consultative Committee on Attendance, Compulsory or otherwise at Continuation Schools*, vol. 1, Report and Appendices, 1909, pp. 272–3.
11 While Rose has extensively used working-class autobiography for his work on Victorian education, my approach of using three specific communities for case studies largely rules out any systematic analysis of working-class autobiographies. See J. Rose, 'Willingly to School: the Working-class Response to Elementary Education 1870–1918', *Journal of British Studies*, 32, April 1993.
12 CRO, CEE/log/15/1, 'St Michael's Church of England School log book', 9 March 1883; 3 March 1897.
13 CRO, CEE/log/20/1, 'Wheatley Street School log book 1 to 1925'.
14 Portsmouth City Archives (PCA), SA/CC/DS/39/3/A/1, 'St Luke's School log book 1867–1939', 17 July 1867, 4 December 1886, 26 September 1887.
15 Leeds City Archive (LCA), LC/ED/160/1/1, 'All Saints' Church of England log book 1872–1901', list of lessons for the year ending December 1893.
16 Penn, *Targeting Schools*, p. 11.
17 Porter, *The Absent-minded Imperialists*, p. 120.
18 A. Thompson, *The Empire Strikes Back? The Impact of Imperialism on Britain from the Mid-nineteenth Century* (Harlow, Longman, 2005), pp. 114–15.
19 *Pall Mall Gazette*, 10 April 1890.
20 For examples see CRO CEE/log/26/4, 'Frederick Bird Boys School'; CEE/log/20/1, 'Wheatley Street School log book', 14 January 1893; 29 June 1896.
21 For example, PCA SA/CC/DS/36/1/1/A/1, 'Portsea Infants' School log book', 28 July 1880; SA/CC/DS/5/2/A/1, 'All Saints' Portsea School log book', 4 May 1897.
22 PCA, SA/CC/DS/39/3/A/1, 'St Luke's School log book'. Short typed history of the school.
23 PCA SA/CC/DS/36/1/1/A/1, 'Portsea Infants' School log book', 23 September 1880; Inspector's report for 1885.
24 PCA, SA/CC/DS/39/3/A/1, 'St Luke's School log book', 1 November 1878.
25 St Luke's was deducted one-tenth of its grant owing to poor instruction and attendance; see PCA, SA/CC/DS/39/3/A/1, 'St Luke's School log book', June 1876.
26 Leeds City Archive (hereafter LCA) LC/ED/62/2, 'St Peter's Square School Board Log Book', 14 September 1894.
27 PCA, AS/CC/DS/5/2/A/1, 'All Saints' Portsea Log Book'. See 24 May 1881; 17 August 1881; 27 June 1890.
28 PCA, SA/CC/DS/39/3/A/1, 'St Luke's School log book', 13 August 1896; LCA, LC/ED/62/2, 'St Peter's Square School Board Log Book', 13 July 1894; CRO, CEE/log/15/1, 'St Michael's Church of England School log book', 18 March 1898.
29 K. Richardson, *Twentieth Century Coventry* (Bungay, Chaucer Press, 1972), p. 250.

30   *Pall Mall Gazette*, 10 April 1890.
31   Thompson, *The Empire Strikes Back?*, p. 117.
32   S. Heathorn, '"Let us remember that we, too, are English": Constructions of Citizenship and National Identity in English Elementary School Reading Books, 1880–1914', *Victorian Studies*, 38, 3, 1995, pp. 395–427.
33   A. Forster, *The Citizen Reader* (London, Cassell, 1886), p. 92.
34   *Practical Teacher*, May 1909, p. 600.
35   CRO, CEE/log/20/1, 'Wheatley Street School log book to 1925', 31 May, 4 June 1897.
36   CRO, CEE/log/20/1, 'Wheatley Street School log book to 1925', 21–5 June 1897.
37   CRO, CEE/log/20/1, 'Wheatley Street School log book to 1925', 3 May 1901; CEE/log/15/1, 'St Michael's Church of England School log book', 30 April 1901.
38   J. Rüger, 'Nation, Empire and Navy: Identity Politics in the United Kingdom 1887–1914', *Past and Present*, 185, November 2004, p. 160.
39   PCA, SA/CC/DS/39/3/A/1, 'St Luke's School log book', 25 September 1902.
40   PCA, SA/CC/DS/39/3/A/1, 'St Luke's School log book', 24 April 1900; SA/CC/DS/5/2/A/1, 'All Saints' Portsea School log book', 9 November 1899; 24 April 1900; 22 May 1900.
41   CRO, CEE/log/20/1, 'Wheatley Street School log book to 1925', 3 May 1901; CEE/log/15/1, 'St Michael's Church of England School log book', 30 April 1901; LCA, LC/ED/62/2, 'St Peter's Square School Board Log Book', 25 May 1900; LC/ED/16/1, 'Czar Street Industrial School log book', 24 May 1900.
42   PCA, SA/CC/DS/5/2/A/1, 'All Saints' Portsea School log book', 17 October 1905.
43   K. Lunn and R. Thomas, 'Naval Imperialism in Portsmouth, 1905–1914', *Southern History*, 10, 1988.
44   Portsmouth Branch WEA, *Childhood Memories*, vol. 2, 1990, p. 4.
45   For an analysis of the Edwardian anxiety over youth culture see B. Beaven, *Leisure, Citizenship and Working-class Men in Britainm 1850–1945* (Manchester, Manchester University Press, 2005), ch. 3.
46   PCA, SA/CC/DS/39/3/A/1, 'St Luke's School log book'. Short typed history of the school, p. 2.
47   PCA, SA/CC/DS/39/3/A/1, 'St Luke's School log book', February 1898.
48   PCA, SA/CC/DS/39/3/A/1, 'St Luke's School log book', June 1898.
49   PCA, SA/CC/DS/39/3/A/1, 'St Luke's School log book', June 1898. Ken Lunn and Ann Day have noted the importance of the 'dockyard ethos in schooling dockyard workers'; see K. Lunn and A. Day, 'Introduction', in K. Lunn and A. Day (eds), *History of Work Labour Relations in the Royal Dockyards* (London, Mansell, 1999), p. xii.
50   PCA, SA/CC/DS/39/3/A/1, 'St Luke's School log book', February 1900.
51   *Hampshire Telegraph*, 27 April 1900.
52   Quoted in Penn, *Targeting Schools*, p. 21.
53   Penn, *Targeting Schools*, p. 24.
54   Quoted in Penn, *Targeting Schools*, pp. 62–3.
55   LCA, LC/ED/62/2, 'St Peter's Square School Board Log Book', March 1903; see also *Yorkshire Post*, 28 March 1903.
56   LCA, LC/ED17/4, 'Darley Street Council School, 1898–1935', log book, 11 June 1904; see also *Jewish Chronicle*, 11 June 1904.
57   G.R. Searle, *The Quest for National Efficiency. A Study of British Politics and Political Thought, 1889–1914* (London, Ashfield Press, 1971, 1990 edn), p. 210.
58   LCA, LC/ED17/4, 'Darley Street Council School, 1898–1935', log book, 6 September 1904; see also *Yorkshire Evening Post*, 5 September 1904.
59   This evidence differs from Lammers's recent interpretations on Jewish immigration that claim that the London County Council was accommodating to Jews in their schooling. B.J. Lammers, 'The Citizens of the Future: Educating the Children of the Jewish East End, *c.* 1885–1939', *Twentieth Century British History*, 9, 4, 2008, pp. 393–418. Chapter 6 discusses this in more detail with relation to Empire Day.
60   *Hampshire Telegraph*, 10 February 1900.

61 Quoted in Penn, *Targeting Schools*, p. 34.
62 J.A. Hobson, *Imperialism a Study* (New York, Cosimo Classics, 1902, 2005 edn), p. 217.
63 G.F. Shee, 'The Deterioration in National Physique', *Nineteenth Century*, 53, May 1903, p. 805.
64 R. Meath, 'The Defence of the Empire', *Nineteenth* Century, 57 May 1905, p. 739; see also Meath's autobiography R. Meath, *Brabazon Potpourri* (London, Hutchinson & Co., 1928), p. 113.
65 *The Times*, 2 November 1900.
66 *Report of the Board of Education*, 1899–1900, vol. III, Appendix to Report, 1900, p. 278.
67 *Evening News*, 23 March 1900.
68 *The Times*, 30 March 1900.
69 PCA, SA/CC/DS/39/3/A/1, 'St Luke's School log book', November 1900.
70 *Hampshire Telegraph*, 10 February 1900.
71 PCA, SA/CC/DS/39/3/A/1, 'St Luke's School log book'. Short typed history of the school, pp. 3–4.
72 PCA, SA/CC/DS/39/3/A/1, 'St Luke's School log book'. Short typed history of the school, pp. 3–4.
73 *The Times*, 2 November 1900.
74 A. Bloomfield, 'Drill and dance as symbols of imperialism', in J.A. Mangan (ed.), *Making Imperial Mentalities* (Manchester, Manchester University Press, 1990), p. 78.
75 *The Times*, 30 March 1900.
76 PCA, SA/CC/DS/39/3/A/1, 'St Luke's School log book', May 1901.
77 LCA, LCED40/1, 'Leyland Board School Logbook, 1893–1919', 29 June 1915; 15 September 1915; CRO, CEE/log/15/1, 'St Michael's Church of England School log book', 14 February 1918; CRO, CEE/log/20/1, 'Wheatley Street School log book 1 to 1925', 11 February 1918.
78 *Evening News*, 14 January 1915.
79 PCA, SA/CC/DS/39/3/A/1, 'St Luke's School log book', 10 January 1917.
80 PCA, SA/CC/DS/39/3/A/1, 'St Luke's School log book', 25 October, 1917.
81 PCA, SA/CC/DS/5/2/A/1, 'All Saints' Portsea School log book', 20 November; 4 December 1918.
82 M.A. Conley, *From Jack Tar to Union Jack. Representing Naval Manhood in the British Empire, 1870–1918* (Manchester, Manchester University Press, 2009), p. 160.
83 Conley, *From Jack Tar to Union Jack*, p. 164.
84 PCA, SA/CC/DS/5/2/A/1, 'All Saints' Portsea School log book', 13 September 1916.
85 CRO, CCE/log/20/1, 'Wheatley Street School log book to 1925', 11 November 1925.
86 LCA, LC/ED/62/2, 'St Peter's Square School Board Log Book', 28 May 1923.
87 *Yorkshire Evening Post*, 29 January 1925.
88 *Evening News*, 3 May 1924.
89 See Chapter 6.
90 PCA, SA/CC/DS/39/3/A/1, 'St Luke's School log book', 28 June 1924; CEE/log/15/1, 'St Michael's Church of England School log book', 10 July 1924.
91 *Yorkshire Evening Post*, 14 April 1924.
92 *Midland Daily Telegraph*, 4 September 1933.
93 *Midland Daily Telegraph*, 1 September 1933.
94 Pathé News's report on the Coventry children's trip to Portsmouth can be viewed at www.britishpathe.com.
95 Coventry Herbert Art Gallery and Museum, 'Coventry school children's educational visit, souvenir programme', and I.A. Steel's essay, 2 September 1933.

CHAPTER SIX

Transmitting the imperial message: Empire Day and the 1924 Wembley Exhibition

By the end of the interwar period, Empire Day had become an established annual event in the British and colonial calendar. First celebrated on 24 May 1903 to mark the late Queen Victoria's birthday, the event continued into the 1950s until it was renamed 'Commonwealth Day'.[1] Surprisingly, for such a long-running event that propagated Britain's Empire, historians have analysed the movement sparingly. Whereas historians have investigated the impact of the Empire Day Movement on colonies such as Australia and New Zealand, analyses of Empire Day in Britain have largely been confined to short passages in larger bodies of work on empire and society. However, for the purposes of this book, the dissemination of Empire Day from the early Edwardian period presents an ideal opportunity to assess an imperial movement's influence in the three communities under investigation. Indeed, the decision to stage Empire Day depended upon the support of the town's civic leaders and often the local teaching profession. This chapter examines the inception, dissemination and development of Empire Day in Portsmouth, Coventry and Leeds and illustrates the contrasting motivations for staging the annual event.

Historians' work on Empire Day is generally contained within broader studies of imperial movements, particularly with regard to the activities of Lord Meath, the movement's founder. For example, John Springhall examined how Meath's fear that masculinity was in perpetual decline through urban degeneration led him to campaign for militarisation youth activities. Another of Meath's aims was to inculcate the young in the values of duty and sacrifice for the British Empire, creating Empire Day as a vehicle for his crusade.[2] John M. MacKenzie noted how Meath's targeting of schools enabled imperial and patriotic events to become institutionalised in both the private and state educational systems.[3] Likewise, Anne Bloomfield argued that Empire Day's inclusion into extra-curricular activities successfully disseminated an imperialist message to the young participants.[4] More recently, Benjamin Lammers has maintained that events such as Empire Day were examples of the inclusive nature of British society and its educational system. He suggests that 'it is quite striking that the education authorities did not see the Jewish pupils in the East End, a potential other, as possessing any impediments to the full enjoyment of Englishness'.[5] Andrew Thompson's research on schooling in the early twentieth century confirmed that Empire Day 'was a firm fixture of the school calendar until at least the mid-1940s'. However, after sampling a range of working-class testimonies, he concludes that while education 'helped to foster a sense of pride in the British Empire, it does not appear to have been very deep-rooted or well-informed'.[6] While most histories of empire and popular culture have merely paused to reflect upon the impact of Empire Day, a recent contribution from Jim English has made the movement the focus of his study. In a detailed investigation, English draws from working-class autobiographies to chart the impact and development of the Empire Day movement in Britain. He argues that the widespread adoption of Empire Day had a greater social influence on British people than historians have hitherto recognised. According to English, Empire Day was able to 'traverse class lines and establish an imperial consciousness in the minds of working-class children' that performed a 'socialising role that upheld a belief in racial superiority and righteousness of the British Empire'.[7] These are strong claims for the importance of Empire Day that are largely based on autobiographical material scattered over Britain. Indeed, these findings contrast sharply with Porter's recent research that, like English, utilises working-class autobiographies but concludes that Empire Day was largely unsuccessful in inculcating an imperial sentiment. While Porter notes that while some, like Robert Roberts, were influenced by the event, most regarded Empire Day as an opportunity for a half-day holiday.[8] Likewise, Jonathan Rose draws evidence from working-class memoirs to conclude that, while Empire Day was often mentioned, it did little to instil a sense of patriotism or nurture a better understanding of the colonies.[9] This chapter takes a different approach and systematically contrasts the influence of the movement in the three communities through the local press, institutions and, where possible, working-class testimony. In contextualising Empire Day within the three communities, the chapter endeavours to contrast experiences between the towns and thereby assess the movement's significance and impact.

Empire Day: the rise of a national movement

Meath's objective was to establish a movement that would exult the 'magnificence and power of the Empire' and create a bond between the four hundred million imperial subjects. In 1905, Meath claimed that six self-governing Colonies, 22 Crown Colonies and schools in nine County Councils, seven District Councils and 23 Borough Councils had observed Empire Day.[10] Viewed nationally, there can be little doubt that during the Edwardian period Empire Day grew to become an annual event in many schools. Taking the Empire Day Movement's own figures, the number of state schools marking Empire Day seems substantial. By 1907, 12,544 out of a total of 20,451 elementary schools celebrated Empire Day and by 1919 only four Local Educational Authorities refused to adopt it.[11] Within a British context, while Meath had been largely successful in writing to local authorities requesting that Empire Day be observed in schools, his campaign to secure the day as an official holiday was met with less enthusiasm by the government. In 1908, the House of Commons rejected the proposal for Empire Day to become an official ceremony and holiday and only in the recruitment crisis of 1916 did it receive government support.[12]

During the interwar period, Empire Day continued to flourish, a development which Jon Springhall found surprising given that there emerged a surge of anti-imperial feeling after the First World War.[13] By the early twentieth century, those on the Left had intellectualised their opposition to empire, linking it to an aggressive form of capitalism. For example, the Independent Labour Party actively campaigned for the dismantling of the British Empire, while the main Labour Party passed a general anti-imperial resolution in 1921. While it must be said that most activists on the British Left were content to create a 'fairer' empire, it is clear that, by the interwar period, events such as Empire Day had become overtly politicised and were liable to attract criticism from factional political groups.[14] Given the emergence of a more sustained criticism of empire, it is perhaps understandable that Empire Day proved resilient as those propagating the movement became determined to counter anti-imperial propaganda. Moreover, MacKenzie has rightly pointed out that the interwar period saw important technological advances in the mass media which were skilfully utilised by proponents of Empire Day to raise the profile of the event and embed it within the state school curriculum and wider society. Thus news reports on Empire Day would play in the new 'picture palaces' and gramophone records, and BBC radio could broadcast the King's Empire Day message directly into schools and homes. These new conduits of the imperial message dovetailed effortlessly alongside more traditional outlets such as the press, imperial exhibitions, juvenile literature and school textbooks in propagating the importance of Empire Day.[15] National perspectives, however, mask the *process* of how Empire Day was implemented in the locality and filtered through the provincial press and civic elites and received by the populous at large. The following sections examines how an international and overtly imperial celebration was received by the three localities in question.

Empire Day in the civic realm

On 17 June 1904, Lord Meath issued a circular to the press outlining the values that underpinned his new Empire Day movement. Within his original declaration, Meath emphasised the importance of instilling a sense of patriotism within the civic realm. He believed that 'patriotism and the sense of civic duty should find their first expression at home, and then afterwards extend themselves to the furthest limits of the Empire'.[16] He added that civic duty could flourish only if class and selfish interests were subordinate to the national interest. The weight placed on civic duty was attractive to local elites who, after all, were charged with implementing Empire Day in their respective communities. In Portsmouth, Coventry and Leeds, Empire Day was adopted but was targeted to address differing civic issues. By the Edwardian period, Portsmouth's civic elite and local press regarded the city with its rich naval heritage as 'the gateway to the Empire'.[17] A successful national campaign by John Fisher, the First Sea Lord, to increase public expenditure on the navy and build the powerful *Dreadnought* battleships in the Portsmouth dockyard, intrinsically linked the town with the expansion and protection of the British Empire.[18] As we have already seen, Portsmouth schools enjoyed a close relationship with the military and were widely perceived as pioneering military drill practices in 1900. With such a significant stake in maintaining the security of the Empire, one might expect Portsmouth's Council schools to have been among the first twelve thousand schools in England to enthusiastically adopt Empire Day in 1905. However, in contrast with Coventry and Leeds, the implementation of Empire Day in Portsmouth met with some resistance and was not systematically adopted until 1913.[19]

From its inception in 1903, Empire Day had struggled to gain a foothold in Portsmouth's Council schools. While the private and religious schools in the town embraced the event, teachers in the Council schools resisted attempts by the municipal authorities to join a civic and military procession for Empire Day. It was significant that the

Grammar School and St Luke's were eager participants in early Empire Days as their respective Cadet Corps and drum and fife band helped stamp a military character over the proceedings. St Luke's began celebrating Empire Day in 1906, when teachers gave lessons on empire and patriotism and pupils then paraded around the playground.[20] However, by 1908, the town's authorities were eager to establish a civic and military ceremony and invited both local schools and military personnel to mark the occasion. According to the Mayor's plan outlined in the local press:

> At three o'clock a procession will be formed and the Cadet Corps with the band playing and colours flying will march to the reserve enclosure on the Common. Arriving at the Arena, the Cadet Corps will fall in line with the School children in alphabetical order from the right. At 3.30, the Cadet Corps will troop the colours at the saluting base, the School children and Cadet Corps will march past and give three cheers and sing 'God Save the King'.[21]

Matters came to a head in May 1908 when the Mayor stated that he had secured permission from the local education committee for all children over ten years of age attending Portsmouth Elementary Schools to take part in the ceremony.[22]

This was the first time that the civic elite had drawn elementary schools into the event, and it was an invitation that was not entirely

4 Empire Day held in Guildhall, Portsmouth, 1912.
By kind permission of the Portsmouth History Centre

5   The long-term effects of the Boer can be seen here during an Empire Day
celebration on Southsea common. A group of Sea Scouts recreate 'Jack'
landing at the Veldt, South Africa in 1913.
By kind permission of the Portsmouth History Centre

welcome. Such was the palpable disquiet among Portsmouth's elementary teachers that the Mayor convened a large, well attended meeting in the Town Hall to discuss the Council Schools' contribution to Empire Day. The Major opened the meeting 'warmly commending the scheme' and hoped the teachers would approve the patriotic and 'inspiring spectacle'. Clearly aware that some teachers were uncomfortable with marking Empire Day in this fashion, the Mayor confirmed that there was no compulsion for teachers to attend, and those not participating were granted a half-day holiday. The teachers unanimously rejected the proposal. On a practical level they complained that the length of the march was too exhausting for the children, with too few refreshment and toilet breaks. The Mayor's attempt to incorporate the town's elementary schoolchildren into the event was also questioned by teachers who reported that 'unhappily many children in the schools of the lower parts of town were insufficiently clothed and had not the foot-gear to make a presentable show at such a display'. The most damning criticism of the programme, and one which perhaps revealed the underlying hostility by some teachers, was aired by one headmistress who believed that 'the spectacle would be lowering to the tone of school life'. Met with this hostility, the Mayor had no choice but to withdraw the elementary school sector from Empire Day parade, though urging that it should be included in the parade in the following year.[23] Portsmouth Council schoolteachers, however, did mark Empire Day in their own way since lessons on Britain and its colonies were taught in the morning prior to the half-day holiday in the afternoon.[24] Moreover, by 1913, teachers diluted the event further by merging it with a prize-giving day for pupils with the best attendance. Prior to the First World War, a militarised civic parade, however, appears to have been a step too far for many Council schoolteachers in the town.[25]

The local press, who along with the civic elite had pressed for the elementary sector's inclusion, did not take too kindly to the Mayor's very public defeat. For the press, Empire Day embodied the values of citizenship, duty and patriotism, qualities that were essential learning for the working-class schoolchild.[26] By 1909, Empire Day was fast becoming an important event in the civic calendar. The key role of the local authorities in arranging the event ensured that Meath's values of citizenship, duty and patriotism designed to instil devotion to the Empire, were filtered through the immediate locality. Thus those refusing to partake in the celebrations snubbed not only their empire but also the civic realm as well. On the eve of the 1909 event, the *Evening News* noted that 'all previous celebrations of Empire Day at Portsmouth will fade into insignificance'.[27] Certainly, Empire Day had caught the imagination of local business, with patriotic adverts placed throughout the local press to commemorate the day. Likewise, the press carried speeches by Meath that estimated that Empire Day was observed by over three million children nationwide, with almost eighteen thousand schools taking part. Significantly, the *Evening News* conflated the Empire with the local when stating that Empire Day 'will strike the moral keynote of a high ideal of imperial civic duty'. Given the importance that the civic elite and local press were beginning to attach to Empire Day, it was a concern that, once again, Portsmouth's elementary schools refused to participate, citing 'practical difficulties'.[28] Furthermore, the militarised character of the event meant that the newly formed Scout troops initially withdrew from the parade since Baden-Powell was keen to disassociate Scouting from military youth movements.[29] After surveying Empire Day around the country, an angry *Evening News* editorial asked:

> And what is Portsmouth doing – Portsmouth, one of the gates of the Empire, proudly boasting that it is the greatest naval port in the world? Well, Portsmouth is not quite sure what it will do on Empire Day. There may be a distribution of prizes in the schools by members of the education committee – if the books are ready in time what is officially con-

sidered rather doubtful. After that the children will have a half-holiday, which they may spend at their sweet will, with no necessary obtrusion of any thoughts of Empire and its meaning. If that is all that Portsmouth is going to do, it certainly falls far short of what Portsmouth might do.[30]

In a thinly veiled attack on the teachers of the elementary schools, the *Evening News* congratulated the Board of Guardians for their patriotism in organising Empire Day events for the workhouse children. The editorial noted that many of the 'inmates' in the home will go on to serve in the military and that 'the inculcation of the Imperial Spirit in them and their fellows now cannot surely be a mistake'.[31] The civic authorities and local press, then, became increasingly frustrated that the vast majority of working-class schoolchildren did not participate in the militarised parades organised to commemorate Empire Day.

In contrast to Portsmouth, Coventry's Empire Day celebrations emphasised the moral duty of the imperial subject, toning down the militarised overtones that were evident in the south-coast town. The absence of military-style parades in Coventry may have been instrumental in avoiding the problems that Portsmouth encountered and was sufficient to placate Council schoolteachers wary of imperialism. In 1907, there were no official activities to mark the event, with only the *Midland Daily Telegraph* noting that thousands of schools in the country were celebrating Empire Day. The newspaper was a lead advocate for the Empire Day movement in Coventry as the editor lamented that 'our children in the present day are taught too little about the Empire as it now exists . . . the introduction of "Empire Day" should lead to the dissemination of wider and more perfect information on our colonies'. However, whereas the Portsmouth press saw Empire Day as a valuable education for children destined for military service, the Coventry newspapers stressed the importance of balancing an imperial education with social welfare at home. The *Midland Daily Telegraph* was alert to contemporary anxieties that industrial strife and poor urban social conditions could adversely effect the future stability of the empire, arguing that 'if there be rot at the core the Empire must pine and perish'.[32] A year later, the newspaper published Lord Meath's telegram to the Mayor, Alderman W. Lee, outlining the values that embodied Empire Day; 'responsibility, duty, sympathy and self-sacrifice'. While the civic authorities had not planned a town parade, in response to these calls Lee ordered that flags be positioned on public buildings and that all Council schoolchildren were to be given a half-day holiday.[33] It was not until 1909 that the Coventry civic authorities organised a comprehensive programme of Empire Day celebrations.[34] The Town Council shunned any form of parade or militarised spectacle through the city and instead private, religious and Council schools followed a similar programme of events. The *Midland Daily Telegraph* described Empire Day as 'largely a children's festival', though there were many more flags displayed on public and private building than the previous year.[35] Schoolchildren would receive a special lesson on the British Empire, followed by a visit and a speech from a local dignitary such as the Mayor, a councillor or member of the clergy. Children would salute the flag and sing 'God save the King', whereupon the Council schoolchildren were granted a half-day holiday. In the speeches delivered to the children, local dignitaries not only outlined the significance of the British Empire but also emphasised the importance of obedience and discipline. In Hale Street School (Church of England), the Reverend E. de B. Saunderson warned pupils against being 'idle, self-indulgent, cruel, disrespectful and disobedient to their parents and those in authority' since 'it was the morality of the people which would be the determining cause of the stability or downfall of the Empire'.[36] At the same time, the *Midland Daily Telegraph* reminded its readers that the key to a stable and prosperous empire was fostering security and social cohesion at home: 'disease and discontent at the centre do not make for the healthfulness and happiness of the peoples on the borderland of Imperial rule'.[37]

The civic elites' stress on obedience and social welfare was perhaps a response to the turbulent industrial relations that had beset Coventry's new staple industries. The city was paralysed by an engineering strike in 1899 and, though official trade unionism was relatively weak, the motor and bicycle sectors were regularly hit by unofficial strikes and industrial disputes throughout the Edwardian period.[38] While the political parties of the Left, such as the Social Democratic Federation and the Independent Labour Party, were small and often detached from the working-class population, they were vocal and generated anxieties among the urban elite.[39] For example, on the same day that the *Midland Daily Telegraph* celebrated Empire Day of 1909, it reported a rousing speech by a socialist councillor calling for a working-class revolution. Councillor Bannington addressed a large and appreciative crowd in the city's market square proclaiming that workers had to work under terrible conditions set by their employers and 'that was the freedom they enjoyed in this great and glorious Empire'. The only solution was for the men to 'sweep away the capitalist system with its miserable poverty for the worker, and take their stand under the banner of revolutionary socialism'.[40] Coventry's rapid industrial and demographic growth in the late nineteenth and early twentieth centuries meant that the city's urban elite struggled to engage with a more militant and migrant population. Empire Day, then, became a useful device to instil loyalty and patriotism not only for the British Empire but also for the institutions that governed their locality.

The development and character of Empire Day in Leeds can also be understood as a reaction to anxieties that were troubling the local urban elite. Leeds elementary schools were some of the first in the country to observe Empire Day since they were already marking the importance of empire before Lord Meath's movement was established. Moreover, the celebration of empire in Leeds was carefully targeted at the Jewish schools in the city and reflected the civic elites' ongoing doubts about the Jewish community's loyalty and patriotism for the imperial cause. Indeed, just as Empire Day in Portsmouth and Coventry attempted to counter local anxieties, the movement in Leeds endeavoured to address concerns about race and political radicalism. For example, the growth of slum conditions in Leyland, the Jewish district of Leeds, was consistently attributed to the racial characteristics of the Jewish community. Commenting on the Jewish quarter of Leeds, Alderman Ward, the Sanitary Committee Chairman, believed that 'the people that work in these sweaters' shops are very filthy. You only have to go into the district where they live to discover this. This is not surprising seeing that they come from parts of Russia which are almost beyond the pale of civilisation.'[41] The Town Council's Inspector for Jewish Workshops helped confirm this view, noting a year later that Jews were 'not notorious for their cleanliness and order'.[42] Alongside a civic consensus that the new Jewish immigrants were responsible for increasing urban squalor, the *Leeds Mercury*, a liberal-leaning newspaper, commented in 1900 that:

> Were it not for the dirt which seems to dog the habitation and life of every Eastern native, and of the Israelite in particular, the Jew would be almost a model citizen. One thing will strike the visitor to any Jewish colony – whether it be in Whitechapel or in Birmingham, or that 'delightful' district of Leeds, the Leylands – and that is the number of children possessed by each family. The streets swarm with little members of the 'Chosen People' to an extent which will simply surprise him.[43]

The assumption that an inferior and uncivilised race was multiplying and perpetuating Leeds's slum districts triggered fears that Britain's urban Anglo-Saxon stock would be irreparably damaged.[44]

The highly concentrated and disease-blighted Jewish district of Leeds produced a hostile reaction from the native populace more intense than in other towns and cities.[45] Furthermore, a significant number of the new Eastern European Jewish immigrants had adopted radical Left-wing politics by the Edwardian period. Joe Buckman argues that Leeds Jewish working-class tailors, influenced by revolutionary ferment in Russia, were particularly driven by socialism. The fresh immigration of Jews from Eastern Europe into late nineteenth-century Leeds, then, provoked unease among a number of social groups in the town. The indigenous working-class trade unions blamed the Jewish sweatshops for undercutting legitimate businesses, while the bourgeois civic elite worried that the new Jewish immigrants could undermine both the political stability and the 'healthy stock' of the nation.[46] To some extent, the established Anglicised Jewish middle class shared these concerns since the radicalism of Eastern European immigrants threatened to weaken their own social and political standing in Leeds.[47] Given these widespread anxieties, the civic authorities looked to the empire to engender a successful social and political assimilation of the Eastern European Jew into English society.

Commenting on the development of Empire Day, the *Yorkshire Evening Post* noted that 'Leeds stands creditably prominent in this matter' as the city's Jewish schools had acted as 'pioneers of the movement'. The pupils of Darley and Leylands Council schools, who were almost entirely Jewish, received intensive instruction on the British Empire far earlier than their contemporaries in other Leeds Council schools. Prior to the Empire Day movement, the pupils of Leyland School received lessons on the empire and were instructed to write letters to children in the Australian, New Zealand, Indian, South African and Canadian colonies. The lessons were designed to cultivate 'loyal and dutiful citizens and true patriots' and 'foster friendship and true understanding between children of the colonies and the mother country'.[48] There was a particular emphasis on race as the Jewish children were instructed that the Anglo-Saxon race possessed 'firmness of ambition, self sacrifice and adventure'.[49] Likewise on Empire Day in 1905, the scholars of Darley Street School assembled to hear an address from the headmaster 'on the Empire and the duty of Jewish children to England'. The headmaster also stressed that the children should appreciate the religious tolerance that the Englishman afforded to them, after which patriotic songs were sung. Thus, in both schools, values that Jewish children should aspire to were cast as racial characteristics of the Anglo-Saxon race. Only by adopting the values of loyalty, duty and patriotism to their adopted country and empire could the Jewish community successfully emulate the English race and assimilate into British society.[50] In supporting the Empire Day movement, the *Yorkshire Evening Post* also reminded readers that it was the innate qualities of the Anglo-Saxon race that were the driving force behind imperial successes. The editor noted that 'the Empire is at once the monument and the living expression of the dauntless courage, the dauntless determination, and the adventuress spirit of the Anglo-Saxon race'.[51]

While the civic elites were preoccupied with the two Jewish schools, the remaining Council schools in Leeds do not appear to have celebrated Empire Day during the early stages of the movement. For example, in 1907, the *Yorkshire Evening Post* noted that Empire Day had 'slipped by practically unnoticed in Leeds', adding that only the two Jewish schools celebrated the event 'by decorating the rooms with Union Jacks' and by 'organising patriotic tableaux'.[52] In the non-Jewish Council school log books surveyed, the first account of Empire Day appears in St Peter's Square Council School in 1916. This is not to claim that Empire Day was not marked in Council schools from 1909, but it was undoubtedly significant that the event did not merit an entry until the First World War. Such was the low-key nature of Empire Day in 1908 that the *Yorkshire Evening Post* decided to investigate whether the working-class man in Leeds was conversant with the event. The first stop for the intrepid reporter was a local public house where he overheard a conversation in which one man consistently misunderstood the purpose of Empire Day. After he mistook it for the opening of a pub or a special 'do' at the Empire Theatre, his friend authoritatively informed him that 'this' ere Empire Day means at we've to celebrate British Empire. Yo knaw t' sun nivver set on it, but there's a danger o' t' foreigner forgettin it.' To the dismay of the journalist, the belief that Empire Day was solely for the 'foreigner' was reinforced at his next port of call, the local barber shop. Believing the city centre barber shop to be the 'original news-vending' profession of local intelligence and gossip, the journalist proudly announced that Empire Day was tomorrow. To the astonishment of the journalist, the barber replied that 'I've nivver heard tell of it'. After the journalist pointed the barber to the item in the local press on the celebration at the Leylands school, he replied, 'yes I did see it, but I thought it was just a bit of a "do" ' at the Jews were havin on their own'. The journalist later noted despairingly that he was 'sufficient of a patriot to remark that we couldn't leave these things entirely to the stranger within the gates though, to judge by the general attitude of the Gentiles, there seemed every likelihood of that being the only way'. After leaving the barber's, the journalist's task of raising awareness of Empire Day did not get any easier. One working-class man inquired whether it would be a good 'kick-up' like the Mafeking do, though he wasn't keen on the flag waving as that was more of a Cockney habit. An Irish man interviewed wanted nothing to do with the celebration and stated, 'I leave that kind o' thing to the children of Israel. There's no Empire that belongs to the ould country. The only thing th' Irishman does is to fight for it, and a man that's busy fightin' hasn't time to spare for shoutin' or flag-wavin'.' To round off the journalist's thoroughly dispiriting day, he then interrogated a businessman who had heard of it but was nonetheless not the least bit interested in it.[53] These dialogues and interviews of various characters in Leeds do reveal a general view that Empire Day was an exercise in providing the Jewish community with an imperial education. Indeed, the Council's preoccupation with Jewish schools suggests that Empire Day was seen as a way of inculcating not only the values of loyalty and patriotism but also the perceived character traits of the Anglo-Saxon race.

The First World War, however, saw Empire Day become a more uniform and established event in all three communities. It was one thing to propagate Empire Day to help address civic issues and another when the nation and empire was at stake in the midst of a world war. Whereas local issues had filtered through and shaped the delivery and content of Empire Day celebrations prior to 1914, wartime conditions made local organisers and schools more receptive to the values of duty, patriotism and self-sacrifice for the sake of nation and empire. Indeed, after over ten years of campaigning, Meath was finally successful in having Empire Day officially recognised by the government in 1916. Flags were now to be flown from government buildings, and schools were granted an official holiday to celebrate the day. In a letter to *The Times*, Meath hoped that 'the few remaining schools that hesitated to mark the day would fall into line with the great majority in the inculcation of patriotic feeling amongst the children committed to their care'.[54] Official recognition of Empire Day did have the affect of formalising the teaching of empire to children in the schools surveyed. For example in 1916, Coventry schools rearranged their timetables to incorporate more instruction on imperial duties, while in Leeds Empire Day activities were noted in some school log books for the first time.[55] Likewise in the same year, the headmaster of All Saints Portsea School, began to address the school on the responsibilities that went with empire and the duty of self-sacrifice. While St Luke's School in Portsmouth had been early enthusiasts, their Empire Day format was enhanced in 1916 so the children could hear a 'stirring speech' by the Reverend B.S. Aldwell on the meaning of empire and the self-sacrifice it demanded. These speeches must have been all the more powerful since these schools relayed to their scholars the roll call of old boys who had been killed throughout the war.[56] Although Meath's original values of duty and self-sacrifice had become the hallmark of Empire Day during the First World War, the event itself had become more sombre.

MacKenzie, however, has argued that it would be a mistake to assume that the First World War put an end to imperial propagation. He has shown that new forms of cultural dissemination assisted the development of a 'moral' notion of empire that was more subtle and shorn of Edwardian arrogance and aggression.[57] Thus, while the intelligentsia increasingly became critical of imperialism, Empire Day continued to flourish during the interwar period albeit in a different socio-economic setting. While empire was perceived as the antidote to a perceived social and biological decline during the Edwardian period, the interwar era saw empire cast as the solution to Britain's economic downturn. The Empire Marketing Board emphasised the economic advantages of the Empire and celebrated the range of exotic goods that could be drawn from the colonies. Established by the Colonial Secretary Leo Amery in 1926, the Board's chief aims were to promote within the trading empire and convince consumers to buy goods produced in the empire.[58] This recasting of imperial objectives was summed up by one journalist who declared that 'our entire economic future is bound up with Empire' and accordingly recommended that the old imperial plan be dropped in favour of 'Empire economics'.[59]

Celebrating empire in the 1920s: the Wembley Exhibition of 1924 and Empire Day

The commercial side of empire, which had always been present in the numerous imperial exhibitions from the 1880s, was showcased in the most extravagant fashion in the Wembley Empire Exhibition of 1924. The exhibition was the greatest, most lavish and most visited of its kind.[60] It encapsulated a growing view that the time was ripe to exploit the British Empire's commercial potential in a spirit of co-operation and tolerance. As one observer remarked, 'Wembley to-day stands as the embodiment of that individual enterprise and faith', adding 'it too stands for the spirit of freedom and tolerance'.[61] Cast as embodying the new spirit of commercialism and international understanding, the exhibition undoubtedly reinvigorated the imperial cause. In addition, it breathed new life into Empire Day since schools from across the country were encouraged to visit Wembley to commemorate the day.[62]

Commenting on the impact of the 1924 Empire Exhibition on the Empire Day movement, the *Midland Daily Telegraph* believed that

> Saturday saw the coming-of-age of Empire Day, and there could not have been a more memorable celebration of that fact. Those who in 1903 worked so well and effectively for the inauguration of this movement could not have foreseen how wonderfully the 21st Anniversary of its being would be observed.[63]

In a rare instance of consensus, historians have been at one in noting the socio-political significance, grand scale and expense of the British

Empire Exhibition at Wembley. Whereas the 1851 Great Exhibition attracted six million visitors and the Colonial and Indian Exhibition of 1886 5.5 million, the 1924–25 Wembley Exhibition received 27 million visitors.[64] MacKenzie described it as the largest and most visited exhibition and speculated that it had the most impact on popular culture, while Richards has described Wembley as the 'culminating exhibition of Empire'.[65] Even those historians who have played down the importance of imperialism in British society have acknowledged the scale and impact of the 1924 Exhibition. Porter has described Wembley as 'the most spectacular example of this [imperial] propaganda'. Likewise Rose concedes that 'reading the memoirs of those who attended, one cannot but help conclude that these [exhibitions] were by far the most persuasive vehicles of imperialist propaganda'. School lessons, he concluded, produced only the haziest memories of empire, but 'once the discussion turns to Wembley, it jumps into sharp and memorable focus'.[66] Certainly, one cannot be but impressed with the huge scale of this publicly and privately funded exhibition. Over a 216 acre site stood Palaces of Industry, Engineering and Art, four conference halls, five restaurants, 28 cafés, churches, a football stadium, dance hall, gardens, a playground and an amusement park. There were 15 miles of roads and two new railway stations serving the exhibition. However, what set this exhibition apart from any other was promise that the visitor could experience any part of the empire without leaving British shores. Pavilions were constructed for the dominions and colonies so that the visitor could explore every corner of the empire.[67] Indeed, on opening the exhibition in front of 110,000 people, King George V declared that 'you see before you a complete and vivid representation of all your Empire. The Dominions, India, the colonies, the protectorates and mandated territories under your care, have joined together in the great task of presenting this picture of our Commonwealth of Nations.'[68] *The Times* described the re-creation of the empire under one roof as nothing less than a 'miracle', and explained how, after the King's speech, the colonial people made their way 'straight for the corner of Wembley that to them stood for their own land'.[69] It was estimated that there were no fewer than 78 'national or racial entities' represented. The British diplomat Sir Henry McMahon wrote that the exhibition 'will show civilisation in almost every stage, from the primitive tribal organisation of the African jungle to the intensive modern national organisation of Canada, Australia and New Zealand'. Thus while commercialism and the principle of colonial 'tolerance' were key driving forces behind the spectacle, racial hierarchies continued to shape the exhibitors' interpretation and presentation of empire in Wembley's pavilions.[70]

The exhibition was also a landmark in radio broadcasting and is a prime example of how new technologies during the interwar period brought the imperial message to towns and cities across the empire. The British Broadcasting Company (BBC), which was established in 1922 with a monopoly and financed through a licence, seized the opportunity to cover the event. The Company had evolved from negotiations between the Post Office, which was anxious to avoid chaotic and unregulated airwaves, and the radio manufacturers. John Reith, the first Director General, saw the BBC's role as educating the public in civil values and disseminating an understanding in public affairs.[71] The public's understanding of empire was very much part of Reith's broadcasting mission, and the 1924 Exhibition provided the first opportunity to cover a major imperial event. Indeed, Reith stated that broadcasting the opening ceremony was easily 'the biggest thing we have done'.[72] K.A. Wright, of the BBC, remarked that the broadcasting of the King's speech at Wembley 'has been an important milestone in the progress of science in this country'. The cultural impact on the transmission was not lost on him either, as he noted:

> It has been demonstrated how an event of vital importance, once seen and heard only by the necessarily limited number of people gathered together in the place of its setting, may now be brought simultaneously to the whole nation. There is absolutely no limit, other than that imposed by the number of receiving sets available.[73]

It also set a precedent for future years, and the Empire became a major theme in BBC broadcasts from the 1920s onwards. However, the nature of 'listening-in' to broadcasts altered fundamentally during the interwar years. Only by the late 1930s, when working-class families could afford radios, did listening to transmissions become a home-centred activity.[74] Since the launch of the exhibition coincided with the early years of broadcasting, the very act of listening to the King's speech was a public affair. The BBC's coverage of the opening of the exhibition was essentially the first attempt to broadcast a major ceremony to the nation, and, with few people owning radios, sponsorship was sought to help bring the transmission to the towns and cities of England. The costs of the installation of large speakers and of the broadcast publicity were met by Marconi and the *Daily Mail* respectively. The *Daily Mail* identified the 'most populous centres' of England to site large Marconi-built loudspeakers (affectionately called 'Uncle Herberts') in civic centres and parks.[75] After striking agreements with civic authorities, the *Daily Mail* listed 26 sites in London alone, plus a further 147 towns and cities that had been selected to receive the loudspeakers.[76] The *Daily Mail* successfully persuaded many civic leaders and employers to grant time off for their staff so that they could listen to the King's speech on the opening of the Wembley Exhibition. The exhibition's opening appears to have been broadcast without any technical difficulties as the *Daily Mail* pronounced the project a 'complete success', estimating that over ten million people listened-in. It added that

> in many towns public bodies adjourned their membership to take advantage of the facilities for listening to the King provided by the *Daily Mail* loud speakers. At Cambridge a Government inquiry suspended a sitting. At Coventry the Board of Guardians postponed a debate on the McKenna duties and at Gateshead the Police court was adjourned.[77]

The national and local press covered the live broadcast in depth, and focused both on the technological breakthrough and on the expectant crowd's response to this new form of communication. Indeed, social commentators eagerly observed the public reaction to outside broadcasts and were quick to recognise the power of radio transmission. In Coventry, the *Midland Daily Telegraph* described in detail how the loudspeakers were assembled on Grey Friars Green. Then, at the moment the King was about to speak, 'suddenly from Uncle Herbert's throat came a groan followed by a shriek' and the speech began. In Leeds, speakers were placed in Victoria Square, and in Portsmouth on South Parade Pier. All three communities attracted crowds of up to three thousand people to listen-in to the broadcast.[78] There was a fairly uniform response to the broadcast from the crowds in Portsmouth, Coventry and Leeds which resembled the *Daily Mail*'s assessment of transmission:

> the unique demonstration of the advancement of wireless science was marked by the sense of 'realness' which characterised the proceedings everywhere. Heads were bared, people stood to attention when the band played the National Anthem at Wembley many miles away . . . people bowed their heads and in some cases knelt for the prayer by the Bishop of London and the Lord's Prayer was repeated by thousands as it was recited in the stadium.[79]

There can be little doubt that the live broadcasts, sponsored by Marconi and *Daily Mail*, raised interest in both the Empire Exhibition and the new technology of radio transmission. The local press in all three localities devoted extensive coverage to the opening ceremony, radio transmissions and travel information for those keen to visit. Furthermore, the daily local press produced reviews and guides to the event aimed at their core working-class readership. These reviews stand in striking contrast to the national press's coverage, which focused on the exotic colonial representations. The national press encouraged the reader to imagine that the exhibition would transport the visitor to glamorous and mysterious corners of the Empire. *The Times*, in depicting the Indian court, wondered whether

> A magician had changed the mosque into a market place. Every court was a blaze of colour; silks tapestries, carpets, precious metals, and ivories all combined to give Oriental splendour to the stalls. Indians in quaint costumes of every colour exhibited their wares to thousands of eager sightseers: the pavilion had, in fact, become a busy corner of an Eastern city.[80]

Similarly, a *Saturday Review* reporter described how 'I set course for the Gold Coast, arriving beneath the sun-baked walls as the first drops of rain fell from a leaden sky' where he witnessed the 'natives engaged in their simple crafts'.[81] The local press's review of the exhibition focused less on the exotic corners of the Empire and instead celebrated their town or city's contribution to the imperial project. For example, after noting that the exhibition would help bond the British people to their empire, the *Midland Daily Telegraph* declared that 'Coventry has its noteworthy part. In the exhibit of the motor and cycle section in the Palace of Engineering some thirty firms of this city are represented' and 'demonstrate the skill of our local artisans forming a goodly proportion of what is a veritable miniature motor show'.[82] After visiting Wembley one journalist was so impressed with the Coventry exhibits that he proclaimed that 'Coventry people are proud that their city ranks high among the great and famous cities of the Empire'.[83] The exhibition also gave the Coventry motor industry an opportunity to enhance its political campaign against the repeal of the McKenna duties which would have removed a tariff on imported components and cars.[84] For the local press, the motor industry's exhibition at Wembley was tangible proof of Coventry's craftsmanship and a reminder of what might be lost if the tariff was abolished.[85] Similarly, the *Evening News* contrived to see the exhibition as much a celebration of Portsmouth as it was of the Empire. The newspaper's guide to the exhibition, which was entitled 'The Wonders of Wembley: Viewed through Portsmouth Glasses', saved its most elaborate depiction of the site for 'the Navy show':

> Of particular interest to Portsmouth will be his Majesty's Government Building which illustrates the various functions of the Home. The Navy, Army and Air Force make their real display in the building. Every visitor from Portsmouth should make a point of visiting the Admiralty Theatre here. The Admiralty has reproduced the history of the Navy for a thousand years by means of models – and very fine models too on a remarkable water stage.[86]

The *Evening News* leader laid claim for Portsmouth's special place in the imperial system by asserting that the Empire's continued prosperity depended upon the strength of Britain's navy and its bases in Portsmouth. The *Evening News* also pressed home a political message too, joining with the Navy League in calling for sufficient naval funding 'for fulfilment of this great purpose'.[87] The coverage of the Empire Exhibition in Leeds proved no exception. The *Leeds Mercury* failed to describe the exhibition in any depth apart from Leeds's contribution to the event. The reporter confidently predicted that 'the woollen and allied textile exhibit will undoubtedly prove one of the greatest attractions at Wembley. It far surpasses both in character and extent anything which has been hitherto attempted.'[88] The rich array of 'differing races of the empire, working on ancient crafts in their natural habitat' that had so interested the national media was ignored by the *Leeds Mercury*. Instead, the newspaper preferred to describe the working Yorkshire looms 'at which Yorkshire lasses will be seen producing the kinds of goods displayed in the parlour'. The reporter concluded that the 'the exhibition will come as a striking revelation to most people outside Yorkshire, few of whom have any conception of the immense range of textile products now turned out'.[89]

As we have seen, in terms of visitor numbers the exhibition was an undoubted success. However, we can never be certain of the exhibition's impact on communities and the motivation that lay behind visitors' excursions to Wembley. For the people of Portsmouth, Coventry and Leeds, the Empire Exhibition was presented to them through a local gaze. The local press placed their own community as a significant player in the exhibition and helped, in the case of Coventry and Portsmouth, to enhance local political campaigns. The live broadcasts of the exhibition reinforced the sense of the local since public transmissions were organised and presided over by town leaders and set in significant civic landmarks such as Leeds's Victoria Square. Accordingly, the exhibition organisers' official objectives of creating a miniature empire that would bond the British with their colonial family was filtered through a local discourse. The fusion of local and national patriotism, the extensive coverage in the press and the excitement of a day trip to the exhibition may well have struck a chord with working-class visitors. Coventry factories and Portsmouth's dockyard organised successful day trips first and foremost to celebrate their own unique contribution to the empire. Exploration of the wider empire appeared to be almost an afterthought. While the sheer distance from Leeds to London largely prohibited the day tripper, the city joined with Coventry and Portsmouth in sending schoolchildren to the exhibition.[90] In a sober reflection on Wembley, the author Edward Shanks wrote in 1925 that there was no doubt that the British Empire Exhibition had ultimately failed. Visitors, he pointed out 'tend to crowd into the Amusement Park and give the Exhibition itself a wide berth'. To compound the problem, the amusement park did little to educate or elevate visitors' engagement with empire and instead indulged in popular vulgarity. He concluded that 'the Amusement Park ought not to be more than a concomitant. The Exhibition proper should be of genuine interest, and apparently it is not'.[91] There was, then, a lingering suspicion that the organisers' attempt to awaken the English citizen's curiosity about empire was falling wide of the mark. Given the opportunity to become intrepid explorers of a miniature empire, working-class visitors appear to have favoured instead a 'pleasure seeking' day trip.

Despite these reservations, the press generally had no doubt about the exhibition's impact on the empire movement and British citizens. While the *Midland Daily Telegraph* editor noted little outward observance of Empire Day in the city, 'Coventry none the less shared in the enthusiasm of pride and patriotism breathing in the heart of Britishers and people of British origin the world over'.[92] On Empire Day in 1924, the editor noted that many people left the city early in the morning for Wembley and positioned reporters on the station platform to capture the public's reaction to the exhibition. One enthusiastic day tripper was reported as proclaiming, 'I went to the Exhibition a Communist and came out an imperialist'. This tale of how the wonders of Wembley fostered a dramatic political conversion circulated in varying forms across the national and local press. The *Evening News* reported that someone in the stadium uttered the same phrase, while the *Daily Express* thought that the King's speech was so effective that it was enough to 'convert all the Communists of the Empire' adding that whereas Communism represented 'fractional chaos' the empire represents 'fraternity and unity'.[93] Thus while undoubtedly the exhibition provided a platform for Empire Day, the spectre of Communism gave imperialists an unremitting drive to promote the Empire Day Movement. The national and local press's reference to the threat of Communism revealed how the old prewar anxieties of national inefficiency had given way to new political worries. Empire, however, remained Britain's salvation. The employment of Empire Day to contest Communism inevitably politicised the movement to a greater degree than in the prewar era. It is the Empire Day Movement's more overt shift to the political arena that we explore in the following section.

Empire Day in the 1930s

For committed imperialists, the interwar years proved an unsettling time. Britain had called upon its empire for men during the First World War and now, after demonstrating a dutiful self-sacrifice, the Empire was demanding greater independence. The Irish Free State was established in 1922, Indian nationalists achieved limited political reforms, and the White Dominions were granted greater autonomy. In addition to this chipping away of imperial authority was a concern from those on the political Right that Communist cells were successfully undermining the British Empire from within.[94] The British Empire Union (BEU), established in 1915, saw Empire Day as a movement that could help eradicate the Communist scourge, especially from the state education sector. The movement was convinced that socialist and Communist teachers had infiltrated elementary schools and mounted campaigns to identify and dismiss Left-wing teachers. From the First World War, the BEU produced between thirty and forty thousand Empire Day medals a year for schoolchildren, though the imperial message was sometimes lost beneath ferocious attacks on the political Left.[95] In May 1924, Reginald Wilson, the BEU's General Secretary, warned readers of the *Saturday Review* that the Young Communist League had formed groups in elementary schools to encourage children to resist the patriotic teaching of Empire Day. According to Wilson, it was the BEU's duty to alert parents, teachers and the clergy 'to the spread of this revolutionary movement among the young'.[96] The Primrose League shared the BEU's concerns and believed that attacks on Empire Day were conspired directly from Moscow. In 1924, the Primrose League Secretary, Reginald Bennett, proclaimed that 'these foul doctrines of Moscow's criminal Government are financed by the Communist International'. He highlighted the Young Communist League's attack on Empire Day and its appeal to school children to 'tell your school mates the truth about the British Empire and protest against its celebration in school'.[97] The belief that socialists were 'nursing assiduously the teaching profession' became firmly entrenched within Right-wing circles during the interwar period.[98] As a result, Empire Day events were carefully scrutinised since they had the potential to expose politically organised resistance to the celebration of empire. This section investigates a controversy over Empire Day that broke out in Coventry in 1932 after a teacher refused to participate in an imperial pageant. The case study is important in two respects. First, it exposes how, by the 1930s, Empire Day had become a highly politicised issue that was beginning to split civic politics down party lines. Moreover, the dispute produced significant local and national interest which generated widespread support for the teacher from the teaching profession. This support reveals how, thirty years after Empire Day's inception, significant numbers of teachers were quietly recasting Meath's original imperial message to align it with their own personal concept of empire.

In May 1932, the Coventry Education Committee circulated its annual request for the city's elementary schools to partake in Empire Day celebrations. The circular allowed schools to arrange the day in the manner they saw fit. The Red Lane Elementary School elected to arrange a pageant and the singing of 'Land and Hope and Glory'. For Beryl Aylward, a young teacher in the school, the event slipped into jingoism and she requested that she should take no part in the celebrations as they contravened her Quaker beliefs.[99] The Red Lane headmistress gave her the option to attend in a non-participatory capacity, but Aylward rejected this on the grounds that 'if I was there, I was taking part in the celebrations, and, as far as anyone else could tell, approving of them'.[100] The headmistress referred her to the Coventry Education Committee, which turned down her request, stating that since she was a servant of the Committee she had no option but to attend the celebrations.[101] After failing to participate, Aylward was summoned by the Committee for an explanation. In her statement to the Committee, Aylward explained that she had been a committed Quaker all her life and her beliefs had revealed the horror of war and the pressing needs of world peace and friendship between nations. These views had been strengthened by her time at Birmingham University where she mixed with international students, an experience that confirmed to her the value of international friendship and co-operation. She continued:

> In England, patriotism has been in the past, and apparently still is, encouraged by pageants showing the greatness of the British Empire and by the singing of such songs as 'Rule Britannia' and 'Land of Hope and Glory'. The whole idea of Empire Day celebrations of this kind is entirely opposed to my up-bringing. I regard such celebrations as encouraging among school-children a belief that Great Britain is the greatest and most important power in the world. Even if it is true, this kind of false pride does not help the spirit of international peace and good-will.[102]

Aylward's statement did little to persuade the Committee and she was dismissed from her post. The decision provoked a national outcry and shattered any illusion that Empire Day was a symbol of political consensus as the controversy exposed the underlying political tensions that had been growing since the 1920s. In a stormy meeting, the City Council voted by two votes for the Education Committee to overturn its original decision and reinstate Aylward. Labour councillors noted that the matter had become of 'nation-wide' importance because of the principles involved and called for the discussion to stay clear of political controversy. This appeal fell on deaf ears as the debate became intensely political and the voting pattern followed party lines, with the Labour councillors demanding Aylward's reinstatement. In an interview with the *Birmingham Post*, the Conservative Mayor, Vincent Wyles, fumed:

> What was the use of being hypocritical and talking about not being a political question, when there was only one political party that had sent resolutions to the Committee, that being the Labour Party? He had received scurrilous and offensive letters, evidently written by people who desired to see the British Empire down and out – people who had no love for their own country but for other countries.[103]

The debate on Empire Day provoked such heated discussion in the Council chamber and the local press that the Mayor received letters stating that he 'ought to be publicly assassinated'.[104] Conservative members of the Council became convinced that religious beliefs were a cover for Aylward's alleged political sympathies with the Left. The Conservative Councillor Payne believed 'that there is something more sinister' than conscientious objection and that there 'is an underlying Socialist element'.[105] Likewise Alderman Lee agreed with his Conservative colleague and believed that she was in league with socialist anti-imperialists who campaigned for the dismantling of the empire. Much was made of Aylward's time at Birmingham University and particularly of her contact with Indian students. According to Lee, fraternising with Indian students had driven her to reject Empire Day and 'undoubtedly there was something more than Quakerism at the back of this'.[106] There may well have been a grain of truth in these allegations since both Aylward and her father seemed to be on first-name terms with leading Coventry socialists and received letters of support from members of the Labour Party and small socialist groups. George Hodgkinson, a Labour local councillor, gave Beryl Aylward support and advice on how to deal with the Education Committee and leading Conservative members on it. Moreover her father Jack received a letter of support from W.A. Stokes, a Communist and leader of the Workers Anti-War Movement, congratulating her on her 'courageous stand' and informing him of a demonstration in Coventry to campaign for his daughter's reinstatement.[107] Indeed, it was reported in *The Worker*, a Communist newspaper, that Stokes's movement had secured over two thousand signatures in support of the reinstatement campaign. The report also accused leading Labour councillors of hypocrisy for supporting both the reinstatement of Aylward and the Empire Day celebrations in general.[108] Over June 1932, the vast majority of letters published in the *Midland Daily Telegraph* supported Aylward and called for her reinstatement. Moreover, of these supportive letters most congratulated Aylward on her anti-imperial position rather than expressing sympathy for her religious conscience. For example, one correspondent called for children to be withdrawn from schools during Empire Day adding that 'we have to dig deeper to get at the roots of a decaying system that is crucifying the world on the cross of capitalistic imperialism'.[109] The *Midland Daily Telegraph* noted that 'the teacher in question stated that she acted on religious grounds, yet the furore which her dismissal has aroused has apparently caused more annoyance to members of the various Socialist party groups than to religious bodies'.[110] The national press was soon to identify the significance of a teacher's refusal to participate in Empire Day and the political implications that would follow. Both *The Times* and the *Manchester Guardian* ran stories, with the latter particularly critical of Coventry's Education Committee's decision of dismissing Alyward.[111] The Empire Day dispute certainly ignited a great deal more political rather than religious controversy and perhaps demonstrates how imperialism had become a political tinder box by the 1930s. The dispute and political climate of the 1930s had placed greater scrutiny on *how* teachers taught Empire Day and, for the imperialists, whether Meath's original message had become diluted. The interwar classroom remains largely opaque for historians, with only school log books shedding light on the topics taught to students. However, the letters of support for Aylward from those in the teaching profession provide an insight into how some teachers recast the imperial message to sit comfortably with their own conscience.

The National Union of Teachers did not offer support to Aylward, noting that by refusing to teach Empire Day she had broken the terms of her contract. Instead Aylward received significant support from teachers across the country who had wrestled with similar dilemmas. The correspondence reveals that, while Education Committees instructed Council schools to observe Empire Day, the tone of the celebration was set by the headmaster or headmistress. For example, one teacher from Surrey wrote:

> You will be interested perhaps knowing that a headmaster of one of our largest Elementary Schools deviated from the usual practice on Empire Day, and being weary of 'flag waving', he took as the text of his address to the boys, the subject of service, through the lives of those missionaries especially David Livingstone.[112]

One teacher recalled that, while working in a Council school in Bedford, he too had taken a stand against Empire Day in 1914. He informed Aylward that he had escaped punishment and 'I am now a Headmaster and keep Empire Day regularly but my authority imposes no special form. I invariably talk about the League of Nations in relation to the British Commonwealth of Nations'.[113] The headmaster's decision to allow teachers a considerable degree of flexibility when observing Empire Day was a policy that appears to have operated in elementary schools elsewhere. Despite being governed by the same Education Committee, one Coventry teacher noted that her head-teacher had taken a more relaxed stance to Empire Day than her counterpart in Aylward's Red Lane School. She wrote 'I was fortunate in this respect as each individual teacher was left to take the celebra-tions in her own class room as she thought best . . . Each nation is suffering so intensely from the malady of national self-sufficiency and isolation that it is essential to get a wider spirit in our class-rooms.'[114] Although Coventry Council refused to reverse its decision, Alyward did secure a teaching post soon after her dismissal in nearby Lutter-worth.[115] The Aylward dismissal exposed the extent to which Empire Day had become a more politicised event and reflected the contempo-rary debates of the interwar period. On one level, Right-wing move-ments and imperialists became anxious that Empire Day had become subjected to challenges by Communist cells eager to convert young minds to their cause. On another level, the domestic and international contexts of the 1930s gave liberal teachers greater scope for teaching more broadly than the British Empire and instead focus on the League of Nations and peacekeeping generally.

Conclusion

The history of Empire Day from its inception in 1903 to the outbreak of war provides an interesting case study on the complexities of endea-vouring to transmit a uniform celebration of empire across the country. Despite its creation through a single national movement led by Lord Meath, local contexts informed and shaped the character and transmis-sion of Empire Day. For example, the celebration in Coventry and Leeds was seized upon by the civic authorities to help resolve per-ceived social problems in their respective cities. In the midst of a national debate to fund the navy, Portsmouth too used Empire Day to further the cause of boosting work in its dockyard. Thus, even with national broadcasts that celebrated the opening of the 1924 Exhibition, the venues used and reports of broadcasts introduced important local dimensions that subtlety changed the meaning of empire for those reading or listening-in. However, not only did local contexts manipu-late Empire Day but also the changing political scene meant that imperialism became a more controversial and politicised phenomenon during the interwar period. The suspicion that the teacher, who was the key to a successful dissemination of the imperial values, diluted

Meath's original message in favour of international conciliation appears well founded. To assume that the creation and Empire Day's impressive adoption by schools in the first quarter of the twentieth century represents a successful inculcation of imperial values underestimates the importance of *how* the event was diffused through differing civic authorities and the teaching profession before reaching the pupil in the classroom. Indeed, the difficulty of measuring the impact of overtly imperial events upon the individual is explored in the final chapter on leisure and imperial societies between 1870 and 1939.

Notes

1 J.O. Springhall, 'Lord Meath, Youth and Empire', *Journal of Contemporary History*, 5, 4, 1970, p. 105.
2 Springhall, 'Lord Meath, Youth and Empire', p. 105.
3 J.M. MacKenzie, *Propaganda and Empire* (Manchester, Manchester University Press, 1984), pp. 232–3.
4 A. Bloomfield, 'Drill and Dance as Symbols of Imperialism', in J.A. Mangan (ed.), *Making Imperial Mentalities* (Manchester, Manchester University Press, 1990), pp. 83–4.
5 B.J. Lammers, ' "The Citizens of the Future": Educating the Children of the Jewish East End, *c*. 1885–1939', *Twentieth Century British History*, 19, 4, 2008, p. 417.
6 A. Thompson, *The Empire Strikes Back? The Impact of Imperialism on Britain from the Mid-nineteenth Century* (Harlow, Longman, 2005), pp. 120, 122.
7 J. English, 'Empire Day in Britain, 1904–1958', *Historical Journal*, 49, 1, 2006, pp. 248, 275.
8 B. Porter, *The Absent-minded Imperialists. Empire, Society, and Culture in Britain* (Oxford, Oxford University Press, 2004, 2006 edn), p. 210.
9 J. Rose, *The Intellectual Life of the British Working Classes* (New Haven, Yale University Press, 2001), p. 338.
10 MacKenzie, *Propaganda and Empire*, p. 232.
11 Thompson, *The Empire Strikes Back?*, p. 118.
12 MacKenzie, *Propaganda and Empire*, pp. 232–3.
13 Springhall, 'Lord Meath, Youth and Empire', p. 107.
14 Porter, *The Absent-minded Imperialists*, pp. 270–1.
15 MacKenzie, *Propaganda and Empire*, p. 233.
16 Earl of Meath, *Brabazon Potpourri* (London, Hutchinson & Co., 1928), p. 99.
17 *Hampshire Telegraph*, 30 July 1926.
18 *The Times*, 24 May 1909.
19 *Portsmouth Times*, 24 May 1913.
20 Portsmouth City Archives (hereafter PCA), SA/CC/DS/39/3/A/2, 'St Luke's School log book 1901–1919', 24 May 1906.
21 *Evening News*, 18 May 1908.
22 *Evening News*, 18 May 1908.
23 *Evening News*, 19 May 1908.
24 PCA, AS/CC/DS/26/36/1/A/2, 'Portsea Infant School log book 1905–1929', 24 May 1908.
25 *Portsmouth Times*, 28 May 1910, 27 May 1911, 25 May 1912, 24 May 1913.
26 For example, the local press such as the *Evening News* and *Hampshire Telegraph* carried speeches by Lord Meath linking the Empire Day with citizenship and duty. See *Evening News*, 21 May 1908.

27 *Evening News*, 22 May 1909.
28 *Evening News*, 13 May 1909.
29 *Evening News*, 22 May 1908.
30 *Evening News*, 7 May 1909.
31 *Evening News*, 7 May 1909.
32 *Midland Daily Telegraph*, 24 May 1907.
33 *Midland Daily Telegraph*, 22 May 1908.
34 A survey of the Coventry Council and Voluntary School log books reveals that there was a co-ordinated programme for Empire Day in May 1909.
35 *Midland Daily Telegraph*, 28 May 1909.
36 *Coventry Herald*, 28 May 1909.
37 *Midland Daily Telegraph*, 24 May 1909.
38 B. Beaven, 'Shop-floor Culture in the Coventry Motor Industry, *c.* 1896–1920', in D. Thoms, L. Holden and T. Claydon (eds), *The Motor Car and Popular Culture in the Twentieth Century* (Ashgate, Aldershot, 1998).
39 B. Beaven and J. Griffiths, 'Urban elites, Socialists and notions of citizenship in an industrial boomtown. Coventry *c.* 1870–1914', *Labour History Review*, 69, 1, April 2004.
40 *Midland Daily Telegraph*, 24 May 1909.
41 *Leeds Mercury*, 11 June 1888.
42 Quoted in J. Buckman, *Immigrants and the Class Struggle. The Jewish Immigrants in Leeds, 1880–1914* (Manchester, Manchester University Press, 1983), pp. 48, 49.
43 *Leeds Mercury*, 8 September 1900.
44 The evidence from Leeds contrasts sharply with Lammers's interpretation of how the authorities perceived the Jewish community. See Lammers, ' "The Citizens of the Future" '.
45 Buckman, *Immigrants and the Class Struggle*, p. xi.
46 For example of a Trade Unionist's critique of Jewish sweat shops see *Leeds Mercury*, 1 May 1900.
47 Buckman, *Immigrants and the Class Struggle*, pp. 162–3.
48 *Yorkshire Evening Post*, 23 May 1907; 22 May 1908.
49 *Yorkshire Evening Post*, 22 May 1908; *Leeds and Yorkshire Mercury*, 25 May 1906.
50 Leeds City Archive (hereafter LCA), LC/ED17/4, 'Darley Street Council School log book 1898–1935', 24 May 1905; 24 May 1906.
51 *Yorkshire Evening Post*, 23 May 1908.
52 *Yorkshire Evening Post*, 24 May 1907.
53 *Yorkshire Evening Post*, 23 May 1908.
54 Meath, *Brabazon Potpourri*, p. 102.
55 For example, Coventry City Archive (hereafter CRO), CEE/log/20/1, 'Wheatley Street School log book to 1925', 24 May 1916, and LCA, LC/ED/62/2, 'St Peter's Square School Board Log Book', 24 May 1916; LCA, LC/ED/160/1/2, 'All Saints Church of England School', 24 May 1916.
56 PCA, SA/CC/DS/39/3/A/2, 'St Luke's School log book', 24 May 1917.
57 MacKenzie, *Propaganda and Empire*, p. 10.
58 MacKenzie, *Propaganda and Empire*, p. 23.
59 A. Harrison, 'The British Empire Exhibition, 1924', *English Review*, November 1922, p. 451.
60 MacKenzie, *Propaganda and Empire*, p. 108.
61 *Saturday Review*, 26 April 1934, p. 428.
62 See *Midland Daily Telegraph*, 24 May 1924; *Yorkshire Evening Post*, 24 April 1924.
63 *Midland Daily Telegraph*, 26 May 1924.
64 J. Richards, *Imperialism and Music. Britain 1876–1953* (Manchester, Manchester University Press, 2001), p. 177.
65 Richards, *Imperialism and Music*, p. 194.
66 Rose, *The Intellectual Life of the British Working Classes*, p. 349.

67 Richards, *Imperialism and Music*, p. 195.
68 Richards, *Imperialism and Music*, p. 195.
69 *The Times*, 24 April 1924.
70 H. McMahon, 'The Fellowship of the British Empire Exhibition', *English Review*, March 1924, pp. 403–4.
71 B. Beaven, *Leisure Citizenship and Working-class Leisure in Britain, 1850–1914* (Manchester, Manchester University Press, 2005), p. 201.
72 Quoted in Richards, *Imperialism and Music*, p. 169.
73 *The School Music Review*, 15 May, 1924, p. 360.
74 Beaven, *Leisure Citizenship and Working-class Leisure in Britain*, pp. 201–6.
75 *Daily Mail*, 23 April 1924.
76 *Daily Mail*, 19 April 1924.
77 *Daily Mail*, 24 April 1924.
78 *Midland Daily Telegraph; Yorkshire Evening Post; Evening News*, 24 April 1924.
79 *Daily Mail*, 24 April 1924.
80 *Times*, 24 April 1924.
81 *Saturday Review*, 17 May 1924, p. 502.
82 *Midland Daily Telegraph*, 23 April 1924.
83 *Midland Daily Telegraph*, 24 May 1924.
84 R. Church, *The Rise and Decline of the British Motor Industry* (Basingstoke, Macmillan Press, 1994), pp. 7, 9. During the interwar period the tariff was temporarily suspended in the year 1925.
85 The local press was dominated by the McKenna Duties repeal; see *Midland Daily Telegraph*, 19, 24–6 April 1924; *The Times*, 19, 24, 26 April 1924.
86 *Evening News*, 24 April 1924.
87 *Evening News*, 23 April 1924.
88 *Leeds Mercury*, 24 April 1924.
89 *Leeds Mercury*, 24 April 1924.
90 *Yorkshire Evening Post*, 24 May 1924.
91 *Saturday Review*, 11 July 1925.
92 *Midland Daily Telegraph*, 24 May 1924.
93 *Evening News*, 24 April 1924; *Daily Express*, 24 April 1924.
94 English, 'Empire Day in Britain', p. 263.
95 University of Warwick, Modern Record Centre, MSS 148/UCW/6/13/42/8, *British Empire Union*, pamphlet (approximately 1933).
96 *Saturday Review*, 17 May 1924, p. 509.
97 *Saturday Review*, 31 May 1924, p. 562.
98 *Saturday Review*, 24 May 1924, p. 534.
99 CRO, PA 1025/38/1/4/1, 'B. Aylward, Quaker Teacher', letter to Harwood, 11 May 1932.
100 CRO, PA 1025/38/1/4/1, 'B. Aylward, Quaker Teacher', Statement to the Sub-Committee, 30 May 1932.
101 CRO, PA 1025, 'B. Aylward, Quaker Teacher', Letter from Frank Harrod (Director of Education) to B. Aylward, 12 May 1932.
102 CRO, PA 1025/38/1/4/1, 'B. Aylward, Quaker Teacher', Statement to the Sub-Committee, 30 May 1932.
103 CRO, PA 1025/40/1/7, 'B. Aylward, Quaker Teacher', *Birmingham Post*, 14 July 1932.
104 CRO, PA 1025/40/1/9, 'B. Aylward, Quaker Teacher', *Reynolds News*, 17 July 1932.
105 CRO, PA 1025/40/4, 'B. Aylward, Quaker Teacher', newspaper cutting, no date or title.
106 *Coventry Herald*, 1 July 1932.
107 CRO, PA/1025/12/1, 'B. Aylward, Quaker Teacher', letter from W.A. Stokes.
108 *The Worker*, 27 June 1932.
109 *Midland Daily Telegraph*, 18 June 1932.
110 *Midland Daily Telegraph*, 18 June 1932.

111 *The Times*, 29 June, 22 July; *Manchester Guardian*, 21, 27, 29 June, 14, 23 July 1932.
112 CRO, PA 1025/10/1, 'B. Aylward, Quaker Teacher', letter of support from Mary Williamson, 16 June 1932.
113 CRO, PA 1025/21/1/1–3, 'B. Aylward, Quaker Teacher', letter of support from F.W. Parrott, Penrith.
114 CRO, PA 1025/6/1, 'B. Aylward, Quaker Teacher', letter of support from G. Jacobs, 10 June 1932.
115 CRO, PA 1025/41/1, 'Report of the Beryl Aylward Committee'.

CHAPTER SEVEN

Mass entertainment, popular culture and imperial societies, 1870–1939

Historians endeavouring to investigate popular engagement with empire have inevitably been drawn to the domain of leisure and recreation. The spectacular depiction of empire on stage and screen, with its colour, pomp and glory, provides historians with an insight into the excitement and interest that performances must have generated. The period between 1870 and 1939 saw tremendous advances in mass entertainment from the singing saloons in the 1860s to the Picture Palaces of the 1930s. Undoubtedly, empire was a genre of entertainment that successfully transferred from the stage to the silver screen, ensuring that filmgoers across the country would have been conversant with the epic imperial films of the 1930s. However, one cannot assume that through reading music hall lyrics or a film script we can identify what empire meant to the audience.[1] This chapter makes the case that entertainment was far from a static entity and that, on stage, performances would change as a result of audience interaction or adapt to the immediate political or social context. Indeed, the theatre or music hall often acted as a conduit for telegraphed news, particularly during an imperial crisis, which often heightened the excitement within a hall. Moreover, in offering a more nuanced approach on the relationship between the performance and the audience, we explore whether imperial sentiment expressed on stage was articulated on the streets during imperial celebrations. In adopting this approach it is argued that in both stage and cinema entertainment a local dimension was an important variant in exploring both the impact and dissemination of mass commercial leisure. Finally, we investigate how the popular entertainment of the late nineteenth century was employed to lure working-class men and women into imperial societies and movements. Indeed, the pattern of development and membership of imperial or anti-imperial movements provides an additional indicator to how working men and women spent their free time.

In 1900, the writer Andrew Wilson toured Britain's music halls and concluded that 'there is no disguising the fact that the music-hall is in its way a social factor of some importance. It represents an "amusement of the people" and in this light alone, its probable influence on social life, manners and morals, is worth studying.'[2] This astute assessment of a key component of popular culture came at the high-water mark of music hall popularity which had grown from the humble origins of the singing saloons and music recitals of the mid-nineteenth century.[3] At its height in 1900, music hall entertainment appeared to dovetail seamlessly with a civilian society that had become increasingly imperial and militarised after the onset of the Boer War.[4] Indeed, both contemporary commentators and subsequent historians have documented the rabid imperialism and jingoism that peppered music hall performances and have lamented the detrimental effects this had upon popular political discourse. The *Morning Post* in the 1880s believed that a combination of enlarging the franchise, popular entertainment and imperial military campaigns had transformed the political landscape. The newspaper declared that

> It is evident that the uneducated factors in the new electorate will be particularly alive to the impulse of the moment. In support of this we may quote the example furnished by what has ironically been called the Music Hall of Politics. During the excitement of 1878 it was abundantly evident that a keen and even combative patriotism pervaded the lower strata of society . . . In these two considerations lies, then, we believe, the key to the conduct of new elections.[5]

Contemporaries, then, were agreed that the music hall carried a significant influence over working people that swayed their political opinion. However, for these observers, the music hall was an alien environment in which they were often ignorant of the protocols between performer and the audience that had developed from the early singing saloons. Indeed, this section both surveys the differing genres staged in the theatre and music hall in Portsmouth, Coventry and Leeds and explores how current affairs and local contexts often shaped the style and content of performance.

The rapid increase in music hall venues in British provincial towns during the late nineteenth century presents the historian with a difficult task in quantifying the variety of entertainment on offer to the working-class Victorian. To gain some insight into the genres offered to the people of Portsmouth, Coventry and Leeds, a month's sample of entertainment was surveyed at ten-yearly intervals between 1870 and 1939. The month of March was selected since music hall programmes would not have been distorted by the Christmas festivities and the summer season in which music hall and theatre audiences tended to dwindle. Through a combination of advertised programmes and reviews, the entertainment was categorised into eight broad genres that included drama, comedy, military, musical and acts with an overtly imperial theme (see Appendix 2). Clearly, the newspaper sources available limit our insight into the dynamics between audience and performer and do not reveal the informal references to empire and imperialism that might have underpinned an act. Jonathan Schneer has shown that, while some music hall or theatrical titles did not contain overtly imperial sentiment, the acts may well have articulated them anyway.[6] Nevertheless, the survey affords an opportunity to identify general trends in the staging of entertainment that occurred in the three communities. Indeed, the survey reveals that audiences in Portsmouth, Coventry and Leeds were exposed to very similar patterns of entertainment that can be broadly categorised into three periods. The first period, 1870 to 1890, witnessed sporadic but spectacular imperial entertainments; the second a more explicit and consistent fusion of imperialism and amusement between 1890 and 1914; and third a less aggressive but revitalised narrative of empire from 1914 to 1939.

Theatre and music hall entertainment: the 'imperial spectacular', 1870–90

Between 1870 and 1890, comic drama, melodrama and music were the most staged forms of entertainment. These figures indicate that, in all three communities, this period witnessed a transition from the popular musical events to the music hall and the 'variety' form of entertainment that characterised it. Prior to the music hall's dominant position, working people could attend 'low theatre' to watch a melodrama or comedy or penny concerts performed by amateur civilian or military bands. The popular concerts in Portsmouth's working-class districts usually presented a wide musical range but invariably included a military band such as the String Band of the Royal Marines.[7] In Coventry, the newly formed Rifle Corps amateur band played to full houses in the 1860s while corporations in large towns and cities such as Manchester, Liverpool, Birmingham and Leeds organised successful organ recitals on Saturday afternoons charging 3d and 6d entrance fee.[8] One commentator, Curwen Spencer, noted in the 1880s that music was fast becoming a popular form of entertainment for urban dwellers as 'the subdivision of labour has made it [work] more monotonous, and has increased the appetite for recreation when work is done'. He observed two particular qualities that made music attractive to the working man. 'First, it can be enjoyed by tired people – it restores the balance to brain or limbs; second, it is social – whether in listening or performing, people are brought together, and thus one of the strongest and most universal instincts is satisfied.'[9] Spencer astutely noted that the same attractions that music had for the working man were embedded in the emerging music hall entertainment where 'music in these places takes its turn with ventriloquism, gymnastics and caricature of all kinds'.[10] Significantly, the drama, music and comedy performed during the earlier sampled period did not overtly convey any imperial issues or matters of empire generally. However, between 1880 and 1890, explicit imperial entertainment begins to appear in the sample and mirrors national trends in theatre and music hall. MacKenzie has argued that, by the late 1870s, 'empire had become its own melodrama', with impresarios striving to produce increasingly more sensational spectacles around an imperial war. Thus, after the 1879 Zulu War, several titles appear such as *The Zulu Chief* and *Cetewayo at Last*.[11] The shows that appear in the three towns typically centred on the re-creation of a recent imperial campaign and endeavoured to produce a spectacular event, casting large numbers of actors. For example in Portsmouth, Ginnett's Hippodrome and Circus staged the 'Afghan War or Fall of Cabul' only two years after the real conflict. The show was described as an 'entirely new Equestrian spectacle' and supported by over one hundred auxiliaries including a detachment of the 69th Regiment. Even within this celebration of empire, the show contained a separate variety element with comics, singers and gymnasts.[12] In 1880, Portsmouth audiences were treated to Zulu shows and the restaging of 'Rorke's Drift'. The *Hampshire Telegraph* described the show as 'certainly one of the most effective and successful displays which has ever been presented to the Portsmouth public' and had been received with 'utmost enthusiasm from crowded houses'. The newspaper's review captures the tone and imperial adventurism that the show endeavoured to generate:

> There are the bands of Zulus, who execute their war dance, and also go through a number of evolutions before attacking the camp at Rorke's Drift. The post is defended by a detachment of British Infantry, whose stubborn resistance kindles the enthusiasm of the spectators. But most exciting of all is the fight with colours. Lieut Melvill is represented on horse-back, endeavouring to save the ensign of the Regiment, being hotly pursued by a band of howling savages . . . then ensues a hand to hand conflict between Melvill and the Zulu hordes. The flag, often torn from his grasp, is however, finally gained possession of, and those enemies who had been harassing his flight being now placed *hors de combat*, the gallant officer wraps the flag around him and dies alongside his steed.[13]

[182]

The reviewer indicated that the soldiers' heroic resistance drew the audience into the spectacle with some enthusiasm and followed a formulaic plotline that stereotyped the show's combatants. The martyrdom of Lieutenant Melvill and the symbolic use of the torn Union Jack reminded the audience that a successful empire required duty, bravery and self-sacrifice. Characterising the Zulus as 'howling savages' afforded imperialism a moral authority, transforming the conflict into a mission to end barbarity and civilise the outer reaches of empire. While the show was staged in a working-class district of Portsmouth, the audiences appear to be mixed, with prices ranging from 3d to 6d. Indeed, a procession of important military figures attended, including the Commander-in-Chief of the Royal Navy.[14] The spectacle continued through the whole of January owing to 'popular demand', while another travelling Zulu show entertained large Portsmouth audiences in September of the same year. In Leeds, a Zulu show was brought to the town by a veteran of the 1879 conflict. The former British soldier had become a 'showman' and 'publicly exhibited' a troupe of Zulus who performed 'national dances, hunting and war songs'.[15] In this show there was less emphasis on recreating an epic imperial war and instead the audience was invited to observe the Zulus as 'noble savages' and exotic exhibits transported to Leeds from a far-flung corner of the Empire. The reviewer noted that 'the women appear coarser in feature as well as stouter in figure than the men; but are all remarkable for symmetry of form and grace and agility of movement'.[16] While Zulus were respected for their noble fighting skills and at the same time condemned as savages, other peoples of the empire were cast in the theatres and music hall as comic figures. In Coventry, audiences flocked to watch a Pygmy tribe, which prompted a local reporter to remark that Swift's 'dream of Lilliput had been realised' and that 'they look more like a troupe of animated dolls than anything else'. In contrast with the dangerous Zulu tribes, the Pygmies were presented as a comic curiosity of the Empire since 'they have more than the average portion of spirits and joviality which nature deals out to her freaks of fancy'.[17] However, when it is considered against the variety of entertainment on offer between 1870 and 1890, audiences were not saturated with overly imperial propaganda in theatres and music halls. The most frequently recorded genres – music, melodrama and comedy – had traditionally been favoured by working-class audiences in the earlier part of the century.[18] However, as we have seen, the 1880s did witness the emergence of a new type of entertainment that was both spectacular and explicitly imperial. Press reports indicate that the sheer scale of the re-enactments of imperial wars, the encouragement of audience participation and the extravagant casting of 'real' Zulus and soldiers did not fail to impress the audiences. Thus, while overt imperial amusement was not a daily or weekly occurrence, the arrival in a town of an 'imperial spectacular' caused excitement in the local press and sold-out to packed houses.

The fusion of popular entertainment and empire, 1890–1914

From the 1890s, issues of empire and imperialism seep more consistently into popular entertainment in all three towns. The survey reveals that the 1890s and early twentieth century saw a gradual increase in imperial or military entertainment. In Portsmouth, for example, at least three different military or imperial dramas were shown in March 1890 alone. This trend perhaps peaked during the Boer War, which received blanket coverage from both the national and the provincial press. As Steve Attridge has argued, the Boer War was an important moment in popular entertainment as 'now the popular taste for the stage conventions of military plays, melodramas and spectators could be used to represent current events'.[19] Indeed, along with these traditional organs of news propagation, the theatre and music hall became significant conduits for current affairs, particularly important if the nation was undergoing a period of imperial excitement. Thus just as earlier imperial wars had initiated lavish re-enactments, the public's thirst for news from the South Africa encouraged a range of Boer War productions. MacKenzie has noted that the Boer War fashioned over a dozen plays including *The Cape Mail*, *The Kimberley Mail*, *The Diamond Rush* and *Britain and the Boer*.[20] In Portsmouth musical entertainment in variety programmes took on a distinctly military flavour. At the People's Hall, the entertainment manager took advantage of the town's drive to instil military drill into the school curriculum by incorporating children into the programme. A reviewer noted that 'among the best of the many good turns is that in which a number of local children take part in a military spectacle entitled "Queen and Country". The way in which they went through their drill and singing last night was extremely creditable.'[21] In addition, the *Evening News* reported that

> With a country in the grip of the 'war fever' it is only expected that there should be an unusually crowded and enthusiastic audience at the Princes Theatre on Monday evening, when a strong company under the direction of Mr Harry Bruce, presented that always popular military drama 'the two Hussars'. The piece throughout is stirring and patriotic, and the representations of the famous charge aroused the audience to great enthusiasm.[22]

Impresarios were desperate to exploit the public's interest in the Boer War, and seized upon new and developing technologies to provide an edge over their competitors. Taking advantage of popular interest in photography and the supernatural, one music hall in Portsmouth staged an exhibition of pictures that included scenes of fighting in South Africa and 'some splendid pictures, notably a spiritual representation of the Cavalry charge at Elands Laagte'.[23] The Boer War also gave an early boost to cinema, and a film or 'bioscope' was often featured as one of the entertainments in a music hall or theatre programme. Following the theatre's spectacular representations of earlier conflicts, the Boer War films were re-enacted and followed their predecessors' pattern of portraying the British as a civilising force fighting a demonised enemy. It has been estimated that the Boer War accounted for up to 40 per pent of the total film production in Britain at this time and it gave film makers an opportunity to document life in the armed forces.[24] The Southsea photographer Alfred West had been experimenting with film in the Portsmouth dockyard in 1897, but only with the onset of the Boer War did he become aware of its commercial potential. He recalled in his autobiography that a Southsea concert agent 'strongly urged me to give a public show of the pictures' and that the agent pledged to organise the venues for him. After a triumphant showing in Portsmouth, in which the local press praised its celebration of both the navy and empire, it had become apparent to imperialists that the film had significant propaganda possibilities. West was approached by the Navy League and recalled that 'It was soon realised that such pictures were of more than local importance and the Secretary of the Navy League invited me to bring them to London, promising good patronage and support'.[25] Through the Navy League's financial support, the film *Our Navy* was shown nationally, prompting the *Polytechnic Magazine* to note that 'West has shown this set of photographs throughout the provinces during the past year, and everywhere they have been received with the utmost enthusiasm'.[26] In Portsmouth, the *Evening News* reported that the film was shown to packed houses and portrayed 'a complete history of a sailor's life from the time when he first joins until he is shaped into the most highly trained fighting man that the world has ever seen'. The film depicted the heroic Blue Jackets' role in relieving Ladysmith along with skirmishes with the enemy and the inevitable retreating Boers.[27] The same film was shown in Leeds and given an enthusiastic billing by the *Leeds Mercury*. The reviewer reported that 'this is the proper time for a patriotic entertainment. The public are prepared to accept and patronise anything where there is an opportunity of demonstrating their patriotism and a glorious chance is given at the Coliseum.'[28] In Coventry, a similar film was exhibited in the Corn Exchange in which 'the latest animated photographs of the Boer War' were shown along with the 'portraits of Roberts, Kitchener, Baden-Powell and all of the celebrities of the day'.[29]

Along with advancing the popularity of cinema in English entertainment venues, the Boer War did more perhaps than any other nineteenth-century conflict to generate new imperial music and song or appropriate existing material to the cause. The liberal-leaning *Coventry Herald* somewhat disapprovingly commented, 'the war in South Africa is responsible for many things: not only has it cost this country valuable lives and much money, but it has added very considerably to the number of patriotic compositions, some of which we could well do without'.[30] The *Daily Mail* commissioned Kipling to produce patriotic verse for the Boer War and he duly obliged in 1899 with the publication of the 'Absent Minded Beggar'.[31] The popularity of this verse spread when Sir Arthur Sullivan set it to music and the piece rapidly became a staple patriotic song in music hall and theatre programmes across the country. Indeed, Kipling's poem spawned not only a song but also a play which involved a Boer villain coveting a heroic British soldier's wife and the relief of Ladysmith. The play included dramatic scenes that recreated 'the rattle of guns and the thunder of the "Long Toms" '.[32] At a local level, new compositions were produced by song writers whose 'latent poetical talents have been brought out by the threatening aspect of affairs in Africa'. The *Coventry Herald* noted that one local music teacher 'produced a song of three verses, with a chorus entitled a "Hot Time in the Transvaal" '. So popular was the song, with 'its very pretty swing', it was played in entertainment venues and 'several hundred' copies of the song-sheet were sold at 6*d* a time.[33] In Leeds, it was reported that in the Grand Music Hall 'terrific cheering' greeted Mr Throne's 'new patriotic song' which had a special reference to the relief of Mafeking.[34] Besides new compositions, impresarios scoured the existing cannon of imperial songs to capture the public's interest in the war. For example, Leslie Stuart's song 'Soldiers of the Queen', originally written for a military themed drama in 1881, was resurrected to become the Boer War signature tune in theatres and music halls. In all three communities 'Soldiers of the Queen' featured in almost all music hall, theatres and soldiers' relief concerts that made reference to the Boer War. In the Leeds Empire Palace, one review reported that the singer 'almost brought the house down' with 'Soldiers of the Queen'.[35] The *Coventry Herald* observed that 'since the outbreak of hostilities war songs have filled the air; in the towns "Soldiers of the Queen" is nightly served up at most places of amusement'.[36] Such was the new popularity of this twenty year old theatrical song, that 'Soldiers of the Queen' was appropriated by the military and played to send off and welcome home Boer War volunteers. The song's journey from an obscure military drama of 1881 to the rallying call of the Boer War demonstrates how a piece of theatrical entertainment became embedded in a wider popular culture and was used for explicitly political purposes.[37]

Song and music, then, had a pervasive quality that did not stay within the confines of a music hall auditorium but became entrenched in everyday life. One Coventry reporter lamented that not only in Coventry streets were the sounds of patriotic songs heard on a nightly basis, but also in Warwickshire 'the solitude of the lanes is broken by the vocal efforts of ploughboys ambitious of thoroughly mastering the musical intricacies of "The British Grenadiers" or "Rule Britannia" '.[38] The theatre and music hall's pervasive influence in popular leisure and their cultural formation in wider society made them a convenient conduit for current affairs. Indeed, audiences were well aware that a visit to a music hall could provide both entertainment and an opportunity to collectively access recently telegraphed war news. Given the extent to which a night's entertainment or song rapidly filtered through a community the following day, the breaking of war news during a performance would likewise swiftly find its way into popular consciousness. The invention of the telegraph and the rise of the popular provincial press meant that news was relayed more efficiently and quickly than ever before.[39] The competition between popular provincial newspapers to announce war news was fierce and could have a significant impact upon sales figures. One Portsmouth *Evening News* reporter recalled how the *Evening Mail* stole a march on his paper during the South African War. 'It was the night of the relief of Mafeking, when, through the premature closing of our private wire system, the "Mail" flooded the town with good news, whilst we were frantically seeking confirmation.'[40] The popular appetite for war news from South Africa can be, to some extent, explained by the newspapers' desire to frame the conflict within a local context. The local volunteers, the associated civic ceremony and reports of their South African campaign in the press had fostered a sense of 'local patriotism' within an imperial context.[41] Music hall and theatre managers also spotted the commercial potential of breaking the war news to audiences. Interrupting the programme to be the first venue to announce war news would heighten the drama and excitement in the hall and add to the overall entertainment on the night. The *Illustrated London News* reported that on the night Mafeking was relieved the news spread quickly from the press to the entertainment venues. 'It was 9 o'clock on Friday night when the telegram reached London, but before ten o'clock it had been announced from the stage of every theatre, and already the suburbs were cheering themselves hoarse over the joyful intelligence.'[42] In the provinces, the rapid relay of news from the newspaper offices to the theatres and music halls was captured by the *Leeds Daily News* when a reporter described how the relief of Mafeking was broken to the public. He noted that the streets were empty until 'a stream of news lads shot from the offices of the *Leeds Daily News* shouting "relief of Mafeking". Then began the carnival. From every hotel, inn, theatre and music hall swept people in their thousands', adding 'the news was received in the theatres and music halls with terrific cheering'.[43] It was reported that the manager of the Theatre Royal in Leeds was

> pretty well first in the field with the news. No sooner had he stepped in front of a convenient and well-timed 'curtain' and announced in but three words 'Mafeking is relieved', than the audience, which had been trying to work up an appreciation for 'Dangers of London', rose to their feet, and with one yell relieved their pent-up feelings. The theatre band struck up the National Anthem, and everybody joined in with a will.

In other Leeds theatres, performers adapted their songs to include 'up-to-date' material of Mafeking, with one comedian at the Grand altering a military song to celebrate Baden-Powell's triumph which provoked another 'outburst' from the audience.[44] The entertainment venues in Portsmouth and Coventry broke the news and celebrated in a similar manner. The theatre or music hall gave audiences the opportunity not only to hear the latest news but also to receive and react to it in a collective fashion. Thus when news broke of an assassination attempt on the Prince of Wales by pro-Boer sympathisers in Belgium, theatres in Portsmouth interrupted their programme to play patriotic songs as a mark of sympathy with Prince Edward.[45] Likewise, when news filtered through that the Boers had signed the Peace Treaty, the manager of the Portsmouth Theatre Royal occasioned a change in the programme to celebrate the 'patriotic feeling'.[46] Theatre performances and audiences enjoyed an interactive relationship, responding to the moment and indicating that popular entertainment was not a static or passive cultural form.

However, while the evidence drawn from the three communities suggests that theatrical popular leisure had become more routinely imperial during the late 1890s and early 1900s, we cannot pronounce with any certainty that audiences expressed a shared enthusiasm for the empire. As has been argued elsewhere, one cannot make assumptions about an audience's engagement with a performance from a song sheet or music hall programme alone.[47] The ritualised relationship between the performer and spectator is the key to understanding the influence of imperial sentiment since meaning is shown in the act of singing rather than in examining song lyrics in cold isolation.[48] Indeed interaction between performer and spectator was fundamental since audiences were not passive consumers but chose their entertainments and participated in fostering the tone and direction of a stage performance.[49] One indication of the extent to which imperial sentiment penetrated recreation may reside in more informal expressions of popular culture. It was commonplace on leaving the theatre for audiences to continue their evening in public houses or the crowded streets, particularly when there was some form of national excitement. Thus, on the night of Mafeking, the *Illustrated London News* reported that 'when the theatres emptied, the audience joined the shouting processions already patrolling the streets'.[50] Here the participants were free from the constraints of a theatre or music hall programme and could appropriate and recite their preferred music, song or dance from popular music hall acts. In assessing the popular scenes of rejoicing at various points during the Boer War, we explore the degree to which the overtly imperial stage entertainment of the late nineteenth and early twentieth centuries manifested itself on the streets.

In Coventry, the relief of Ladysmith was the signal for bicycle factories to close, whereupon 'many people instinctively made for the licensed houses'.[51] The relief of Mafeking was, however, more dramatic and had long been anticipated by a public hungry for news. Once news was received by the *Coventry Standard* at 9.50 pm, staff immediately posted 'Mafeking Relieved' on the office window. The empty streets were soon filled as 'instantly, as if by magic, people swarmed into Broadgate' from the theatres, music halls and public houses. Significantly, the patriotic singing of 'Soldiers of the Queen' gave way to an impromptu street torchlight pageant led by the Deputy Mayor, the city fire brigade and leading bicycle and car firms.[52] The leading role of Coventry's civic elite and the procession of bicycle and car firms gave a prominent sense of local patriotism to the celebration of Mafeking's relief. Thus, the crowds were invited to celebrate the relief of Mafeking through a civic pageant-style parade that showcased the city's leading role in the motor and bicycle industries. The following day did not produce as much excitement, though most workers stayed away from their factory without the sanction of an official holiday. Talk in the streets appeared to have been a mixture of relief that Mafeking had been reprieved and the celebrations of the previous night. The *Coventry Standard* reported that the procession 'was talked about with evident satisfaction by all who took part. "I would not have been out of it for any money," said one individual to another, and apparently this was the sentiment of all.'[53] The signing of the Boer

Peace Treaty also triggered a popular carnival in the centre of the town. After the public house and music hall had closed, thousands took to the streets, whereupon 'everyone sang – young and old, they sang in groups, they sang en masse'; 'sentimental, comic, patriotic – every kind of song was started'. The singers were joined by people replicating popular music hall acts on the street:

> A very appreciative crowd gathered round a youth who cleverly performed the 'Cobblers Dance', the audience whistling the accompaniment, and at the close vociferously applauding him; another man charmed his audience with acrobatic feats; and a third, with more or less success, essayed the principal part in 'Jack the Giant Killer,' the spectators very funnily interpolating the creepy and guttural 'ha! ha! ha!'[54]

What is quite remarkable about this spontaneous street entertainment was the almost total absence of references to the Boer War. Only with the arrival of a 'small but valiant army' from the local barracks who sang the praises of General Butler did the entertainment strike an imperial tone. Indeed, the following day, the journalist suspected that the joy of peace was mixed with the desire for an unofficial holiday. He noted that 'of course many workmen wanted another holiday – and most of them got it' and, when some employers refused, 'the men had their holiday'.

> At one factory, which employs 600 or 700 hands, less than a dozen turned up, and naturally the place was closed. The same thing happened elsewhere, with the consequences that at nine o'clock there were thousands of girls, boys and men ready to enter upon the day's festivities with light and gleeful hearts. At 10 o'clock there were hundreds of people gathered in Broadgate and reinforcements continued to arrive every few minutes.[55]

The second day of festivities was more organised and included a Mayoral torchlight parade through the city and patriotic singing. The journalist noted that, unlike the previous night, the streets and buildings were awash with Union Jack flags and bunting.[56] The prearranged celebrations marking peace, then, conveyed a clearly patriotic and imperial agenda and one which attracted thousands of people on to the Coventry streets to revel in the end of hostilities and an additional holiday. Significantly the more spontaneous celebrations revealed a real mix of street entertainment ranging from the imperial to the music hall comic and reflected a desire for enjoyment rather than blindly replicating jingoistic material.

In Leeds, the town's evolving civic culture meant that public celebrations were carefully organised. For example the Mafeking celebrations, which have largely been viewed in Britain as spontaneous popular celebrations, were orchestrated in advance by the civic and business elite.[57] The *Leeds Times* observed that, prior to the relief of Mafeking and in preparation of the celebration, the streets were festooned with decorations:

> At the town hall additional flags staffs have been erected, and most large warehouses and many shops seem to be getting out poles in readiness for the inevitable display of bunting. The decorations and bunting manufacturers have never been busier, and we may therefore expect such an outburst of enthusiasm as will completely overshadow the Ladysmith rejoicings.[58]

In decorating the streets, the civic elite and local businesses clearly signalled to the populace that an extravagant carnival was about to commence. This both legitimised the event and embedded an imperial character to the proceedings that were absent in Coventry's initial celebrations. Public fervour for the empire was, indeed, more evident in Leeds at this time. One newspaper noted that 'everybody was wild with enthusiasm' since the 'streets were thronged with men and women carrying banners, marching in procession and singing patriotic songs'.[59] Local politics in Leeds had been consumed with the South African War since there was a strong tradition of Liberal opposition to imperial conflicts led by leading industrialists. Indeed, on the night of the Mafeking celebrations, a group of 'demonstrators' made their way to the house of Arnold Lupton, a prominent Liberal and a member of the local South African Conciliation Committee, and cheered, 'hooted' and smashed windows. Lupton was forced to call upon mounted police to finally clear the protesters from his premises.[60] Thus the heated political debate in Leeds, aligned with the jingoism from the stage, was perhaps the principal agent that nurtured more animated Mafeking and peace celebrations in the city.

In Portsmouth, the steady increase in public naval spectacles such as Fleet Reviews and navy days from the late nineteenth century had already established a militarised flavour to popular leisure. During the Boer War, the heavy presence of sailors and troops on the streets undoubtedly intensified the military and imperial feel to popular leisure in the town. Once the news of the relief of Mafeking had reached Portsmouth, the music halls emptied and 'impromptu concerts' were held in the town in which 'for hours the populace sang patriotic songs'. Both the national and local press reported 'wild excitement' and marked out the activities of sailors and soldiers for special attention. 'Sailors and soldiers were hoisted shoulder high and carried about in the crowd by their comrades. Several sailors climbed the electric lamp columns and waved small Union Jacks amid hearty cheers.'[61] The reporter added that 'the scene was entirely unprecedented and demonstrates the intense interest and anxiety which has been felt in Portsmouth'. On leaving their respective entertainment venues, then, the Portsmouth crowd appear to have received the news in subtly different ways to their Coventry and Leeds counterparts. The formal celebrations did not draw upon popular music hall acts that had little to do with the war, as was the case in Coventry, nor were they intensely politicised as they were in Leeds. Reports suggest that large contingents of sailors and soldiers dominated the street celebrations since, for these people, the war naturally had a more tangible impact on their lives. Indeed, it is perhaps significant that press reports of Coventry and Leeds rejoicing do not repeatedly describe a sense of 'war anxiety' that hung over Portsmouth at this time.

The survey of entertainment shown in theatres and music halls between 1870 and 1914 undoubtedly shows that a more militarised and imperial form of entertainment appeared on the stage in all three communities. However, the more qualitative evidence reveals that the dissemination of imperial entertainment from the stage to the streets was more mixed and largely depended upon a town's political and social milieu. Dominant civic cultures were fused with imperial celebrations, giving the diffusion of music hall and theatre entertainment from the stage to the streets a local dimension. Thus the assumption that celebrations of Mafeking or other imperial events show simply a town's populace blindly replicating the jingoism of the music halls is somewhat wide of the mark.[62]

War, its aftermath and the imperial epic, 1914–39

The music hall and theatre continued to be important in both entertaining the masses and providing a significant conduit for news from the Edwardian period through to the First World War. During the Great War, recruitment speeches and rallies were added to music hall programmes and, as with the Boer War, entertainment programmes were changed to reflect the popular mood.[63] Indeed, music hall entertainment was one of the main cultural references for soldiers leaving their town for the front. One military musician noted that the ordinary soldier's musical preference was shaped by 'the barrel organ, the gramophone, the cinematograph orchestra and the music hall'.[64] In a similar trend to the Boer War, the Great War saw the resurrection of old songs to suit the new militarised climate. Old favourites such as 'Soldiers of the Queen' and 'Good-bye Dolly Gray' were among over a dozen marching songs adopted by battalions across the country. In a striking similarity to the media's propagation of 'Soldiers of the Queen' in the

Boer War, 'It's a Long Way to Tipperary' had little to do with the immediate hostilities and was not well known when it was performed in the music hall prior to the war. However, Lord Northcliffe was aware of the propaganda potential of this sentimental song and published the music in the *Daily Mail*. By November 1914, it had been released as a gramophone record and over two million copies of the sheet music had been sold.[65] Nick Hiley has rightly argued that despite these fluid cultural exchanges between the music hall and wider society, to focus on these well-known early tunes would exaggerate the propagating potency of the music hall. He has shown that the soldiers 'relished the constantly changing pattern of commercial popular songs, and took from it what they needed to express their different moods'. The wistful 'Tipperary' gave way to the escapist 'Pack up Your Troubles' and the more cynical and war-weary 'Carry Me Back to Dear Old Blighty' as the war progressed.[66] Likewise, on the home front, the survey of entertainment during the war period shows that, while military and imperial drama was more widespread than in peacetime, the dominant genre of entertainment remained the comic drama or melodrama. Indeed, even during imperial conflicts and the Great War, these two genres dominated popular entertainment between 1900 and 1939 (Appendix 1).

A similar preference for comedy and melodrama was found in the cinema. The cinema's transformation from a music hall curiosity to the most dominant form of mass entertainment began in the Edwardian period and reflected the most popular forms of entertainment found on the stage. As was the case with the theatre and music hall, the First World War brought a more militarised flavour to the cinema, particularly through 'documentaries' or 'news' items that restaged battles in a favourable light. However, the public's thirst for depictions of the First World War was not, it seems, as great as for smaller imperial conflicts. Certainly, for the soldiers on the front line, war films were the last genre of preference. In Portsmouth, the *Evening News* reported an interview with a cinema manager who had arranged for films to be shown to troops for a halfpenny in a disused grain house behind the firing line in France. The manager remarked that 'we specialise, of course, in comics, particularly Charlie Chaplin. That is what the boys come and see. They like anything but the war.'[67] There was also a similar aversion to military or imperial musical propaganda on the front line. One solider recalled that soldiers 'did not particularly want to be reminded of what had become the routine of daily life' and he 'was not moved by any more patriotic appeals of denunciations of the enemy'. He added, that when the solider was on leave at home 'he wanted to get away from all that [the war]'.[68]

At home there was more interest in war news depicted through 'documentaries' that celebrated the navy or restaged recent battles on the continent in places such as Salisbury Plain.[69] However, these films were dwarfed in number by the staple genres of comedy and melodrama that continued to dominate cinema schedules. Surprisingly, the British government had yet to see the potential of using film as wartime propaganda since it was perceived as a fleeting novelty that would have little impact upon the populace at large.[70] It was not until November 1917 that the War Office began releasing official war films.[71] Moreover, it is questionable how effectual silent film propaganda would have been given the audiences' tradition, learned in the music halls, of interacting with their entertainment. In answering the question of why people went to the theatre in wartime, Portsmouth's *Evening News* drew upon recent research that claimed

> that all classes like motion picture plays because each person puts into their mouths of the silent actors the exclamations, words and lines that he himself would use under the circumstances. The spectator tells the unspoken story to himself and there is no possibility of artificial, strained or incomprehensible dialogue. To one who watches Hamlet with Yorick's skull, the words of the play may come 'Imperial [*sic*] Caesar dead and turn'd to clay. Might stop a hole to keep the wind away'. To another's imagination Hamlet says 'well, we all gotta come to it'.[72]

However, with the widespread circulation of 'talkies' in Britain by the early 1930s, the audiences' ability to reinterpret films to coincide with their own frame of reference would have been somewhat reduced. During the interwar period, comedy and melodrama were the most frequently shown and continued a pattern of popular taste that had been set in late nineteenth-century music halls. However, while Appendix 1 indicates that there were fewer films on empire shown, one should not underestimate the popularity of the Hollywood epic of Britain's imperial past. The popularity of films depicting the empire in a positive light has led historians to argue that the 1930s saw a new era in cinema propaganda in which working-class audiences developed a renewed affection for empire that had been tainted by the horrors of the First World War. For example, by the 1920s, the public appeared to have regained their appetite for thrillers in which the enemy threatened to bring down the empire. The 1924 film *Silent Commander* inevitably found favour in Portsmouth and was described as a 'thriller set in high seas' and a naval mystery in which 'patriotism and heroism combine to thwart the unscrupulous plotters'.[73] Indeed, Robert James has shown that this film was part of a wider pattern of popular taste in Portsmouth as he contends that cinema managers responded to popular demand for naval epics during peacetime.[74] As we have seen, as early as 1898 senior figures in the navy had supported Alfred West's early films and had helped generate interest among their fellow ser- vicemen. As James has pointed out, the navy and dockyard were Portsmouth's largest employers and had a considerable impact on cinema demand in the town.[75] While the popularity of naval and empire film was particularly marked in Portsmouth, there was undoubtedly a nationwide spike in the popularity of imperial films. For Stuart Ward, the cinema was a 'prime vehicle for the diffusion of an imperial outlook', while Andrew Thompson has argued that, while the quality of imperial films was uneven, 'it would be difficult to deny the British public's enthusiasm for this genre of film'.[76] Imperial films provided swashbuckling excitement that found favour even with those hostile to imperialism. For example, Jeffrey Richards cites Bertolt Brecht's reflections on having seen the epic *Gunga Din* (1939) to illus- trate the powerful effect of film. Brecht wrote:

> In the film *Gunga Din* . . . I saw British occupation forces fighting a native population. An Indian tribe . . . attacked by a body of British troops stationed in India. The Indians were primitive creatures, either comic or wicked: comic when loyal to the British and wicked when hostile. The British soldiers were honest, good humoured chaps and when they used their fists on the mob and 'knocked some sense' into them the audience laughed . . . I was amused and touched because this utterly distorted account was an artistic success and considerable resources in talent and ingenuity had been applied in making it.[77]

Clearly, Brecht's firm opposition to imperialism would not have faltered as a result of enjoying one film. Nevertheless, Richards specu- lates that the picture may have had an 'immense' impact on those cinemagoers who had no previous knowledge or opinion of empire. However, the theory that cinema helped engender a social cohesion or imperial fervour in British society through the messages embedded in popular films tends to underestimate the audience's power of choice. Cinemas and film makers were, after all, commercial institutions that relied on popular support. Social surveys noted that working-class audiences were drawn towards certain genres of film that were essen- tially escapist in narrative. Indeed, the desire for an escapist adventure might well be a reason why imperial epics were so popular during the 1930s. Films with an imperial theme regularly featured in the top 50 British films throughout the 1930s, with almost all of them celebrating the imperial cause.[78] As Richards has suggested, you did not need to know a great deal about the workings of imperialism to enjoy a film on empire since for most people 'the Empire was the mythic landscape of romance and adventure. It was that quarter of the globe that was coloured red and included "Darkest Africa" and the "mysterious East". In short it was "ours." [79] Furthermore, cinemagoers were not only treated to adventures in the far-flung reaches of the British Empire, they were also often transported back to the pomp and glory of the Victorian and Edwardian eras – a far cry from depression-ravaged Britain of the 1930s. As MacKenzie has rightly argued, although cinema was a new technology it was disseminating material that had first been popular in the late nineteenth century. For example, although Kipling's reputation underwent a damaging re-evaluation after the First World War, the appetite for Kipling stories in the cinema went unabated in the interwar period and beyond. The film *Elephant Boy* (1937) was followed by *Gunga Din* (1939), *The Jungle Book* (1942) and *Kim* (1951). Other Victorian or Edwardian novels transferred to cinema included Rider Haggard's *King Solomon's Mines* (book 1885; film 1937), A.E.W. Mason's *Four Feathers* (book 1902; film 1939) and Edgar Wallace's *Sanders of the River* (book 1911; film 1935). Similar imperial films such as the account of *Rhodes of Africa* (1936), *Lives of a Bengal Lancer* (1936) and *We're Going to Be Rich* (1938) that celebrated a past imperial age were all written in the 1930s.[80] Given the success of these films it would be difficult to argue with MacKenzie's assessment that

> The public remained set in the late nineteenth-century view of the world, and popular preoccupations – military and naval adventure, oriental fascinations, racial condescension, deference to royalty and patriotic symbols – survive from decade to decade, stimulated rather than stifled by warfare. The 1930s represented an extraordinary renaissance of the imperial adventure tradition, made all the more potent by Hollywood's eager participation.[81]

The empire film, then, along with melodrama and comedy formed the staple diet of cinema entertainment in Britain during the 1930s. While demand for naval adventures may have been a little more apparent in Portsmouth, the imperial film proved durable in both Coventry and Leeds particularly during peacetime in the first quarter of the twentieth century. However, the uncertainty of audience engagement with film renders it difficult to estimate in any meaningful way the extent to which a film's imperial values overly influenced an individual's outlook or behaviour.[82] The close relationship between music hall and spontaneous street theatre, apparent during the Boer War, did not survive into the 1930s. Suburbanisation and more privatised leisure patterns removed the symbolic significance of the main thoroughfares of city centres and with it the elaborate civic and popular urban ritual of the late nineteenth and early twentieth centuries.[83] For a leisure pursuit that generates a less ambiguous relationship between the individual and imperial propaganda we need to turn to other forms of recreation. Perhaps the most explicit example of an individual embracing or challenging the imperial message is their joining imperial or anti-imperial societies. Indeed, imperial societies often staged popular forms of entertainment to draw working people into their movement.

Entertaining the masses through imperial societies

For some time historians have argued that while imperial societies mushroomed in Britain between 1880 and 1914 their impact upon the public was limited. MacKenzie has challenged this notion by insisting that their wider influence on schooling and curriculum design should be taken into account. Here, he argues, societies were successful in inculcating an 'imperial world view, replete with racial, cultural and economic values'.[84] Thompson, however, offers a more sceptical view and suggests that schooling, particularly during the late nineteenth century, was not an efficient conduit for imperial dissemination because of widespread poor attendance rates.[85] The societies that we focus upon here are those which professed a desire to engage with the working classes in urban Britain. Their success or otherwise in establishing a presence in Portsmouth, Coventry and Leeds may provide an indication of their capacity to penetrate differing urban English contexts between 1870 and 1939.

The Primrose League, established in 1883, was undoubtedly an imperial society intent on recruiting support for the empire in Britain's major cities. Lord Salisbury claimed that the Primrose League was instrumental in rousing popular support for the Empire in the second half of the nineteenth century. In the midst of an upsurge of enthusiasm for the Boer War he declared that 'this remarkable change in public opinion is almost synchronous with the birth and of the development of the Primrose League'.[86] Although its founder, Lord Randolph Churchill, originally envisaged the society as an elitist imperial movement costing members one guinea a year to join, by 1890 the Primrose League claimed to have proletarian support and a membership of one million. Indeed, by the 1890s one of the Primrose League's aims was 'to instruct working men and women how to answer the arguments of Radicals and Socialists and the Atheists in the workshops and in the public houses, and at the street corners'.[87] The official history of the Primrose League acknowledged that popular support for the society in urban areas was mixed. In Bolton it was reported that meetings regularly generated crowds four thousand strong consisting almost entirely of artisans and factory workers, while in Birmingham enthusiasm for the Primrose League was comparatively weak. Clearly, Bolton's staple textile industries were heavily reliant on imperial trade and may explain, to some degree, the widespread popular interest in the society.[88] However, the Primrose League did not refrain from staging 'low' forms of racist and jingoistic entertainment to attract popular interest. When answering criticism of a Primrose League handbill that read 'Primrose Day – Don't forget the Grand Negro Entertainment', Lord Salisbury retorted 'Vulgar? Of course it is vulgar! But that is why we have got on so well.'[89] Typical entertainment included jugglers, ventriloquists, conjurers and 'oriental illusions'. Admission fees were low and attracted working-class men and women, particularly in northern England. J.H. Robb, the official historian, has contended that 'much of the political propaganda of the League was cleverly disguised with a coating of popular entertainment, or was so surreptitiously introduced into the evening's gaiety as to be almost unnoticed'. Indeed, the entertainment certainly was popular in character and, just as in the music halls, there was a fluidity between performer and the audience. For example, the Primrose League had difficulty in explaining one incident in which the audience burnt an effigy of a local vicar for protesting that the entertainment regularly continued into the early hours of the morning.[90]

In Coventry, the Primrose League failed to make an early impression in the city's political landscape. Despite its forming a branch in 1884, membership was confined to the elite Conservatives of the town. In a similar scenario to Birmingham, the Primrose League did not ignite popular enthusiasm in its first political test, the 1885 General Election.[91] It found more support in the midland shires since it was reported in same election that 'the Primrose badge was very conspicuous and the "Dames" of the League were particularly active in the contest'.[92] By the mid-1890s membership had grown in the Coventry branch to over one thousand, though the activists remained middle-class Conservatives. Moreover, a significant number had connections with the city's bicycle trade and the Primrose League became a vehicle to promote overseas trade even beyond the boundaries of the British Empire.[93] In Leeds, there was a more concerted effort to attract working-class membership through staging popular entertainments. One correspondent to the *Leeds Mercury* was shocked at the depths to which the Primrose League would plummet in recruiting popular support. Describing himself as a 'Yorkshire Vicar', he complained that the League organised

> Amusement rather than instruction, pleasure in preference to thought, catering for men and women's weaknesses instead of offering opportuni-

ties for self-improvement and the acquisition of knowledge, are evidently the lines upon which the Primrose Club is working. 'Give us your votes, and we will supply you with pleasures: eat, drink, dance, and be jolly, and don't bother your heads about politics, except to keep Conservatives in office', appears to be about the sum-total of the teaching of the Primrose League.[94]

Despite attempts to capture working-class support with events such as staging football and skittle entertainment, membership of the Primrose League was still largely drawn from the Conservative-supporting middle class in the 1890s.[95] In Portsmouth, while 'Primrose Day' was celebrated in the Conservative clubs in the town, there appears to have been little in the way of a proactive campaign to enlist working-class support.[96] Indeed, by 1915, the Primrose League could boast only just over two hundred members in Portsmouth, largely drawn from the existing branches of the Tory Party. Indeed, the Primrose League's demand for conscription during the First World War did little to galvanise support from outside a narrow field of Conservative political activists.[97]

An organisation that claimed to be less politically partisan and have a more penetrating impact upon daily life, particularly with regard to schoolchildren, was the Navy League. The leading members of the Navy League, such as Charles Beresford, had also been 'prime movers' in the Primrose League and the two organisations would often share lantern lectures on the navy and empire.[98] Indeed, it was the Primrose League rather than the Navy League that convened a large Town Hall meeting in Portsmouth on the future of the British navy in 1909. Illustrating the interdependency between navy and empire, the speaker, Sir John Comb, declared that 'the Empire could only be maintained by our unquestioned supremacy over the sea'.[99] The Navy League, however, was much more organised in disseminating imperial maps and literature to schoolchildren than in organising entertainment, and regarded education as an important conduit for propagating the Empire.[100] A focus was placed on working-class children as the League urged the government to introduce in all Board Schools a 'service class' which would train children for a military career.[101] Accordingly, the Navy League was founded in 1895 with a mission to educate working men on the importance of empire. However, the movement suffered from a weak start since, although it had 34 branches in 1899, membership was largely middle-class.[102] In its first four years, then, the League had failed in its objective in enticing substantial working-class support. A Leeds branch was established in 1898 and succeeded only in attracting middle-class members, while in Coventry there was no Navy League presence recorded in the city's trade directories.[103] The Navy

League did have some notable successes in Britain's urban areas in the early twentieth century. Branches in Bristol and Liverpool generated considerable enthusiasm for the cause and a number of imperial philanthropic enterprises were established. For example, the League opened a home for orphans that would train and send the boys to sea as a way of reducing the reliance on foreign nationals in the British navy. Frans Coetzee suggests that the League's success in these two cities was due to their rich nautical heritage and a long tradition of philanthropy.[104] This explanation may go some way in explaining why the Navy League, rather surprisingly, occupied a fairly low profile in Portsmouth. Since the Admiralty was the town's largest employer, Portsmouth did not have a substantial local manufacturing class, a group which was often the source of a philanthropic culture in a town. Perhaps more significantly, however, Portsmouth was synonymous with navy culture and so perhaps the League deemed a campaigning local presence was unnecessary. Certainly the local press in Portsmouth championed the Navy League's ideals without need of prompting. The major newspapers, including the liberal-leaning *Evening News*, carried supportive reports, congratulating the Navy League for establishing a presence outside of the naval dockyard towns and for applying pressure on the government to increase spending on the Royal Navy.[105] At the outbreak of the First World War, the editor of the *Evening News*, William Gates, explicitly aligned the Navy League's objectives with Portsmouth's identity and interests:

> Under all circumstances the British Empire must maintain as the basis of imperial policy, the command of the seas . . . that the teaching of naval history and the lessons it conveys should be made an especial feature of elementary education throughout the Empire. To each of these points we in this town and district can subscribe with all our hearts.[106]

Gates's enthusiasm for the Navy League was matched in Portsmouth's elementary schools as the League made regular visits to the town's local schools. Significantly, a number of state-run schools in Portsmouth had a substantial number of governors with naval backgrounds.[107] In St Luke's, a Church of England school, the Navy League actively shaped the curriculum by setting essays on 'The British Navy in the Great War'.[108] However, while the Navy League had close ties with Portsmouth schools, the branch in Leeds appears less successful since no examples of school visits were recorded in the log books sampled. Portsmouth, then, was possibly the exception to the rule in the League's attempt in gaining widespread and unequivocal support from a provincial town. This, together with the fact that Coventry did not possess a Navy League branch, suggests that the League was more successful in lobbying national rather than local institutions between 1895 and 1918. Indeed, by 1914 and with a predominantly rural membership, the Navy League had concluded that it had failed to attract sufficient lower middle-class and working-class members.[109]

The period 1918 to 1939 saw a change in focus and strategy for imperial societies and movements. The attempt to gain mass support through 'low' or popular leisure events was deemed outdated, as was the attempt by societies to claim they campaigned for non-politically partisan objectives. During the interwar period, popular discourse on empire became enmeshed with distaste for jingoism in the postwar aftermath and a growing anxiety among conservatives about revolution on the international stage. In such an unstable period it is perhaps no surprise that the interwar period spurned heavily politicised movements either supporting or opposing the Empire. For most imperial societies such as the Primrose and Navy Leagues, the lobbying for empire became fused with the fight against the 'Bolshevik menace'. Indeed, the Empire was cast as the bulwark against the spread of Communism in Europe and the rest of the world. For example, in 1924, the Secretary of the Primrose League wrote to the sympathetic *Saturday Review* outlining the League's attempts to confront the Bolshevik threat:

> For several years the Primrose League has been combating pernicious doctrines of Socialist and Communist Sunday Schools, and in some of the industrial centres we have been successful in establishing branches of the Primrose League. But many more branches are necessary if the influence of the Young Communist Movement is to be effectively opposed.[110]

The Primrose League's national objectives were certainly disseminated through the Portsmouth branch, which organised a gathering of over five hundred children or 'buds' on Southsea Common to sing 'Land of Hope and Glory'. The Secretary of the League praised the Portsmouth branch for 'making a gallant and successful effort to save the children and youths of Portsmouth from the subversive doctrines of Socialism and Communism'. Significantly, the event had the approval of the local educational authority as the children were given a half-day holiday to attend the rally.[111] The Primrose League, however, was one of the few overtly imperial societies to survive in Portsmouth after the First World War. Perhaps unsurprisingly, Portsmouth's interwar societies were dominated by naval veteran clubs and benevolent societies. During the mid-1930s, only one overtly imperial society was listed – the City Empire Social Club – but it failed to make an impression and was absent from the 1939 trade directories.[112] Indeed, apart from the major political parties and Trade Unions, the 1939 directories do not list any specific imperial or anti-imperial organisation. The meagre scattering of political clubs in Portsmouth indicates that working people elected to spend their free time in the plethora of naval and dockyard social and sporting societies that dominated the town. In Coventry, the city's trade directories reveal that prior to the First World War the Primrose League and Conservative Party were out numbered by Left-leaning organisations such as the ILP, Fabian Society, Labour Party, the United Irish League and the Social Democratic Federation. However by 1919, only the Conservative, Liberal and Labour Parties were listed, suggesting that most of the societies had dual members and few had substantial roots in Coventry's political and cultural landscape. Indeed, the Primrose League does not appear after 1912, though by the end of the 1930s there is a mushrooming of political societies once more. Of the 15 societies listed, only one, The Junior Imperial League, was formed to further the cause of empire. Most societies were splinter groups of the Left and included the Communist Party, Left Book Club, Labour Women, the League of Nations Union and the Labour Party League of Youth. The list, however, should not be taken to mean that there was a strong and active socialist or anti-imperial movement in the city. Membership between these societies was fluid and it is questionable whether these activists made inroads into the political culture of the factory floor. The political societies pale into insignificance when contrasted with social and sporting clubs that formed in Coventry factories. By 1939, Coventry boasted over seventy social and sporting clubs, the vast majority linked to the workplace, providing an indication of how workers spent their free time. Unfortunately, the trade directories for Leeds are less revealing since the leading publication was not consistent in the institutions it selected to list, making it difficult to trace a pattern of the growth of political societies during the early twentieth century.[113]

However, when contrasted with Portsmouth and Coventry, Leeds undoubtedly possessed Left-wing and anti-imperial societies with deeper roots in their local community. By 1914, the Leeds Labour Party, according to one historian, 'represented a labour movement stronger and more confident than at any time since the Chartist era'. The movement had successfully developed its own retail co-operative, leisure societies and newspaper in the working-class districts of Leeds.[114] However, the working class in Leeds were also targeted by imperial societies after the First World War, and the British Empire Union (BEU) achieved some success in establishing a branch in the town in 1920. Of all the postwar imperial societies, the BEU was perhaps the most aggressive in its targeting of the working class in a bid to fend off the threat of socialism. The movement was founded in

London in 1915 to 'work against the revolutionaries on behalf of industrial peace', adding that its aim was to 'arouse in British people an appreciation of their responsibilities and privileges in being citizens of the greatest Empire the World has ever known'. Significantly, despite proclaiming to be a society of empire, the clear emphasis of the movement was to guard against socialist agitation at home. In a pamphlet designed for wealthy and sympathetic industrialists, the BEU outlined how they could inculcate their workforce with imperial sentiment and cultivate a hostility to socialism.

> One of the best means of countering the growth of Socialism is by means of outdoor meetings at which trained speakers, preferably working men and women, can impress upon their audience the fallacies of Socialism and how workers are the greatest sufferers by supporting its policy. The British Empire Union has a body of trained and capable working-men speakers, who have proved their ability to defeat Socialism, whom you can employ and who will fight your battle for you.[115]

The Leeds branch was established by a consortium of manufacturers, largely from the engineering industries, and followed the BEU's national guidelines in holding open-air rallies with trained working-class speakers. The Leeds branch reported that 'all meetings were conducted in those parts of the town where there is a working-class population and where the need for counter-revolutionary propaganda is very great'.[116] However, given that the appeal of this movement to manufacturers was to drive socialism from the workplace, it is questionable how far the imperial message was disseminated through the Leeds populous. Moreover by the interwar period, while the political momentum in Leeds had certainly shifted towards Labour from the Liberals, the range of the city's political societies reflected that of Portsmouth and Coventry. The smaller pressure groups agitating for or against empire failed to make a sustained mark on Leeds's political landscape, which was dominated by the established political parties.[117]

Conclusion

This chapter has shown that popular leisure patterns in Britain underwent a number of broad changes in how imperial entertainment and imagery were disseminated and engaged with by the public. Prior to the Great War, music halls and theatres had become an important conduit of news, and imperial intelligence in particular proved a popular and exciting addition to a performance. Indeed, the celebration of news from an imperial war could be effortlessly integrated into a show with songs and music that was instantly recognisable to the audience. These institutions and their entertainment programmes, then, ought as not to be viewed static entities but as reactive to their particular environment. Furthermore, this chapter has argued that the particular social and political locale of a town had an important bearing on the extent to which imperial sentiment in shows spilled over into the post-performance 'street theatre' and entertainment in the main thoroughfares of a town. However, by the interwar period, the symbolic significance of popular entertainment in the main streets of a city diminished with greater suburbanisation and more privatised leisure patterns epitomised by the rapid expansion of the suburban cinema. Furthermore, a town's work culture – be it the Portsmouth dockyard or Coventry's engineering factories – also impacted upon the nature of popular societies and clubs in the late nineteenth and early twentieth centuries. The growth of overtly political societies of the late nineteenth century, which had succeeded in recruiting few working-class members, became significantly outnumbered by the growth of factory sporting and leisure clubs that had began to mushroom in a town's suburban areas.

Notes

1   B. Beaven, *Leisure, Citizenship and Working-class Men in Britain 1850–1945* (Manchester, Manchester University Press, 2005), pp. 52–3.
2   A. Wilson, 'Music Halls', *Contemporary Review*, 78, July 1900, p. 134.
3   Beaven, *Leisure, Citizenship and Working-class Men in Britain*, ch. 3.
4   B. Porter, *The Absent-minded Imperialists. Empire, Society and Culture in Britain* (Oxford, Oxford University Press, 2004, 2006 edn), p. 199.
5   *Morning Post*, 12 December 1884.
6   J. Schneer, *London 1900. The Imperial Metropolis* (New Haven, Yale University Press, 1999), p. 95.
7   *Portsmouth Times*, 6 March 1880.
8   *Coventry Times*, 26 April 1861; C.J. Spencer, 'The Progress of Popular Music', *Contemporary Review*, 52, August 1887, p. 240.
9   Spencer, 'The Progress of Popular Music', p. 236.
10 Spencer, 'The Progress of Popular Music', p. 245.
11 J.M. MacKenzie, *Propaganda and Empire* (Manchester, Manchester University Press, 1984), p. 49.
12 *Portsmouth Times*, 6 March 1880.
13 *Hampshire Telegraph*, 24 January 1880.
14 *Hampshire Telegraph*, 24 January 1880.
15 *Leeds Mercury*, 1 March 1880.
16 *Leeds Mercury*, 24 February 1880.
17 *Midland Daily Telegraph*, 28 February 1898. Coventry audiences were also treated to 'spectacular events' such as 'Great Britain's glorious victory in the Soudan' which included '1,200 men, women and mules'; see *Midland Daily Telegraph*, 6 April 1900.
18 L. Rutherford, ' "Harmless nonsense": the Comic Sketch and the Development of Music-hall Entertainment', in J.S. Bratton (ed.), *Music Hall Performance and Style* (Oxford, Open University Press, 1986), p. 131.

19   S. Attridge, *Nationalism, Imperialism and Identity in Late Victorian Culture. Civil and Military Worlds* (Basingstoke, Palgrave, 2003), p. 22.
20   MacKenzie, *Propaganda and Empire*, p. 49.
21   *Evening News*, 27 March 1900.
22   *Evening News*, 6 February 1900.
23   *Evening News*, 10 April 1900.
24   A. Thompson, *The Empire Strikes Back? The Impact of Imperialism on Britain from the Mid-nineteenth Century* (Harlow, Longman, 2005), p. 89. For example, see *Leeds Times*, 13 January 1900.
25   A.J. West, 'Seasalts and Celluloid', unpublished autobiography, 1936, pdf version, p. 16, www.ournavy.org.uk. Accessed 4 July 2011.
26   *Polytechnic Magazine*, vol. 1, XXXV, 11 October 1899, pp. 173–4, extract retrieved from www.ournavy.org.uk. Accessed 4 July 2011.
27   *Evening News*, 27 March 1900.
28   *Leeds Mercury*, 10 April 1900.
29   *Midland Daily Telegraph*, 31 March 1900.
30   *Coventry Herald*, 2 February 1900.
31   MacKenzie, *Propaganda and Empire*, p. 56.
32   Schneer, *London 1900*, p. 96.
33   *Coventry Herald*, 2 February 1900.
34   *Leeds Daily News*, 19 May 1900.
35   *Leeds Daily News*, 2 January 1900.
36   *Coventry Herald*, 2 February 1900.
37   Attridge, *Nationalism, Imperialism and Identity*, p. 32; MacKenzie, *Propaganda and Empire*, p. 56.
38   *Coventry Herald*, 2 February 1900.
39   Attridge, *Nationalism, Imperialism and Identity*, p. 22.
40   *Evening News*, 13 January 1934.
41   See the Boer War Volunteers, Chapter 3.
42   *Illustrated London News*, 26 May 1900.
43   *Leeds Daily News*, 19 May 1900.
44   *Leeds Mercury*, 19 May 1900.
45   *Evening News*, 6 April 1900.
46   *Hampshire Telegraph*, 7 June 1902.
47   Beaven, *Leisure, Citizenship and Working-class Men*, p. 52.
48   Attridge, *Nationalism, Imperialism and Identity*, p. 22.
49   Schneer, *London 1900*, p. 93.
50   *Illustrated London News*, 26 May 1900.
51   *Coventry Herald*, 2 March 1900.
52   *Coventry Standard*, 25 May 1900.
53   *Coventry Standard*, 25 May 1900.
54   Coventry City Archives, 'Lowe Newspaper Cuttings', vol. 26, p. 245.
55   'Lowe Newspaper Cuttings', vol. 26, p. 246.
56   'Lowe Newspaper Cuttings', vol. 26, p. 246.
57   R. Price, *An Imperial War and the British Working Class. Working-class Attitudes and Reactions to the Boer War, 1899–1902* (London, Routledge, 1972), p. 132.
58   *Leeds Times*, 19 May 1900.
59   *Leeds Mercury*, 19 May 1900.
60   *Leeds Mercury*, 19 May 1900.
61   *Evening News*, 19 May 1900.
62   For a discussion of this see Porter, *The Absent Minded Imperialists*, p. 212.
63   G. Robb, *British Culture and the First World War* (Basingstoke, Palgrave, 2002), ch. 6.
64   Quoted in N. Hiley, 'Ploughboys and Soldiers: the Folk Song and the Gramophone in the British Expeditionary Force 1914–1918', *Media History*, 4, 1, 1988, p. 65.
65   Hiley, 'Ploughboys and soldiers', p. 66.
66   Hiley, 'Ploughboys and soldiers', pp. 66, 68.

67   *Evening News*, 17 January 1916.
68   Quoted in Hiley, 'Ploughboys and soldiers', p. 68.
69   *Evening News*, 11 September 1915.
70   National Archives, HO 45/10960/340327, 'Cinema and the War'.
71   MacKenzie, *Propaganda and Empire*, p. 75.
72   *Evening News*, 28 January 1916.
73   *Evening News*, 22 April 1924.
74   R. James, *Popular Culture and Working-class Taste in Britain, 1930–39* (Manchester, Manchester University Press, 2010), ch. 8.
75   James, *Popular Culture and Working-class Taste*, p. 182.
76   Quoted in Thompson, *The Empire Strikes Back?*, p. 94.
77   J. Richards, 'Boy's Own Empire: Feature Films and Imperialism in the 1930s', in J.M. MacKenzie (ed.), *Imperialism and Popular Culture* (Manchester University Press, 1986), p. 144.
78   Thompson, *The Empire Strikes Back?*, p. 92.
79   Richards, 'Boy's Own Empire', p. 143.
80   British Film Institute, On-line Film data base, www.bfi.org.uk.
81   MacKenzie, *Propaganda and Empire*, p. 91.
82   Beaven, *Leisure, Citizenship and Working-class Men*, ch. 6.
83   Beaven, *Leisure, Citizenship and Working-class Men*, ch. 4.
84   MacKenzie, *Propaganda and Empire*, p. 149.
85   Thompson, *The Empire Strikes Back?*, p. 113.
86   *The Times*, 9 May 1900.
87   J.H. Robb, *The Primrose League 1883–1906* (New York, AMS Press, 1942), pp. 49–50.
88   Robb, *The Primrose League*, p. 60.
89   Robb, *The Primrose League*, p. 87.
90   Robb, *The Primrose League*, p. 89.
91   *Birmingham Daily Post*, 19 April 1895.
92   *Birmingham Daily Post*, 25 November 1885.
93   *Birmingham Daily Post*, 19 April 1895.
94   *Leeds Mercury*, 3 May 1888.
95   *Leeds Mercury*, 26 November 1888; 24 August 1891.
96   *Evening News*, 22 April 1893.
97   *Evening News*, 23 November 1915.
98   Robb, *The Primrose League*, pp. 206–7.
99   *Evening News*, 6 May 1909.
100 Thompson, *Empire Strikes Back?*, p. 113.
101 *Navy League Journal*, 1 July 1895.
102 F. Coetzee, *For Party or Country: Nationalism and the Dilemmas of Popular Conservatism in Edwardian England* (Oxford, Oxford University Press, 1990), pp. 22, 29.
103 Coetzee, *For Party or Country*, p. 29; Coventry Directory editions 1901, 1931 to 1939 (Curtis and Beamish, Coventry); *Spennells Annual Directory of Coventry* editions 1911 to 1920.
104 Coetzee, *For Party or Country*, p. 28.
105 *Evening News*, 18 May 1908.
106 *Evening News*, 21 October 1914.
107 *Hampshire Telegraph*, 24 April 1907.
108 Portsmouth City Archives, SA/CC/DS/39/3/A/2, 'St Luke's School log book 1901–1919', 25 October 1917.
109 Coetzee, *For Party or Country*, pp. 111–15.
110 *Saturday Review*, 31 May 1931.
111 *Hampshire Telegraph*, 23 July 1926. See also Coetzee, *For Party or Country*, p. 142.
112 Portsmouth Local Studies, *Kelly's Portsmouth Directory 1934–5/1939*.

113 Leeds Local Studies, *Kellys Directory for Leeds*. This set of directories tended to focus on elite institutions such as opera houses rather than music halls and major political parties rather than splinter or smaller movements.

114 T. Woodhouse, 'The Working Class', in D. Fraser (ed.), *A History of Modern Leeds* (Manchester, Manchester University Press, 1980), p. 377.

115 University of Warwick, Modern Record Centre (MRC), MSS 148/UCW/6/13/42/8. British Empire Union Pamphlet (n.d.).

116 University of Warwick, MRC, MSS 15c/5/7/1, 'British Empire Union. Its branches and what they are doing', n.d.).

117 Woodhouse, 'The Working Class', p. 384.

Conclusion

This book has constructed an alternative narrative of empire from the local margins and assessed the centrality of imperial identity to those living in urban communities between 1870 and 1939.[1] With the city as the centre piece of analysis, the book has sought to transcend national narratives of imperialism that have characterised the historiography of popular culture and empire. Only by viewing imperial ideas and attitudes through the prism of urban elites and communities can we appreciate the layered and filtered process of its dissemination. Undoubtedly, in exploring the ebb and flow of daily urban life, national contexts and trends impinged upon how those governing and living in English cities viewed matters of empire. Moral panics that gripped the nation, such as the sensational reporting in London of the 'jungle-like slums', seeped out into the provinces, influencing local perceptions of urban degeneration. Likewise, in all three communities the relative absence of imperial lessons and songs in the classroom until the 1890s and the launch of Empire Day in 1903 seem to confirm that national anxieties over international competition had driven efforts to imperialise the school curriculum. However, while the confirmation of national trends in Portsmouth, Coventry and Leeds may provide a *general* overview of the existence of imperial propaganda and attitudes in a community, it does little to understand *how* an imperial hegemony was transmitted and received by the larger population. These general trends have led 'new imperial' historians to assume that there was a shared sense of empire among the English regardless of class, gender and locale.[2] This book has shown this approach to be misleading and instead revealed distinct differences in how the imperial project was presented to the public. Imperial culture was neither generic nor unimportant but was instead multi-layered and recast to capture the concerns of a locality. For example, while we can acknowledge that all three communities began to address matters of empire in the classroom, the nature and objectives of imperial teaching were closely linked to local anxieties. In Coventry it was to produce an efficient workforce, in Portsmouth it was to instil masculinity for those destined for the navy and in Leeds fears of Jewish disconnection with the Empire drove aspects of the educational policy. The log books surveyed all recorded imperial lessons beginning around the 1890s but tone, direction and target audience all differed significantly in the three communities. Moreover, those who read the local daily press in Portsmouth, Coventry and Leeds were informed of the importance of empire in relation to their *own* city. Thus the meaning of empire was closely related to tangible local affairs that would, they were told, have a direct bearing on the economic, political or civic reputation of their town or city. Thus a national spectacle such as the Empire Exhibition at Wembley in 1924 was reported through a local perspective. The most exciting exhibitions were not, as the national press reported, the exotic recreations of an African village, but the exhibitions that included products from Coventry, Leeds or Portsmouth. The local daily press in particular was subject to intense competition at the turn of the twentieth century and was keen to conform to readership demands. Indeed, it was the new daily press's recognition of the popularity of local news and sport that helped editors construct a relationship with their reading public. In examining the importance and relationship between local identity, civic elites and the working class, this book has explored why men volunteered for two imperial wars during the late nineteenth and early twentieth centuries. The civic platform alone, however, was insufficient in encouraging popular local patriotism as working-class communities were also developing their own urban identity. The Boer War came during a time in which working people began to carve out a civic identity through sporting teams and to take an intense interest in neighbourhood affairs. The appeal for local volunteers saw important synergies develop between civic pride and an imperial war that struck a chord in working-class communities. This fusion of civic identity and an imperial war offers an explanation as to why working-class enthusiasm for empire often appeared ephemeral. In many respects the Boer War was a unique phenomenon as it marked the convergence of a genuine local patriotism, a popular press and an imperial adventure. It was an exceptional set of circumstances that not even the great propaganda machine of the First World War could recapture. With memories of the Boer War still fresh, it seems that the most enthusiastic volunteers were the middle-class Pals who were still committed to the civic project. For working people in all three communities, their attachment to a civic identity had become weakened by cultural, political and economic issues that seemed to sharpen social divisions. This book has argued that, between 1870 and 1939, the 'imperial message' was neither uniform nor static but was filtered through local elites and communities where it became altered and adapted to address local anxieties, enhance civic reputations and engage the local populace. To overlook this process is to overlook a significant dimension in imperial dissemination and, ultimately, how empire was received and consumed by the wider public.

Notes

1 The recognition that local case studies have an important bearing on historiography is explored in a number of recent studies such as P. Purseigle, 'Beyond and Below the Nations: Towards a Comparative History of Local Communities at War', in J. Macleod and P. Purseigle (eds), *Uncovered Fields: Perspectives in First World War Studies* (Leiden, Brill, 2003); H.B. McCartney, *Citizen Soldiers: The Liverpool Territorials in the First World War* (Cambridge, Cambridge University Press, 2005).
2 A. Burton, 'Who Needs Nation? Interrogating "British" History', *Journal of Historical Sociology*, 10, 3, September 1997.

Principal newspapers in Portsmouth, Coventry and Leeds c. 1800–1940

Table 4 Principal newspapers in Portsmouth, Coventry and Leeds, 1800–1940

Newspapers	Political stance	Ownership
Traditional newspapers		
Coventry Herald	Liberal	1830–1940 purchased by Midland Daily Telegraph in 1915
Coventry Standard	Conservative	1836–1969
Hampshire Telegraph	Liberal	1802–1976 purchased by Evening News 1905
Leeds Mercury	Liberal	1738–1939 incorporated with Evening Post
Leeds Times	Liberal	1837–1901
Portsmouth Times	Conservative	1850–1928 incorporated with Hampshire Telegraph
Yorkshire Post	Conservative	Est 1874
'New' journalism		
Athletic Reporter	Conservative	1885–1886
Evening News (Portsmouth)	Liberal	1877 to date
Evening Mail (Portsmouth)	Conservative	1884 purchased by Evening News in 1905
Evening Star (Portsmouth)	Conservative	1884–1885
Leeds Daily News	Conservative	1872
Midland Daily Telegraph	Liberal 1891–1897 then Conservative	1891 to present (from 1941 Coventry Evening Telegraph)
Yorkshire Evening Post	Conservative	1890 to date established by Yorkshire Post
Yorkshire Weekly Post	Conservative	1882–1937 established by Yorkshire Post

Source: British Library Newspaper Library Colindale: newspaper catalogue

A sample of theatre, music hall and cinema entertainment in Portsmouth, Coventry and Leeds, 1870–1939

Table 5: Theatre and music hall entertainment in Portsmouth, March 1870–March 1939

	Comic drama	Melodrama/ drama	Military/imperial drama	Military exhibition	Military musical	Musical	Musical rational recreation	Variety
March 1870	3	3	0	0	0	3	1	1
March 1880	1	4	1	0	2	3	0	2
March 1890	1	4	1	0	2	1	0	1
March 1900	0	5	0	1	2	3	0	3
Sept* 1910	0	3	1	0	1	4	0	3
March 1920	3	4	1	0	0	2	0	1
March 1930	2	1	0	0	0	0	0	1
March 1939	1	1	0	0	0	0	0	1

* Microfilm unavailable for March 1910

Table 6: Cinema in Portsmouth, 1911–1939

	Comic	Crime	Documentary/news	Drama	Military/imperial drama
1911	0	0	1	0	1
1920	2	0	2	8	0
1930	1	0	2	1	0
1939	6	4	0	15	1

Table 7: Theatre and music hall entertainment in Coventry, March 1870–March 1939

	Comic drama	Melodrama/ drama	Military/imperial drama	Military exhibition	Military musical	Musical	Musical rational recreation	Variety
March 1870	0	4	0	0	2	1	1	1
March 1880	2	0	2	0	0	1	0	
March 1890	0	0	0	0	0	6	0	4
March 1900	0	4	2	1	1	1	0	12
March 1910	1	3	1	0	0	4	0	6
March 1920	1	4	1	0	0	2	0	1
March 1925	2	5	0	0	2	2	0	4
March 1930	0	2	0	0	0	0	0	1
March 1935	0	1	0	0	0	2	0	3
March 1939	1	3	0	0	0	2	0	6

Table 8: Cinema in Coventry, 1910–1939

	Comic	Crime	Documentary/news	Drama	Military/imperial drama
1910	2		3	5	2
1920	3		1	5	
1930	3		2	13	
1939	2		1	6	

Table 9: Theatre and music hall entertainment in Leeds, March 1870–March 1939

	Comic drama	Melodrama/ drama	Military/ imperial drama	Military exhibition	Military musical	Musical	Musical rational recreation	Variety	Other
March 1870	1	3			3	3		2	1
March 1880	2	2	3	1		2		1	
March 1890	2	2	4	2		2		3	
March 1900	3	3				1		5	
March 1910	2	3	2		2	1		9	4
March 1925	3	1	1			1		4	1
March 1939	6	3						6	

Table 10: Cinema in Leeds, 1910–1935

	Comic	Crime	Documentary/news	Drama	Military/imperial drama
1910	2		2		2
1918	1			4	
1925	5		2	26	
1935	3			23	

REFERENCES

Primary sources

Newspapers

Athletic Reporter
Birmingham Post
Coventry Graphic
Coventry Herald
Coventry Standard
Coventry Times
Daily Mail
Evening News (Portsmouth)
Hampshire Telegraph
Illustrated London News
Leeds Daily News
Leeds Mercury
Manchester Guardian
Morning Post
Midland Daily Telegraph
North Leeds News
Portsmouth Times
Pall Mall Gazette
The Times
Yorkshire Evening Post

Journals

Aeroplane
British Medical Journal
English Review
Fraser's Magazine
Household Words
Jewish Chronicle
London Quarterly Review
Navy League Journal
Polytechnic Magazine
Practical Teacher
Reynolds News
The School Music Review
The Speaker
The Worker

REFERENCES

Trade directories Coventry
Coventry Directory 1874, 1886, 1892, 1901, 1932, 1940 (Curtis and Beamish, Coventry).
Coventry Official Guide 1909 (Coventry, 1909).
Spennell's Annual Directory of Coventry and District 1912, 1919 (no publisher or location identified).

Trade directories Portsmouth
Butcher and Co Borough of Portsmouth Directory, 1874–5 (London, 1875).
Chamberlain's Directory 1881–2 (Portsmouth, 1882).
Kellys Directory of Portsmouth 1892, 1900, 1909–10, 1913–14 (London).

National Archives
CAB/24/34, 'The Labour Situation', 5 December 1917.
HO 45/24551, 'File relating to Jews being refused entrance into public houses in Leeds', 20 February 1908.
MUN 5/53/300/99, The shop steward movement. Intelligence Division, Ministry of Labour, February 1920.
NA, Kew, Mun 5/55/300/47, Intelligence and statistics section weekly labour notes, 20 September 1918.
NATS 1/398, 'Approximate number of recruits raised daily'.

Coventry History Centre
PA 1025/38/1/4/1, 'B. Aylward, Quaker Teacher and Empire Day controversy'.
Acc 1417/1/1, S. Bettmann, 'Struggling' (unpublished autobiography, no date).
T. Collins, 'Brief reflections suggested to those persons who patronized the procession at Spon Street Wake July 8th 1844' (Coventry, Stephen Knapp, 1845).
Acc 135, Roland Barrett, 'Socialism made plain'.
Acc 835/2, Hugh Farren, 'newspaper cuttings'.
CEE/log/26/4, 'Frederick Bird Boys School log books'.
'Lowe Newspaper Cuttings'.
CEE/log/15/1, 'St Michael's Church of England School log books'.
CEE/log/20/1, 'Wheatley Street School log books'.

Portsmouth History Centre
Portsmouth Branch WEA, *Childhood Memories*, vol. 2, 1990.
1350A/1, 'John Mear's War Diary'.
SA/CC/DS/36/1/1/A/1, 'Portsea Infants School log books'.
SA/CC/DS/39/3/A/1, 'St Luke's School log books'.
11A/J/5, R.N. Shutte, 'Mission of the Good Shepherd, Portsea', 1870.

Leeds City Archive
LC/ED/160/1/1, 'All Saints' Church of England log books'.
LC/ED17/4, 'Darley Street Council School, 1898–1935, log books'.
LCED40/1, 'Leyland Board School Logbook'.

LC/ED/62/2, 'St Peter's Square School Board Log Books'.
WYL 707/1813, 'Diaries of Cecil Rhodes'.

Modern Record Centre, University of Warwick
MSS 148/UCW/6/13/42/8, *British Empire Union*, pamphlet (approximately 1933).
MSS 240/R/3/71, A.R. Rollins Collection, 'Leeds Jewry'.

British Parliamentary Papers
Board of Education. *Report on the Consultative Committee on Attendance, Compulsory or otherwise at Continuation Schools*, vol. 1, Report and Appendices, 1909.
Parliamentary Papers, *Inter-Departmental Committee on Physical Deterioration*, vol. II, 1904.
Inter-Departmental Committee on Physical Deterioration, vol. II, 1904.
Report of the Board of Education, 1899–1900, vol. III, Appendix to Report, 1900.

Contemporary publications

Arnold, M. 'Up to Easter', *Nineteenth Century*, XXI, 1887, pp. 638–9.
Besant, W. *East London* (London, Chatto and Windus, 1899, 1903 edn).
Booth, W. *In Darkest England and the Way Out* (London, Salvation Army, 1890, 1970 edn).
Clayton, J. *Father Dolling. A Memoir* (London, Wells, Gardner, Darton & Co., 1902).
Dolling, R.R. *Ten Years in a Portsmouth Slum* (London, S.C. Brown, Langham & Co., 1896, 1903 edn).
Dyche, J.A. 'The Jewish Workman', *Contemporary Review*, 73, January 1898.
Dyche, J.A. 'The Jewish Immigrant', *Contemporary Review*, 75, March 1899.
Forster, A. *The Citizen Reader* (London, Cassell, 1886).
Gates, W. *Portsmouth and the Great War* (Portsmouth, Evening News, 1919).
Harrison, A. 'The British Empire Exhibition, 1934', *English Review*, November 1922.
Hobson, J.A. *The Psychology of Jingoism* (London, Grant Richards, 1901).
Hobson, J.A. *Imperialism a Study* (Cosimo Classics, New York, 1902, 2005 edn).
London, J. *The People of the Abyss* (London, Thomas Nelson and Sons, 1903, 1916 edn).
McMahon, H. 'The Fellowship of the British Empire Exhibition', *English Review*, March 1924.
Masterman, C.F.G. *The Heart of Empire. Discussions of Problems of Modern City Life in England* (London, Fisher Unwin, 1901).
Meath, R. 'The Defence of the Empire', *Nineteenth Century*, 57, May 1905.
Meath, R. *Brabazon Potpourri* (London, Hutchinson & Co., 1928).
Osborne, C.E. *The Life of Father Dolling* (London, Edward Arnold, 1903).

Shee, G.F. 'The Deterioration in National Physique', *Nineteenth Century*, 53, May 1903.

Spencer, C.J. 'The Progress of Popular Music', *Contemporary Review*, 52, August 1887.

Wells, H.G. *The Time Machine* (London, Heinemann, 1895).

White, A. 'A Typical Alien Immigrant', *Contemporary Review*, 73, February 1898.

Wilson, A. 'Music Halls', *Contemporary Review*, 78, July 1900.

Secondary sources

Armytage, W.H.G. *Four Hundred Years of English Education* (Cambridge, Cambridge University Press, 1964).

Ashworth, G.J. *Portsmouth's Political Patterns 1885–1945* (Portsmouth, Portsmouth City Council, 1976).

Attridge, S. *Nationalism, Imperilaism and Identity in Late Victorian Culture. Civil and Military Worlds* (Basingstoke, Palgrave, 2003).

August, A. *The British Working Class 1832–1940* (Harlow, Longman, 2007).

Beaven, B. 'Custom, Culture and Conflict. A Study of the Coventry Ribbon Trade in the First Half of the Nineteenth Century', *Midland History*, 15, 1990.

Beaven, B. 'Shop-floor Culture in the Coventry Motor Industry, *c.* 1896–1920', in D. Thoms, L. Holden and T. Claydon (eds), *The Motor Car and Popular Culture in the Twentieth Century* (Aldershot, Ashgate, 1998).

Beaven, B. *Leisure, Citizenship and Working-class Men in Britain, 1850–1945* (Manchester, Manchester University Press, 2005).

Beaven, B. 'Challenges to Civic Governance in Post-war England: the Peace Day Disturbances of 1919', *Urban History*, 33, 3, 2006.

Beaven, B. and J. Griffiths. 'Urban Elites, Socialists and Notions of Citizenship in an Industrial. Boomtown: Coventry *c.* 1870–1914', *Labour History Review*, 69, 1, April 2004.

Beresford, M. 'The Face of Leeds', in D. Fraser (ed.), *A History of Modern Leeds* (Manchester, Manchester University Press, 1980).

Bloomfield, A. 'Drill and Dance as Symbols of Imperialism', in J.A. Mangan (ed.), *Making Imperial Mentalities* (Manchester, Manchester University Press, 1990).

Boone, T. *Youth in Darkest England. Working-class Children at the Heart of Victorian Empire* (London, Routledge, 2005).

Boyce, D. 'Harmsworth, ACW', *Oxford Dictionary of National Biography*, Oxford University Press, on-line edition (www.oxforddnb.com).

Brodie, M. *Politics of the Poor: The East End of London 1885–1914* (Oxford, Clarendon Press, 2004).

Brown, J. 'Charles Booth and Labour Colonies', *Economic History Review*, 21, 2, August 1968.

Buckman, J. *Immigrants and the Class Struggle. The Jewish Immigrants in Leeds, 1880–1914* (Manchester, Manchester University Press, 1983).

REFERENCES

Burton, A. 'Who Needs Nation? Interrogating "British" History', *Journal of Historical Sociology*, 10, 3, September 1997.

Cannadine, D. 'The Transformation of Civic Ritual in Modern Britain: the Colchester Oyster Feast', *Past and Present*, 94, 1982.

Carr, F. 'Municipal Socialism: Labour's Rise to Power', in B. Lancaster and T. Mason (eds), *Life and Labour in a 20th Century City. The Experience of Coventry* (Coventry, Cryfield Press, 1986).

Caunce, S. 'Yorkshire Post Newspaper Ltd: Perseverance Rewarded', in J. Chartres and K. Honeyman (eds), *Leeds City Business 1893–1993: Essays Marking the Centenary of Incorporation* (Leeds, Leeds University Press, 1993).

Checkland, S.G. *The Rise of Industrial Society in England 1815–1885* (London, Longman, 1964).

Church, R. *The Rise and Decline of the British Motor Industry* (Basingstoke, Macmillan Press, 1994).

Coetzee, F. *For Party or Country: Nationalism and the Dilemmas of Popular Conservatism in Edwardian England* (Oxford, Oxford University Press, 1990).

Colls, R. and R. Rodger. *Cities of Ideas: Civil Society and Urban Governance in Britain 1800–2000. Essays in Honour of David Reader* (Aldershot, Ashgate, 2004).

Conley, M.A. *From Jack Tar to Union Jack. Representing Naval Manhood in the British Empire, 1870–1918* (Manchester, Manchester University Press, 2009).

Connell, E.J. and M. Ward. 'Industrial Development', in D. Fraser (ed.), *A History of Modern Leeds* (Manchester, Manchester University Press, 1980).

Croll, A. *Civilizing the Urban. Popular Culture and Public Space in Merthyr c. 1870–1914* (Cardiff, University of Wales, 2000).

Cunningham, H. 'Jingoism and the working classes, 1877–78', *Bulletin of the Society for the Study of Labour History*, 19, 6–9, 1969.

Cunningham, H. *The Volunteer Force: A Social and Political History, 1859–1908* (London, Croom Helm, 1975).

Cunningham, H. *The Children of the Poor. Representations of Childhood since the Seventeenth Century* (Oxford, Blackwell, 1991).

Day, A. 'A Spirit of Improvements: Improvement Commissioners, Boards of Health and Central-local Relations in Portsea', in R.J. Morris and R.H. Trainor (eds), *Urban Governance. Britain and Beyond 1750* (Aldershot, Ashgate, 2000).

Doyle, B. 'Mapping Slums in a Historic City: Representing Working Class Communities in Edwardian Norwich', *Planning Perspectives*, 16, 2001.

Driver, F. *Geography Militant. Cultures of Exploration and Empire* (Oxford, Blackwell, 2001).

Driver, F. and D. Gilbert (eds). *Imperial Cities* (Manchester, Manchester University Press, 2003).

Dunae, P.A. 'Boys' Literature and the Idea of Empire, 1870–1914', *Victorian Studies*, 24, 1980.

Englander, D. 'Booth's Jews: the presentation of Jews and Judaism in *Life and Labour of the People of London*', in D. Englander and R. O'Day (eds), *Retrieved Riches. Social Investigation in Britain, 1814–1914* (Aldershot, Scolar Press, 1995).

Englander, D. 'Comparisons and Contrasts: Henry Mayhew and Charles Booth as Social Investigators', in D. Englander and R. O'Day (eds), *Retrieved Riches. Social Investigation in Britain, 1840–1914* (Aldershot, Scolar Press, 1995).

English, J. 'Empire Day in Britain, 1904–1958', *Historical Journal*, 49, 1, 2006.

Field, J. 'Wealth, Styles of Life and Social Tone amongst Portsmouth's Middle Class 1800–75', in R.J. Morris (ed.), *Class, Power and Social Structure in British Nineteenth Century Towns* (Leicester, Leicester University Press, 1986).

Fraser, D. *Urban Politics in Victorian England* (London, Macmillian, 1976).

Garrard, J. *Leadership and Power in Victorian Industrial Towns, 1830–80* (Manchester, Manchester University Press, 1983).

Gliddon, P. 'The Political Importance of Provincial Newspapers, 1903–1945: the Rowntrees and the Liberal Press', *Twentieth Century British History*, 14, 1, 2003.

Griffiths, J.R. 'Civic Communication in Britain: a Study of the *Municipal Journal*, c. 1893–1910', *Journal of Urban History*, 34, 2008.

Gunn, S. *The Public Culture of the Victorian Middle Class. Ritual and Authority in the English Industrial City, 1840–1914* (Manchester, Manchester University Press, 2000).

Haggerty, S., A. Webster and N.J. White (eds). *Empire in One City? Liverpool's Inconvenient Imperial Past* (Manchester, Manchester University Press, 2008).

Hall, C. (ed.). *Cultures of Empire. Colonizers in Britain and the Empire in the Nineteenth and Twentieth Centuries: A Reader* (Manchester, Manchester University Press, 2000).

Hampton, M. *Visions of the Press in Britain 1850–1950* (Chicago, University of Illinois Press, 2004).

Hartigan, J. 'Volunteering in the First World War: the Birmingham experience, August 1914–May 1915', *Midland History*, 24, 1999.

Heathorn, S. ' "Let us remember that we, too, are English": Constructions of Citizenship and National Identity in English Elementary School Reading Books, 1880–1914', *Victorian Studies*, 38, 3, 1995.

Hiley, N. 'Ploughboys and Soldiers: the Folk Song and the Gramophone in the British Expeditionary Force 1914–1918', *Media History*, 4, 1, 1988.

Hill, J. 'Rite of Spring: Cup Finals and Community in the North of England', in J. Hill and J. Williams (eds), *Sport and Identity in the North of England* (Keele, Keele University Press, 1996).

Hobsbawm, E.J. *The Age of Empire, 1875–1914* (London, Abacus, 1997 edn).

Hoggart, R. *The Uses of Literacy* (Harmondsworth, Penguin, 1957).

Holt, R.J. 'Football and the Urban Way of Life in Nineteenth Century Britain', in J.A. Mangan (ed.), *Pleasure, Profit and Proselytism. British Culture and Sport at Home and Abroad, 1700–1914* (London, Frank Cass, 1988).

REFERENCES

James, R. *Popular Culture and Working-Class Taste in Britain, 1930–39* (Manchester, Manchester University Press, 2010).

Jones, A. *Powers of the Press. Newspapers, Power and the Public in Nineteenth Century England* (Aldershot, Scolar Press, 1996).

Keating, P. (ed.). *Into Unknown England, 1866–1913. Selections from the Social Explorers* (Glasgow, Fontana, 1976, 1981 edn).

Koven, S. *Slumming. Sexual and Social Politics in Victorian England* (Princeton, Princeton University Press, 2004).

Lammers, B.J. ' "The Citizens of the Future": Educating the Children of the Jewish East End, c. 1885–1939', *Twentieth Century British History*, 19, 4, 2008.

Lancaster, B. 'Who's a Real Coventry Kid? Migration into Twentieth Century Coventry', in B. Lancaster and T. Mason (eds), *Life and Labour in a 20th Century City. The Experience of Coventry* (Coventry, Cryfield Press, 1986).

Luckin, B. 'Revisiting the Idea of Degeneration in Urban Britain, 1830–1900', *Urban History*, 33, 3, 2, 2006.

Lunn, K. and A. Day. 'Introduction', in K. Lunn and A. Day (eds), *History of Work Labour Relations in the Royal Dockyards* (London, Mansell, 1999).

Lunn, K. and R. Thomas. 'Naval Imperialism in Portsmouth, 1905–1914', *Southern History*, 10, 1988.

McCartney, H.B. *Citizen Soldiers: The Liverpool Territorials in the First World War* (Cambridge, Cambridge University Press, 2005).

MacKenzie, J.M. *Propaganda and Empire* (Manchester, Manchester University Press, 1984).

MacKenzie, J.M. (ed.). *Imperialism and Popular Culture* (Manchester, Manchester University Press, 1986).

MacKenzie, J.M. ' "The second city of the empire". Glasgow – Imperial Municipality', in F. Driver and D. Gilbert (eds), *Imperial Cities* (Manchester, Manchester University Press, 1999).

MacKenzie, J.M. 'The Press and the Dominant Ideology of Empire', in S. Potter (ed.), *Newspapers and Empire in Ireland and Britain* (Dublin, Four Courts Press, 2004).

MacKenzie, J.M. 'Irish, Scottish, Welsh and English Worlds? A Four-nation Approach to the History of the British Empire', *History Compass*, 6, 5, 2008.

McLaughlin, J. *Writing the Urban Jungle. Reading Empire in London from Doyle to Eliot* (Charlottesville, University of Virginia, 2000).

McLeay, P. 'The Wolverhampton Motor Car Industry 1896–1937', *West Midlands Studies*, 2, 1969.

Marriott, J. *The Other Empire. Metropolis, India and Progress in the Colonial Imagination* (Manchester, Manchester University Press, 2003).

Marwick, A. *The Deluge. British Society in the First World War* (London, Bodley Head, 1965).

Mayne, A. *The Imagined Slum: Newspaper Representations in Three Cities, 1870–1914* (Leicester, Leicester University Press, 1993).

Meadowcroft, M. 'The Years of Political Transition', in D. Fraser (ed.), *A History of Modern Leeds* (Manchester, Manchester University Press, 1980).

Meath, Earl of. *Brabazon Potpourri* (London, Hutchinson & Co., 1928).

Messinger, G. *British Propaganda and the State in the First World War* (Manchester, Manchester University Press, 1992).

Miller, S.M. 'In support of the "Imperial Mission"? Volunteering for the South African War, 1899–1902'. *Journal of Military History* 69, 3, July 2005.

Miller, S.M. *Volunteers on the Veld. Britain's Citizen Soldiers and the South African War, 1899–1902* (Norman, Oklahoma Press, 2007).

Milner, L. *Leeds Pals. A History of the 15th (Service) Battalion (1st Leeds). The Prince of Wales Own (Yorkshire Regiment), 1914–18* (London, Leo Cooper, 1991).

Morgan, C.J. 'Demographic Change 1771–1911', in D. Fraser (ed.), *A History of Modern Leeds* (Manchester, Manchester University Press, 1980).

Morgan, K.O. 'The Boer War and the Media (1899–1902)', *Twentieth Century British History*, 13, 1, 2002.

Morris, A.J.A. 'J.P. Edwards: Newspaper Proprietor and Philanthropist', *Oxford Dictionary of National Biography*, Oxford University Press, on-line edition (www.oxforddnb.com); *Evening News* 27 April 1977.

Morris, R.J. 'Middle-Class Culture, 1700–1914', in D. Fraser (ed.), *A History of Modern Leeds* (Manchester, Manchester University Press, 1980).

Morris, R.J. *Class, Sect and Party. The Making of the British Middle Class, Leeds 1820–1850* (Manchester, Manchester University Press, 1990).

Osborne, J.M. 'Defining Their Own Patriotism: British Volunteer Training Corps in the First World War', *Journal of Contemporary History*, 23, 1988.

Pelling, H. *Popular Politics in Late Victorian Society* (London, Macmillan, 1968).

Penn, A. *Targeting Schools. Drill, Militarism and Imperialism* (London, Woburn Press, 1999).

Porter, B. *The Absent-minded Imperialists. Empire, Society and Culture in Britain* (Oxford, Oxford University Press, 2004, 2006 edn).

Porter, B. 'Further Thoughts on Imperial Absent Mindedness', *Journal of Imperial and Commonwealth History*, 36, 1, March 2008.

Price, R. *An Imperial War and the British Working Class. Working-class Attitudes and Reactions to the Boer War, 1899–1902* (London, Routledge, 1972).

Price, R. *Labour in British Society* (London, Croom Helm, 1986).

Price, R. 'One Big Thing: Britain, Its Empire and Their Imperial Culture', *Journal of British Studies*, 45, July 2006.

Purseigle, P. 'Beyond and Below the Nations: Towards a Comparative History of Local Communities at War', in J. Macleod and P. Purseigle (eds), *Uncovered Fields: Perspectives in First World War Studies* (Leiden, Brill, 2003).

Reeder, D. 'Representations of Metropolis: Descriptions of the Social Environment in *Life and Labour*', in D. Englander and R. O'Day (eds), *Retrieved Riches. Social Investigation in Britain, 1840–1914* (Aldershot, Scolar Press, 1995).

Richards, J. 'Boy's Own Empire: Feature Films and Imperialism in the 1930s', in J.M. MacKenzie (ed.), *Imperialism and Popular Culture* (Manchester University Press, 1986).

Richards, J. *Imperialism and Music. Britain 1876–1953* (Manchester, Manchester University Press, 2001).

Richardson, K. *Twentieth Century Coventry* (Bungay, Chaucer Press, 1972).

Riley, R. *Portsmouth: Ships, Dockyard and Town* (Stroud, Tempus, 2002).

Riley, R.C. *The Industries of Portsmouth in the 19th Century* (Portsmouth: Portsmouth Papers, 1976).

Robb, G. *British Culture and the First World War* (Basingstoke, Palgrave, 2002).

Robb, J.H. *The Primrose League 1883–1906* (New York, AMS Press, 1942).

Roberts, M. 'Constructing a Tory World-view: Popular Politics and the Conservative Press in Late Victorian Leeds', *Historical Research*, 79, 2006.

Rose, J. 'Willingly to School: the Working-class Response to Elementary Education 1870–1918', *Journal of British Studies*, 32, April 1993.

Rose, J. *The Intellectual Life of the British Working Classes* (New Haven, Yale University Press, 2001).

Rüger, J. 'Nation, Empire and Navy: Identity Politics in the United Kingdom 1887–1914', *Past and Present*, 185, November 2004.

Rüger, J. *The Great Naval Game. Britain and Germany in the Age of Empire* (Cambridge, Cambridge University Press, 2007).

Russell, G. 'Entertainment of Oddities', in K. Wilson (ed.), *A New Imperial History: Culture, Identity and Modernity in Britain and Empire 1660–1849* (Cambridge, Cambridge University Press, 2004).

Rutherford, L. ' "Harmless nonsense": the comic sketch and the development of music-hall entertainment', in J.S. Bratton (ed.), *Music Hall Performance and Style* (Oxford, Open University Press, 1986).

Said, E. *Culture and Imperialism* (London, Vintage, 1993).

Savage, M. and A. Miles. *The Remaking of the British Working Class, 1840–1940* (London, Routledge, 1994).

Schneer, J. *London 1900. The Imperial Metropolis* (New Haven, Yale University Press, 1999).

Searle, G.R. *The Quest for National Efficiency. A Study in British Politics and Political Thought, 1899–1914* (London, Ashfield Press, 1971, 1990 edn).

Silbey, D. *The British Working Class and Enthusiasm for War 1914–16* (London, Frank Cass, 2005).

Simon, B. *Education and the Labour Movement, 1870–1920* (London, Lawrence and Wishart, 1965).

Smith, A. and D. Fry. *Godiva's Heritage: Coventry Industry* (Coventry, Simanda Press, 1997).

Smith, F. *Coventry Six Hundred Years of Municipal Life* (Coventry, Coventry Evening Telegraph, 1945).

Springhall, J.O. 'Lord Meath, Youth and Empire', *Journal of Contemporary History*, 5, 4, 1970.

Stacey, M. *Tradition and Change: A Study of Banbury* (London, Oxford University Press, 1960).

Steele, E.D. 'Imperialism and Leeds Politics, c. 1850–1914', in D. Fraser (ed.), *A History of Modern Leeds* (Manchester, Manchester University Press, 1980).

REFERENCES

Taylor, A.J. 'Victorian Leeds: an Overview', in D. Fraser (ed.), *A History of Modern Leeds* (Manchester, Manchester University Press, 1980).

Taylor, M. *The Association Game. A History of British Football* (Harlow, Longman, 2007).

Thomas, R. 'Empire, Naval Pageantry and Public Spectacles', *Mariners Mirror*, 88, 2, May 2002.

Thompson, A. *The Empire Strikes Back? The Impact of Imperialism on Britain from the Mid-nineteenth Century* (Harlow, Longman, 2005).

Thompson, F.M.L. 'Town and City', in F.M.L. Thompson (ed.), *The Cambridge Social History of Britain 1750–1950*, 3 vols (Cambridge, Cambridge University Press, 1990).

Thompson, J. 'Modern Britain and the New Imperial History', *History Compass*, 5, 2, 2007.

Thoms, D. and T. Donnelly. *The Motor Car Industry in Coventry since the 1890s* (Chatham, Croom Helm, 1985).

Thoms, D.W. and T. Donnelly. 'Coventry's Industrial Economy', in B. Lancaster and T. Mason (eds), *Life and Labour in a 20th Century City. The Experience of Coventry* (Coventry, Cryfield Press, 1986).

Trainor, R.H. *Black Country Elites. The Exercise of Authority in an Industrialized Area 1830–1900* (Oxford, Clarendon Press, 1993).

Valverde, M. 'The Dialect of the Familiar and Unfamiliar: "The Jungle" in Early Slum Travel Writing', *Sociology*, 30, 3, August 1996.

Vaughan, L. and A. Penn. 'Jewish Immigrant Settlement Patterns in Manchester and Leeds 1881', *Urban Studies*, 43, 3, March 2006.

Vincent, D. *Testaments of Radicalism. Memoirs of Working Class Politicians 1790–1885* (London, Europa, 1977).

Waites, B. *A Class Society at War. England 1914–1918* (Leamington Spa, Berg, 1987).

Walkowitz, J.R. *City of Dreadful Delight. Narratives of Sexual Danger in Late Victorian London* (London, Virago Press, 1992).

Walton, J.K. 'The north west', in F.M.L. Thompson (ed.), *The Cambridge Social History of Britain 1750–1950*, Vol. 1 (Cambridge, Cambridge University Press, 1900).

Washington, E.S. *Local Battles in Fact and Fiction: The Portsmouth Election of 1895* (Portsmouth, Portsmouth City Council, 1985).

Watson, A. and P. Porter. 'Bereaved and Aggrieved: Combat Motivation and the Ideology of Sacrifice in the First World War', *Historical Research*, 83, February 2010.

White, B.J. 'Volunteerism and Early Recruitment Efforts in Devonshire, August 1914–December 1915', *Historical Journal*, 52, 3, 2009.

Williams, J. 'One Could Literally Have Walked on the Heads of the People Congregated There', in K. Laybourn (ed.), *Social Conditions, Status and Community, 1860–c. 1920* (Stroud, Sutton, 1997).

Woodhouse, T. 'The Working Class', in D. Fraser (ed.), *A History of Modern Leeds* (Manchester, Manchester University Press, 1980).

Wright, A.W. *G.D.H. Cole and Socialist Democracy* (Oxford, Clarendon Press, 1979), 63–5.

REFERENCES

Yates, J.A. *Pioneers to Power: The Story of the Ordinary People of Coventry* (Coventry, Coventry Labour Party, 1950).

Zeitlin, J. 'Emergence of the Shop Steward Organisation and Job Control in the British Car industry', *History Workshop*, 10, 1980.

Theses

Beaven, B. 'The Growth and Significance of the Coventry Car Component Industry, 1895–1939' (unpublished PhD thesis, De Montfort University, 1994).

Carr, F.W. 'Engineering Workers and the Rise of Labour, 1914–1939' (PhD thesis, University of Warwick, 1978).

Denyer, R. 'The Bitter Cry of Outcast Portsmouth: Poverty and Crime 1860–1900' (BA dissertation, University of Portsmouth, 2004).

Fulda, V. 'Space, Civic Pride, Citizenship and Identity in 1890s Portsmouth' (unpublished PhD thesis, University of Portsmouth, 2006).

Websites

British Film Institute, On-line Film data base, http://www.bfi.org.uk

www.britishpathe.com

Charles Booth on-line Archive, Police note books; http://booth.lse.ac.uk/note-books/b357/jpg/23.html

www.VisionofBritain.org.uk; Statistics for Coventry, Leeds and Portsmouth

Victoria County History, Warwickshire vol. VIII, on-line: www.british-history.ac.uk

West, A.J. 'Seasalts and Celluloid', unpublished autobiography, 1936, pdf version, p. 16, ww.ournavy.org.uk

INDEX

Note: literary works can be found under authors' names

EU authorised representative for GPSR:
Easy Access System Europe, Mustamäe tee 50,
10621 Tallinn, Estonia
gpsr.requests@easproject.com